Environmental Human Rights

The nature of environmental human rights and their relation to larger rights theories has been a frequent topic of discussion in law, environmental ethics and political theory. However, the subject of environmental human rights has not been fully established among other human rights concerns within political philosophy and theory.

In examining environmental rights from a political theory perspective, this book explores an aspect of environmental human rights that has received less attention within the literature. In linking the constraints of political reality with a focus on the theoretical underpinnings of how we think about politics, this book explores how environmental human rights must respond to the key questions of politics, such as the state and sovereignty, equality, recognition and representation, and examines how the competing understandings about these rights are also related to political ideologies.

Drawing together contributions from a range of key thinkers in the field, this is a valuable resource for students and scholars of human rights, environmental ethics, and international environmental law and politics more generally.

Markku Oksanen is a Senior Lecturer in Philosophy at the University of Eastern Finland.

Ashley Dodsworth is a Senior Teaching Associate in Politics at the University of Bristol, UK.

Selina O'Doherty at the University of South Wales, UK.

Routledge Explorations in Environmental Studies

For a full list of titles in this series, please visit www.routledge.com/Routledge-Explorations-in-Environmental-Studies/book-series/REES

Environmental Human Rights

A Political Theory Perspective

Edited by Markku Oksanen,
Ashley Dodsworth and
Selina O'Doherty

LONDON AND NEW YORK

from Routledge

First published 2018 by Routledge

2 Park Square, Milton Park, Abingdon, Oxfordshire OX14 4RN
52 Vanderbilt Avenue, New York, NY 10017

Routledge is an imprint of the Taylor & Francis Group, an informa business

First issued in paperback 2019

British Library Cataloguing-in-Publication Data
A catalogue record for this book is available from the British Library

Library of Congress Cataloging-in-Publication Data
A catalog record for this book has been requested

ISBN: 978-1-138-73258-2 (hbk)
ISBN: 978-0-367-24463-7 (pbk)

Typeset in Goudy
by Apex CoVantage, LLC

Contents

Table

Contributors

Ted Benton is emeritus professor of sociology at University of Essex. He has written extensively on social theory and philosophy, arguing for the continuing relevance of Marxian approaches and also for rethinking the relation between social and life sciences. He has developed this theme most thoroughly in relation to the ecological conditions and consequences of contemporary capitalist socio-economic dynamics. He has also written on the applicability of concepts of rights and justice both within and across the boundary between the human species and others (*Natural Relations: Ecology, Animal Rights and Social Justice* (Verso, 1993). S. Moog & R. Stones (ed) 2009 *Nature, Social Relations and Human Needs: Essays in Honour of Ted Benton* (Palgrave) includes discussion of the range of his contributions to social theory. More recently he has written an intellectual biography of Alfred Russel Wallace, co-founder of the theory of evolution by natural selection, and is author of many books on natural history, including two award-winning monographs in the HarperCollins New Naturalist series (*Bumblebees* (2006), *Grasshoppers and Crickets* (2012). He is a founding member of the Red-Green Study Group and honourary president of Colchester Natural History Society.

Daniel P. Corrigan is a PhD candidate in philosophy at the University of Miami. His research is in human rights, political and legal philosophy, and applied ethics. In particular, his work has focused on business and human rights and environmental human rights. As of autumn 2017, he will be Arsht Ethics Initiatives Post-Doctoral Associate in Business Ethics and Bioethics at the University of Miami School of Business Administration.

Ashley Dodsworth is a Senior Teaching Associate at the University of Bristol. Her PhD, on the past conceptions of environmental rights, was completed at the University of Leicester and she has published work on Gerrard Winstanley's understanding of labour and rights and on the rhetoric of the Green Party with reference to fracking.

Eike Düvel is a PhD candidate at the Karl-Franzens-University of Graz and a member of the interdisciplinary doctoral programme "Climate Change" of the Austrian Science Fund (FWF). His research focusses on risk ethics and inter-generational ethics.

Petra Gümplová holds a PhD in sociology from The New School for Social Research, New York, US. She works as a Fellow at Max Weber Kolleg at the University of Erfurt, Germany. Her research is focused on international law, justice, state sovereignty, natural resources, and human rights. Her book *Sovereignty and Constitutional Democracy* was published in 2011.

Anne Kumpula is Professor of Environmental Law at the University of Turku, Finland.

Selina O'Doherty is a PhD candidate at the University of South Wales. Her thesis examined the responsibility to pre-emptively protect future generations from climate change. She has presented her work widely, on the rights of future people, and on the concepts of duty, responsibility, and harm in international relations. Her current research focuses on civil society, the duty of resistance, and transnational governance.

Markku Oksanen is a Senior Lecturer in Philosophy at the University of Eastern Finland. He has co-edited *Philosophy and Biodiversity* (Cambridge 2004) and *Ethics and Animal Re-creation and Modification* (Palgrave 2014) and published articles on green political theory and environmental ethics.

Hubert Schnueriger is a Lecturer in Philosophy at the University of Basel, Switzerland.

Marcel Wissenburg is Professor of Political Theory at Radboud University, Nijmegen, the Netherlands, and Head of its Department of Public Administration and Political Science. He co-edited *Political Animals and Animal Politics* (Palgrave Macmillan 2014) and published articles on various aspects of environmental political theory, from the Anthropocene to population policy.

Kerri Woods is lecturer in political theory at the University of Leeds, UK. She is author of *Human Rights and Environmental Sustainability* (Elgar 2010) and *Human Rights* (Palgrave 2014). She has published articles on environmental human rights, climate justice, and cosmopolitan political philosophy.

Acknowledgements

The groundwork for this volume was laid on two separate occasions in Manchester Political Theory Workshops ("Mancept") in 2015 and 2016. We would like to thank our contributors and other workshop participants for stimulating and fruitful debates. Special thanks are due to Kerri Woods, with whom Markku organised the first workshop.

Markku Oksanen
Ashley Dodsworth
Selina O'Doherty

Introduction
Environmental human rights and political theory

Ashley Dodsworth, Selina O'Doherty and Markku Oksanen

Introduction

Human rights are one of, if not the, most dominant concept within contemporary politics and ethics. Claiming that something is a right, or that an action violates rights, ensures a certain level of attention and gravity because human rights–centered approaches have a strong rhetorical appeal. As Tom Campbell points out 'the discourse of rights is pervasive and popular in politics, law and morality. There is scarcely any position, opinion, claim, criticism or aspiration relating to social and political life that is not asserted and affirmed using the term "right"' (2006, 3). Few public debates or political campaigns do not draw upon the concept of rights for support and the notion of a human right shapes our moral discourse. As a result, it is not surprising that environmental scholars and activists have framed their claims in the language and vocabulary of human rights.

Though human rights are a legal concept, references to human rights often serve political purposes, addressing power relations and acting as both expressions of moral disapproval and calls to action. Whilst there may be little legal bite to these claims, they can have immense normative weight and therefore are able to bring about legal and political reform. This has been particularly true with regard to environmental concerns, where legislation was universally either non-existent or weakly implemented, and so the urge to equip 'rights' with the attributes 'human' and 'environmental' in order to promote action is understandable given the emergence of these concerns. This is comparable to the early stages of the United Nations' human rights work. Prior to the Universal Declaration of Human Rights (UDHR) on 10 December 1948, there was only the political will and the call for accessible and timely moral standards, on the basis of which state-led atrocities would be criminalised as crimes against humanity. Thus, including the environment expands the scope of legitimate human interests that are or should be protected in terms of rights. Whether the environment, and all those who depend upon it, will then be adequately protected by this measure is, however, a matter of debate.

In this collection, the concept of environmental human rights will be explored from a political theory perspective. Political theory, as an academic subdiscipline, escapes definitions that are short, precise and firm. As John Dryzek, Bonnie Hönig and Anne Phillips characterize it, 'political theory is an interdisciplinary endeavor whose center of gravity lies at the humanities end of the happily still undisciplined discipline of political science' (2006, 4).

It follows then that the focus of these chapters is not solely on human rights legislation, international covenants and legal cases that would typically be the prime sources for legal studies. Nor is there a predominate focus on case studies surrounding the campaigns for environmental human rights or analysis of whether these rights have secured environmental sustainability, as with a political science volume. Instead the focus is on the conceptual, justificatory and normative issues revolving around the concept of environmental human rights.

Rights and human rights

Rights are one of the central, dominant concepts within political theory yet there is still debate over just what they actually are. In this, rights are similar to other key concepts within political theory, such as freedom, democracy and power – indeed the debate over just what is meant by these terms is often the point. W.B. Gallie argues that such concepts are therefore 'essentially contested' (Gallie 1955–1956) as no precise definition is available and instead there are many appealing but mutually excluding or contradictory definitions and usages, with manifold conflicts between the different understandings. An uncontested, universally agreed upon definition is therefore not possible, but this may be no bad thing, for the tensions between the different understandings leads to 'un-disciplinarity', that is, to creativity, imaginative analysis and the potential for a wider application of rights, as this collection of articles illustrates.

Whilst each chapter draws on its own understanding of rights, certain points are common to all: the justification of rights, human rights vs natural rights, the link between rights and duties, the question of the state and the ambiguity of rights.

The first question is that of the basis of rights, or why do subjects have rights? What is the justification for rights? The standard answer is that subjects are said to have rights because they have needs that require protection – there are things which we must have if we are to survive and flourish and rights ensure that we have access to these goods. People therefore have environmental rights because without our environment we would not survive. Two key accounts of rights have been put forward: will theory (also known as choice theory) and interest theory (also known as benefit theory). Although both theories have a descriptive and justificatory dimension of rights, they proffer opposing accounts on the function and nature of rights. Both approaches have their advantages and weakness. That subjects need rights to protect themselves is clear; what is being protected and why is less so.

According to the will theory, rights provide a space for us to assert our agency and make our own choices. It positions itself in defense of rights necessitating control over the duties of others. From a will theory approach, the primary purpose of rights is to afford the rights-holder the autonomy to control duties which are owed to her by others, thereby protecting individual autonomy (Hart 1982; Wellman 1995). Will theorists argue that no right can exist unless it has a recognisable subject who holds the option of enforcing or waiving the duty correlative to the right. This therefore excludes any subject without autonomous agency from being entitled to or capable or having rights. For example, in addition to the non-existent future subjects, as discussed in Schnueriger's chapter, a will theory application of human rights also excludes minors and the infirm (Steiner 1994). As a result of this exclusion the will theory of rights as a justificatory analysis has come under severe scrutiny. Wellman does however defend, or attempt to neutralise, the exclusionary nature of will theory conceptualisations of rights by claiming that a paternalistic sense of moral duty still provides agency-less and rights-less non-subjects protection, as 'non-autonomous human beings are the beneficiaries of a stringent set of moral duties borne by all members of the community of autonomous agents' (1995, 127).

The interest theory instead argues that the primary function of rights is to secure for their holder certain benefits or interests (see Feinburg 1980; Jones 1994; Campbell 2006; Shorten 2016, 281–288). Interest theory accounts or understandings of rights are not primarily concerned with presuming or defining either what rights there are or what kinds of entities can be rights-holders. The focus instead is on the protection rights offer to the rights-bearer's core interests. Rather than being applicable only to subjects holding the agency or sentience to waive or refuse their rights, as with will theory, interest theory instead holds that any subject which possesses or is capable of possessing interests may bear rights, as long as the corresponding interest is sufficiently important to justify ascribing duties onto others. Due the lack of priority or scale prescribed between differing interests, this approach draws criticism for being individually focused, permitting self-interest and for undercutting the agency of the rights holder. However conceptualising rights as interests is the closest mainstream interpretation in the political process and practice of human rights.

The term rights can refer to human rights or it can refer to natural rights, a distinction that carries weight for all it seeming to be small. Human rights are linked to the development of the UDHR and the post–World War Two development of rights, whereas natural rights have a much longer history which encompasses the great canonical works of political theory, such as Locke's *Two Treatises of Government*. This distinction also partly overlaps with the separation of legal and moral rights – between rights that are morally said to be held by all individuals and those that are legally recognised and enforced. Moral rights were the subject of Bentham's infamous critique that they are nothing but 'nonsense upon stilts' (Bentham [1816] 1987) because they were not rooted in law and practice. But moral rights provide a way to critique current laws and existing institutions, providing a guide to aim for and a goal to aspire to. The case of environmental human rights represents such a critique since the earlier lists of human rights were devoid of specific environmental rights and the environmentalist interpretations of established rights were non-existent. One constant thread of the human rights debates has concerned the feasibility of the expansion and revision of rights to better reflect the development of societies and international politics. In this volume, some chapters focus mainly on moral rights, others more on legal rights. Because of the tendency of human rights to expand and to be revised, to be in flux, the nature of the moral-legal divide is a matter of constant reflection and disagreement. The chapter by Oksanen and Kumpula on human rights and landscape exemplifies the nature of such a debate, as does Corrigan's chapter.

Exploring the difference between human and moral rights leads to the role of the state. The traditional sense of human rights has been as protection of individuals against the power of the state. For example, an assault by another citizen is a crime; an assault by an agent of the state, such as a police officer as an abuse of human rights (if the state does not prosecute the citizen who committed the crime, that could also be an abuse of human rights). The scope of human rights has expanded to cover acts of non-state actors, in cases where the state does not prosecute the citizen who committed the crime. In other words, human rights require that the state actively enforce them. This opens up the question of the duties of other citizens, even if their duties are to support and create a state that respects human rights. When the transboundary nature of environmental harm is considered, the relationship between rights and the state becomes more complicated.

What is clearer however is the correlation between rights and duties. If one person has a right, then someone else must bear the duty to ensure that right is fulfilled. If a person has the right not to be tortured, or to be provided with an education, then that places an obligation on others to either refrain from torture or provide an education and this is an obligation they must fulfil. Whether the state bears this duty directly, or is responsible for ensuring that others carry out their duties may depend on the right and the relationship between the state and the citizens in a particular context. A society committed to a 'minimal government' for example may have a private police forces or private education systems in which the state is responsible for overseeing these actors and ensuring they fulfil their contracted duties. In a society that takes a more expansive view of the role of the state, it may be that it is the state itself which retains this responsibility. But in any case, that there is an actor under a duty to ensure these rights is clear. Indeed when Nickel (1993) sets out the criteria that any proposed right must meet, one of the criteria is that there must be an identifiable duty-bearer.

The debate over negative and positive rights grows out of this link between rights and duties. Negative rights are said to be rights that requires the duty bearer to refrain from action, whilst positive rights require individuals and collective actors to fulfil a specific task.[1] This makes the question of identifying a duty-bearer harder. If there is a positive right against the state, then the answer is clear, but for rights that require a large number of people to refrain from taking action, then things become more complicated. That rights impose duties is obvious – which rights impose which duties, and upon whom those duties are imposed, is more complicated, especially with regard to the complex relationship between people and their environment, as both Schnueriger and O'Doherty's chapters note (and see also Shue's discussion in *Climate Justice*).

While many key concepts in political theory are 'essentially contested', the debate over rights is particularly extensive and has crucial implications for who gets to be a rights-holder, what that enables them to claim and from whom. Nickel argues that this vagueness is not a problem, but rather a strength, as it enables each society and legal body to define rights in the way that best fits their practices and needs and the vagueness within the UDHR enables it to be universally applied (1993). However, when trying to tackle a global problem like climate change and environmental catastrophe, or when facing such a multifaceted problem that requires a variety of action and inaction if humanity's most vital and basic needs are to be secured, more consensus is needed. The chapters in this volume seek to provide a response.

Environmental rights in political theory

With the concept of rights in general introduced, an explanation of environmental rights is needed. Again this section will be structured around the key questions that are asked regarding such rights and to which the chapters in this volume present different answers.

The first key question concerns the relationship of environmental rights and rights in general. A position called human rights minimalism argues that protecting bodily security against intentional cruelty and acts of torture, rape, beating and killing should be the main, if not only, aim of human rights (see Ignatieff 2001, 173). This reflects Maurice Cranston's argument regarding the inflation of rights discourse, which worries that if there are too many rights claims, to too many different goods, than the power of these claims will be reduced and watered down (Cranston 1967). This position raises doubts over the applicability of human rights language to environmental concerns. In response Michael Anderson points out that there are three ways of combining environmental concerns with rights (Anderson 1996, 4–10). Firstly, a specified quality of environment could be a requirement of rights in general. Secondly, specific existing rights could be said to require a stable environment. The rights to life and health are often referenced here and Jan Hancock suggests that the rights to freedom from hunger and self-determination would also require control over natural resources (Hancock 2003). Rights against discrimination would also prevent rights-holders from being excluded from using and accessing their environment along with others. This approach is taken by O'Doherty and Gümplová within this volume. But other scholars such as Oksanen and Kumpula and Dodsworth argue the benefits that the environment brings stretch beyond the mere fulfilment of any individual rights such as life or health. Instead it encompasses all aspects of human life. In recognition of this fact, the third option is the creation of specific rights to the environment, so that environmental access is secured directly, as opposed to being subsumed or implied by other rights.

If environmental rights are to be classed as a distinct category of rights on their own, then the question of what they are rights to is raised. Again, two kinds of rights can be identified: substantive and procedural rights. Substantive rights are rights to a specific good, so in the case of substantive environmental rights this would be rights to specific natural resources, or to the environment as a whole. Procedural rights enable their holder to take part in the decision-making process and to play a part in collective governance. Eckersley provides the most expansive explanation of what procedural environmental rights would be, suggesting that they include:

> a right to environmental information and a corresponding duty on the part of the state to provide regular state of the environment reports, the right to be informed of risk generating proposals, third-party litigation rights, a right to participate in environmental impact assessment processes and the right to environmental remedies when harm is suffered.
>
> (Eckersley 2004, 137)

Such rights would enable individuals to be informed of the state of the environment in a timely and comprehensible way and to have the means to adjust their threshold levels accordingly, as well as providing recourse when the threshold is not met. Sax claims that 'the first environmental right is the right to choose' what quality and quantity of natural resources we should be entitled to access (Sax 1990–1991, 97). He argues that environmental rights do not mean that their holders are entitled to an untouched, unchanged environment, but rather that they should be able to decide for themselves how and in what ways their environment is used. Sax explicitly ties the 'basic right not to be left to fall below some minimum level of substantive protection against hazard' (Ibid., 100) to procedural rights, arguing that each society must be able to use its procedural rights in order to decide what the 'appropriate level of protection' is. Procedural environmental rights reflect concerns regarding the use of pesticides and other health-affecting chemicals in the environment but, as Oksanen and Kumpula (2013) have argued in nature conservation there are reasons for limiting public access to databases: sometimes the best conservation policy is that the locations of bird nests and valuable orchids are undisclosed. There are also other areas where the justifiability of full disclosure and openness of databases is contentious (e.g. in flood mapping, see O'Neill and O'Neill 2012).

There is a tension within these procedural or democratic environmental rights, namely collective myopia or the danger of short-term trade-offs through the prioritisation of other values, such as economic development over environmental concerns, such as in the aptly named economy-ecology debate. This holds that if environmental human rights are to be adequately protected, the necessary actions will negatively affect socio-economic development and stability. To fully address this problem, authors such as Eerik Lagerspetz (1999) and Tim Hayward (2004) have proposed that environmental rights should be constitutionalised because environmental concerns need to be lifted above day-to-day politics and short-term decision making. Though there is agreement as to the importance of decision making, endeavouring to balance the need for consultation and choice against the fundamental importance of the environment creates tension.

This tension also manifests in the relationship between environmental rights and democracy and also with the liberal tradition as a whole. The 'green' credentials of liberalism have been repeatedly questioned, defended and reinterpreted with reference to the history of that ideology and its key figures, and it has frequently been found wanting (Dobson 2007, 149–158; Stephens 2016). Marcel Wissenburg argues that while 'there were once good grounds to suspect liberalism of at the very least a certain indifference towards ecological challenges – yet this attitude is changing dramatically' and that liberalism is 'greening' (Wissenburg 2006, 20). Wissenburg's chapter in this volume develops this argument further, but it is possible to ground environmental rights within other traditions. A more conservative approach, which sees rights as specific to the society they are in and designed to ensure continuity and stability, would be able to support environmental rights, especially if rooted in traditional practices and uses of resources. This could be seen in the British conservative thinker Roger Scruton's arguments regarding the dangers of the international human rights regime:

> Increasingly, in Europe, the idea of human rights is being used . . . to cancel national traditions and undermine managed environments, in the interest of internationalist ideals that are imposed without counting the cost to those who must conform to them.
>
> (2013, 374)

An emancipatory approach, perhaps growing out of Marx's critique of rights (Benton 1993) or the feminist critique (Bunch 1990; Binion 1995), both of which aim to move away from individualistic, atomistic rights towards a more holistic approach that sees rights as empowering and transformative, could also engage with claims to natural resources. Liberalism, and the rights tradition that is associated with it, may not be as opposed to environmentalism as it seems and even if it were to be so, there are other traditions and other understandings of rights.

The debate over liberalism also questions whether environmental values are compatible with, or can be reconciled with, democracy, a contentious question particularly since the publication of Garrett Hardin's polemical essay 'The Tragedy of the Commons' (1968) and its authoritarian message regarding reproductive rights. Democracy is committed to an open-ended procedure in which all can participate and has no set outcome, while environmentalism has specific aims and ends that are required to meet and sustain them. Indeed this is why scholars such as Hayward argued for constitutional environmental rights, as he believed environmental protection needed to be lifted above day-to-day politics and protected from the trade-offs that democracy requires. Eckersley however takes a different, more optimistic position, believing that environmental rights could prove a bridge between environmental and democratic concerns. She asks whether 'a reformulated rights discourse, grounded in a prima facie respect for the autonomy of all life forms, [could] also serve as a linchpin between green values and democracy?' (Eckersley 1996, 214) and concludes that 'rights discourse . . . [could be] enlisted as a means of connecting democratic concerns and ecological concerns at the level of principle' (Ibid., 214). The regulation and restrictive legislation that is required for environmental protection and to tackle climate change is therefore transformed from the authoritarian dictates of Hardin's response to the commons, to the self-government of peoples protecting their rights. Through recognising the importance of the environment to all human life and securing it against trade-offs via rights status, environmentalism and democracy are reconciled.

Eckersley may be right, and environmental rights might be the solution to linking democratic processes with environmental protection and values. Yet if this is true, it will only work at the state, or perhaps the regional level. The link between states and rights was set out in the earlier section and there we noted the problem that the environmental crisis is global – pollution is transboundary and climate change will affect every part of the world, albeit in different ways. Environmental rights therefore interact with the debates surrounding global justice (Hayward 2005; Shue 2014). When thinking about the environment we therefore need to not only consider all the people (or living beings) across the globe but also across time. As the chapters in this volume by O'Doherty, Schnueriger and Düvel show, both temporal and spatial justice is therefore required.

Finally, there are questions regarding the conceptual coherence of environmental rights, concerns that even proponents of environmental rights raise. Various authors such as John Barry and Kerri Woods (Barry and Woods 2012; Woods 2010, 2016) and Helen Batty and Tim Gray (1996) have questioned 'the assumed compatibility between human rights and the environment' (Woods and Barry 2012, 384). This critique is most strongly made by Batty and Gray, who argue that environmental rights are 'theoretically problematic . . . [because] the language of rights is not appropriate to the environment and that, while there may be a duty to protect the environment, there is no corresponding right to an adequate environment' (1996, 150). As previously shown, rights and duties are interlinked, making the identification of a duty-bearer synonymous with the identification of a rights-holder. The inability to do so in the case of environmental rights is linked to the variety of actions that are required by so many actors – for example preventing climate change will involve millions of people around the world reducing their carbon usage. Can we say that all are under the duty to do so? Furthermore, not everyone would have to reduce their limits to meet the required targets, so how do we decide who should be obliged and duty-bound to do so? Though there are responses to this problem, for example Shue's distinction between luxury and subsistence emissions (Shue 2014, 47–67, originally 1993) and O'Doherty's chapter in this volume, the implementation of this has yet to be tried. Batty and Grey offer further reasons for their scepticism, including the problem of defining environmental rights, especially with regard to whether they are liberty rights or welfare rights and the different duties these rights impose, and the problem of enforcing environmental rights world-wide. All of these problems stem from one key criticism, which says environmental rights 'require a fresh philosophical foundation' (Batty and Grey 1996, 154).

Woods has also 'question[ed] the presumed harmony between human rights and environmental sustainability' (Woods 2010, 25). This critical questioning has led Woods to suggest that while a rights-based approach to the environment does have its advantages, these are offset by persistent tensions between the two concepts:

> The idea of environmental human rights has much to recommend it, if and only if, human rights as human rights are not taken as they are but are instead reinterpreted so as to address the problem of underfulfilment of human rights and so as to recognise the ecological as well as the social embeddedness of human life. The human rights framework, however, has only limited utility from an environmental perspective.
>
> (Ibid, 150)

Arguing that not enough attention has been paid to the inherent incompatibility of rights and finite environmental resources (Ibid., 128), she suggests that an awareness of the problems and contradictions within environmental rights must be brought to the fore. And it is these problems and contradictions that the chapters in the volume explore and offer solutions to.

Details of this volume

This volume is rooted within political theory which, as noted earlier distinguishes it from the other collected works on environmental rights such as Anderson and Boyle's *Human Rights Approaches to Environmental Protection*, which is rooted in legal theory, and Grear and Kotzé's *Research Handbook on Human Rights and the Environment*, which sits at the intersection of law and politics. Our focus is primarily that of political theory, on the theories that consider the negotiation of power and of compromise between people and which help us decide who gets what and why, to paraphrase Lasswell (1936). Environmental rights can answer this question by providing a way of assigning environmental resources to subjects which must be respected, and it is only through an engagement with these questions that these rights can be understood.

There are other works on environmental rights that take a political theory approach, namely Jan Hancock's *Environmental Human Rights*, Tim Hayward's *Constitutional Environmental Rights*, Richard Hiskes' *The Human Right to a Green Future* and Kerri Woods' *Human Rights and Environmental Sustainability*. These monographs have helped shape and develop the field, and the contributions to this volume build on these works, showing how our understanding of environmental human rights has developed and the new frontiers of the discipline, whilst also exploring a wider range of perspectives than these texts were able to do.

We believe that these chapters will speak to scholars from different disciplines. The severity and the extent of the environmental challenges that we all now face means that we will need to draw on a multitude of disciplines to provide the tools to equip ourselves and respond. Environmental rights as a concept also sits at the nexus of different fields – they are linked to the practice and theory of the law for example and their implementation is a question of comparative politics. The understanding of rights and who should be classed as a rights-holder has philosophical implications, as the work from Woods, O'Doherty and Düvel shows. Meanwhile the argument regarding the need to explore the context of these rights, as made by Dodsworth and Wissenburg, reflects the work of environmental historians. Students and researchers from these disciplines will therefore find much to interest them in these works and the authors featured here hope that this volume contributes to the larger, multidisciplinary conversation that is required to advance environmental rights and so respond to the environmental crisis as a whole.

Kerri Woods' work on human rights seeks to reorient our understanding of rights around the fact that humanity is ecologically embedded, dependent on the natural world for our very survival. Noting that human rights have long been contested and used to challenge dominant power structures, she argues that they both can and have been adapted to recognise our reliance on non-human nature. She ends by exploring this implication for the rights of future generations and the need to continue to develop our conceptualisation of what environmental human rights will entail and for whom.

Ashley Dodsworth's chapter shows how problematic the concept of rights to natural resources is in the Anthropocene era. If humanity's impact on the environment has been so extensive as to warrant the beginning of a new geological epoch, then surely there can be little 'natural' resources left. Yet this chapter argues that problematising what is meant by natural highlights why rights to these resources are needed.

Ted Benton's chapter explores the limits of the sustainable development framework with regard to the relationship between humanity and the natural world. He shows how the dominance of this approach has closed down other avenues which could provide a more sustainable relationship, and shows the strengths and weaknesses of these alternatives, particularly those grounded in rights.

In his chapter Marcel Wissenburg also considers environmental human rights as rights to nature. Through a close reading of the political canon, he distinguishes two ideal-typical theories of original ownership and acquisition. The first is the 'orthodox' perception associated with right-libertarianism and classical liberalism that understands nature as 'unowned' before individual appropriation. The second is a more 'lenient' tradition, which interprets nature as a common asset of humanity. Although this seems to suggest that what is good for nature (per se) is bad for the environment, and therefore also for environmental human rights, he argues that in fact, an orthodox conception of original non-ownership is a necessary condition for any legitimate theory of environmental human rights, precisely because it is a safeguard against short-sightedness.

One of the most contested areas of environmental rights is that relating to the environmental rights of future generations. The increasing threat of climate change and the fact that people not yet living will bear the consequences of actions taken by present generations presents a conceptual and normative tension. Three of the chapters in the volume engage with the problem of the rights of future people to their environment. The first comes from Hubert Schnueriger, whose work answers an 'ontological worry' of whether people in the future have claims against agents living today. Rejecting both the non-existence objection and the future-rights-of-future-people approach, Schnueriger proposes an alternative that draws upon interests to defend the rights of those yet to come.

Selina O'Doherty's chapter also considers the rights of future people through considering whose responsibility it is to take pre-emptive action to ensure environmental human rights are provided. Where there are rights, there are duties, and this chapter takes an interest theory approach to rights and addresses questions of the responsibilities correlated to environmental human rights. From a moderate cosmopolitan premise and presuming an English School conception of international society, O'Doherty's chapter suggests there is a chain of collective responsibility including individuals, civil society, states and supra-state actors who must all fulfil certain duties in order to provide and protect environmental human rights.

Eike Düvel's chapter (also) considers the implications of rights for future generations. Düvel's work however focuses on the problems of aggregation, considering risk and the uncertainty surrounding precautionary measures. This chapter shows how these problems can be answered in order to justify adaption and mitigation action on behalf of rights of future generations.

Daniel Corrigan's work explores how environmental rights can be fulfilled and enforced. Drawing on the work of Allan Buchanan, Corrigan challenges those who defend an exclusive focus on the constitutional approach to environmental rights, such as May and Daly. Instead his chapter shows how international environmental rights can provide several key benefits, such as providing support for domestic legislation, developing a global framework for a global crisis and responding to a weakness within democracy at the state level.

Petra Gümplová's chapter explores the historical affinity and tension between the international law of human rights and the rights of states to natural resources. She argues that the chief purpose of human rights is to provide a universal standard for regulating the behaviour of states, to limit their sovereignty for the sake of promoting welfare and protecting the equal moral status of individuals. The key point of the argument in this chapter is to show that due to their historical co-originality and due to the transformative impact human rights have had on state sovereignty, international human rights law has direct implications for how we should interpret the scope and extent of states' rights to natural resources.

The rise of environmental concerns has also given a rise to new specific topics in the human rights debates. One of these new issues is how to conceptualise the political significance of landscapes and detect its links to human rights. In their article, Markku Oksanen and Anne Kumpula ask such questions as: Can there be a human right to cultural landscape? How can such a right be justified? And whose duty is to provide or secure landscapes of cultural kind? The protection of landscape is in the public interest requiring land-use regulation since landscapes are typically not singly owned areas. Landscapes considered to have a recognisable cultural character are usually not a product of any single cultural community but an accumulation of traces from several human generations and different cultural communities. Therefore, the authors conclude that the idea of human right to landscape has a dimension of the politics of identity strongly linked to procedural rights.

For all the strengths of this volume, there are some limitations. The main limitation of this work is the lack of explicit discussion of the Global South, with only Petra Gümplová's discussion of sovereignty in post-colonial states, explicitly engaging with the distinction between environmental resources/access across the globe. This reflects a recurring critique that the discipline of political theory and the discourse of rights are both too western-centric and so this work will share the limitations of the approaches it explores.[2] Gümplová's chapter suggests ways in which the issues of the Global South could be addressed further and more work in this area would be useful to broaden the scope of the field. Another area that has been underexplored is that of gender. The discussions of rights in these chapters are designed to apply to all genders and when the term human is used it refers to all people. However, this gender-blindness can overlook the differences and discrimination that female-identified people face. Any discussion of future generations in particular needs to consider the role of sex and gender in creating said generations and the unequal burden that is placed on those who have and raise children, and further work on this topic is needed.

There is also the problem of anthropocentrism. This criticism can apply to all accounts of environmental rights (Shelton 1991–1992, 104, 108; Redgewell 1996, 71) because, as Anderson puts it 'a human right to environmental protection, no matter how ambitious in its protective objectives is still at base a human right and is very different from a right bestowed upon nonhuman species or upon natural resources' (Anderson 1996, 14). Conceptions of rights to the environment will be anthropocentric if they regard the environment as a site and means for human labour and activity, as a thing to be distributed to people, and a volume on environmental human rights is particularly open to this critique. Yet not all environmental rights do this, for examining the rights of humanity to their environment need not automatically over-ride the rights of non-humans, as Eckersley, Hayward and Woods point out (Eckersley 1996; Hayward 2005; Woods 2010) and as the chapters by Benton and Oksanen and Kumpula in this volume make clear.

There are two reasons why this is so. The first is because environmental rights represent a concern for all humanity, rather than the political interests of a powerful minority. Hayward argues that many of the atrocities that have been attributed to the anthropocentric position, such as over-fishing or the destruction of the rainforest, are not committed in order to benefit all humanity, but to benefit specific groups of humans (Hayward 1998). Indeed, as Hayward made clear, these supposedly 'anthropocentric' actions are often *opposed* by many people and cause great harm to others. This point is followed up, albeit often implicitly, in many of the chapters in this book – Gümplová, Dodsworth and Corrigan for example all draw attention to the unequal use of environmental resources that privileges some over others. Environmental rights are a recognition of our contested environment with competing actors (such as, but not limited to, individuals, communities, or states), fighting over it through political relationships of power and equality. Such rights help navigate these relationships, drawing attention to the differences between actors and breaking down the universalist presumption inherent in *anthropo*centric.

The second and stronger point is that environmental human rights can provide common ground for a consensus between different groups and between the ecocentric and human-centered approaches. The discussions of the necessity, justification and form of environmental rights, as seen in this volume and other works, break down the presumed human/nature divide to show that humans exist within not outside nature. In recognising the variety of ways in which people interact with the non-human world and how humans are dependent on their environment, these rights reflect the central ecocentric claim. The rights-based approach also complements and strengthens animal rights claims. This is not to downplay the differences in these positions, or to suggest that they offer an identical response, but to instead highlight the areas of shared concern and agreement, and the way in which environmental rights reflect this.

There is also a pragmatic element here for, as Kiran Kaur Grewal points out, 'whether we like it or not human rights are currently the main game in town' (2017, 4). Environmental rights can be used as an effective means to secure the goals that are shared by these groups – that they do not have all goals in common, or the same reasons for wanting to achieve these aims does not mean that they should abandon this approach. Instead the overlapping consensus that environmental rights provide is therefore a practical and theoretical advantage that is open to all who wish to challenge environmentally unsustainable and disrespectful practices and should be embraced as such.

Conclusion

This collection explores the tensions and possibilities within environmental human rights from a political theory perspective. Thinking through the definitional, normative, justificatory and conceptual aspects of these rights, they provide new solutions and fresh insight into this concept. Environmental human rights will remain 'essentially contested' but this volume will hopefully help scholars and students alike to have greater clarity and understanding on a concept that is essential to facing the climate crisis that we now face.

Notes

1 Hayward points out the line between positive and negative rights is blurred, that the duty not to do something may require action, as in his example of the negative right not to be tortured, and requires that the state refrain from using such practices but may also require them to take action, e.g. training their agents not to do so and actively prosecuting those who do use torture (Hayward 2005).
2 Hancock and Woods are central exceptions within the existing literature on environmental rights.

References

Anderson, M. (1996) "Human Rights Approaches to Environmental Protection: An Overview" in Boyle, A. and Anderson, M. eds, *Human Rights Approaches to Environmental Protection*. Oxford University Press, Oxford, 1–23.

Barry, J. and Woods, K. (2012) "The Environment" in Goodhard, M. ed, *Human Rights Politics and Practice*, Second Edition, Oxford University Press, New York, 380–395.

Batty, H. and Gray, T. (1996) "Environmental Rights and National Sovereignty" in Caney, S., George, D. and Jones, P. eds, *National Rights, International Obligations*. Westview Press, Oxford, 149–165.

Bentham, J. (1987 [1816]) "Anarchical Fallacies" in Waldron, J. ed, *Nonsense Upon Stilts: Bentham, Burke and Marx on the Rights of Man*. Methuen, London and New York, 46–75.

Benton, T. (1993) *Natural Relations: Ecology, Animal Rights and Social Justice*. Verso, London.

Binion, G. (1995) "Human Rights: A Feminist Perspective" *Human Rights Quarterly*, 17(3), 509–526.

Bunch, C. (1990) "Women's Rights as Human Rights: Toward a Re-Vision of Human Rights" *Human Rights Quarterly*, 12(4), 486–498.

Campbell, T. (2006) *Rights: A Critical Introduction*. Routledge, London.

Cranston, M. (1967) "Human Rights, Real and Supposed" in Raphael, D. D. ed, *Political Theory and the Rights of Man*. Indiana University Press, Bloomington, 43–53.

Dobson, A. (2007) *Green Political Thought*. Fourth Edition. Routledge, London.

Dryzek, J., Honig, B. and Phillips, A. (2006) "Introduction" in Dryzek, J., Honig, B., and Phillips, A., eds, *The Oxford Handbook of Political Theory*. Oxford University Press, New York, 3–41.

Eckersley, R. (1996) "Greening Liberal Democracy: The Rights Discourse Revisited" in Doherty, B. and de Geus, M. eds, *Democracy and Green Political Thought*. Routledge, London, 212–236.

Eckersley, R. (2004) *The Green State*. MIT Press, Cambridge, MA.

Feinburg, J. (1980) *Rights, Justice and the Bounds of Liberty*. Princeton University Press, Princeton.

Gallie, W. B. (1955–1956) "Essentially Contested Concepts" *Proceedings of the Aristotelian Society*, 56, 167–198.

Grear, A. and Korté, L. J. eds. (2015) *Research Handbook on Human Rights and the Environment*. Edward Elgar, Cheltenham.

Hancock, J. (2003) *Environmental Human Rights: Power, Ethics and Law*. Ashgate, Aldershot.

Hardin, G. (1968) "The Tragedy of the Commons" *Science* 162, 1243–1248.

Hart, H. L. A. (1982) *Essays on Bentham: Studies in Jurisprudence and Political Theory*. Oxford University Press, Oxford.

Hayward, T. (1998) *Political Theory and Ecological Values*. Polity Press, Oxford.

Hayward, T. (2005) *Constitutional Environmental Rights*. Oxford University Press, Oxford.

Hiskes, R. P. (2009) *The Human Right to a Green Future*. Cambridge University Press, Cambridge.

Ignatieff, M. (2001) *Human Rights as Politics and Idolatry*. Princeton University Press, Princeton.

Jones, P. (1994) *Rights*. Macmillian, Basingstoke.

Kaur Grewal, K. (2017) *The Socio-Political Practice of Human Rights*. Routledge, Abingdon.

Lagerspetz, E. (1999) "Rationality and Politics in Long-Term Decisions" *Biodiversity and Conservation*, 8, 149–164.

Lasswell, H. (1936) *Politics: Who Gets What When and How*. Whittlesey House, New York.

Oksanen, M. and Kumpula, A. (2013) "Transparency in Conservation: Rare Species, Secret Files, and Democracy" *Environmental Politics*, 22, 975–991.

O'Neill, J. and O'Neill, M. (2012) *Social Justice and the Future of Flood Insurance*. Joseph Rowntree Foundation. www.jrf.org.uk/sites/files/jrf/vulnerable-households-flood-insurance-summary.pdf

Redgewell, C. (1996) "Life, the Universe and Everything: A Critique of Anthropocentric Rights" in Boyle, A. E. and Anderson, M. R. eds, *Human Rights Approaches to Environmental Protection*. Clarendon Press, Oxford, 71–87.

Sax, J. (1990–1991) "The Search for Environmental Rights" *Journal of Land Use and Environmental Law*, 6, 93–105.

Scruton, R. (2013) *Green Philosophy: How to Think Seriously about the Planet*. Atlantic Books, London.

Shelton, D. (1991–1992) "Human Rights, Environmental Rights and the Right to Environment" *Stanford Journal of International Law*, 28, 103–138.

Shorten, A., (2016) *Contemporary Political Theory*. Palgrave, London.

Shue, H. (1980) *Basic Rights: Subsistence, Affluence and U.S. Foreign Policy*. Princeton University Press, Princeton.

Shue, H. (2014) *Climate Justice: Vulnerability and Protection*. Oxford University Press, Oxford.

Steiner, H. (1994) *An Essay on Rights*. Blackwell, Oxford.

Stephens, P. (2016) "EPT and the Liberal Tradition" in Gabrielson, T., Hall, C., Meyer, J. M. and Schlosberg, D. eds, *The Oxford Handbook of Environmental Political Theory*. Oxford University Press, Oxford, 57–71.

Wellman, C. (1995) *Real Rights*. Oxford University Press, New York.

Wissenburg, M. (2006) "Liberalism" in Dobson, A. and Eckersley, R. eds, *Political Theory and the Ecological Challenge*. Cambridge University Press, Cambridge, 20–34.

Woods, K. (2010) *Human Rights and Environmental Sustainability*. Edward Elgar, Cheltenham.

Woods, K. (2016) "Environmental Human Rights" in Gabrielson, T., Hall, C., Meyer, J. M. and Schlosberg, D. eds, *The Oxford Handbook of Environmental Political Theory*. Oxford University Press, Oxford, 333–345.

1 The rights of humans as ecologically embedded beings

Kerri Woods[1]

Introduction

Humans are ecologically embedded beings, that is to say, we are dependent upon, and in important ways vulnerable to, the non-human environments in which we live. We need air to breathe, water to drink, soil to grow food. We also need shelter from natural phenomena such as hostile weather, extremes of cold and heat, and we try to protect ourselves from viruses and bacteria. In short, our materiality renders us vulnerable to our environment (Grear 2013). We are said to have human rights in virtue of our humanity. Rights are a social phenomenon; we do not, and could not, have rights against weather or viruses. We have rights against other human beings, or, more specifically, against human institutions. For the most part, human rights are codified such that we have rights against our own governments. Human rights tell us much about what we understand human beings to be, both individually and in relation to one another.

Historically, human rights law and practice has had comparatively little to say about the rights, and much less any associated duties, that humans hold with respect to their environments. Indeed, while human rights have recognised the materiality of human beings to a degree, it is nevertheless clear that the vision of the human at the centre of human rights has not paradigmatically been an ecologically embedded being, that is, one whose dependence upon the non-human environment is central to the self-conception of the human. However, this historical omission need not lead us to reject human rights as a framework for addressing urgent environmental challenges. For a brief study of the history of human rights also tells us that, in both law and in political practice, human rights are malleable. While critics have worried that the 'protean' character of human rights is evidence of their ultimate meaninglessness (Glendon 1994), social movements have proven that the enduring appeal of human rights presents an opportunity to harness a dominant normative language to advance new causes.

In the process of adopting human rights, social movements have also served to redefine them (Stammers 1999). In redefining human rights, we begin to challenge the dominant idea of the human, and of the community, which practices of human rights affirm. Thus, the remarkable dominance of human rights as a global legal and political framework presents a strategic opportunity from an environmental point of view to foster a view of the human as an ecologically embedded being, and to fully articulate the rights and the duties that such a vision of the human might entail.

In this chapter, I begin by commenting briefly on the history of human rights, not to give a full account of how human rights came to be accepted as dominant norms, but rather to highlight the ways in which human rights practice has simultaneously defined and challenged dominant normative visions of what it is to be a human being and who falls within the scope of the community of justice demarcated by these rights. I endorse Henry Shue's (1990) notion that human rights as codified in international law after World War II were enacted to protect the human against 'standard threats'. In the second section, I outline some of the ways in which widely accepted human rights are severely threatened by environmental issues both now and in the future. This being accepted, there is a *prima facie* case for either an extensionist defence of environmental human rights, or the articulation and recognition of new, distinctly environmental human rights. I then proceed to a discussion of recent developments in human rights legal practice that point tentatively towards an emergent body of environmental human rights. Finally, I reflect on what these emerging trends suggest about the ways in which we understand the human and the scope of the community of rights.

The human in the history of human rights

There is a tendency in legal and political thought to downplay the historicity of human rights. For example, Charles Beitz's (2009) influential analysis of human rights takes as its point of departure the advent of human rights institutions in the post–Second World War settlement. Yet, as historians and sociologists have long noted, human rights can trace their origins at least to the 18th century declarations of rights in revolutionary America and France, and to the texts and movements which shaped those events (Hunt 2007; Ishay 2008; Stammers 1999). Seventeenth- and eighteenth-century natural rights theorists had a palpable influence on the content of the rights proclaimed by the American and French revolutionaries. The anti-slavery movements, feminist movements and workers' rights movements of the 19th century also profoundly shaped 20th-century understandings of human rights.

Human rights declarations are written by human beings in a particular historical and social context. It should not surprise us, then, that despite the purported universalism of human rights, they vary at times, as they are shaped by circumstance, time and place. Nor need it follow from this that human rights are not in an important sense true: We may accept as true the claim that there are certain forms of treatment that ought never to be visited on any human being anywhere, or that there are certain thresholds of well-being below which no human being should be permitted to fall, whilst at the same time affirming that particular legal or political declarations of rights have not accurately captured that truth (Woods 2014).

It is not always easy to identify the subject of human rights. There are national and international human rights laws, there are philosophical debates about what kinds of rights human beings (should) have and why, and there are political claims advanced by social movements and political actors who appeal to human rights as a moral standard. I take human rights practice to be the sum of all of these processes, and possibly more.

Understood in this way, the history of human rights is a history of contestation. For example, the Declaration of the Rights of Man and the Citizen which was proclaimed in France in 1791 was universalistic in its ambition – note it refers to the rights of 'man', so potentially all men. It was written by privileged men who had read the natural rights theorists, who were both excited by the ideas of the Enlightenment and caught up in the exhilaration and zeal of a revolutionary movement. It proclaimed many rights that we continue to recognise as human rights – rights against torture and political despotism, rights to freedom of conscience and assembly – but it restricted these rights to white men who were Catholics. Neither women, nor non-Europeans, nor Protestants, nor Jews were considered to belong within the community of justice demarcated by the status of rights-bearer. Vigorous debate ensued, within the National Assembly and in the wider public and press. Within months the community of justice was expanded to include all Christian men, and subsequently Jews. Yet claims for the rights of women, powerfully articulated by Olympe de Gouges, who was herself a significant political figure at the time, were dismissed, as were the rights of non-Europeans (van Kley 1994; Hunt 2007).

This process of contestation gives rise to a worry, that human rights are 'protean' in character – that they can be re-shaped to fit new demands as they arise, and that in fact they invite new demands. New claims that are comparatively trivial are presented in the same language, and thus on the same moral terms, as grave wrongs such as torture. Human rights, we are told, are inalienable and indivisible, but, the sceptic asks, is the right to freedom from discrimination on the grounds of gender really so very urgent and important as the right not to be tortured?[2] Persons previously considered to be outside the moral community demarcated by the status of rights-bearer demand a place within the community of rights. Hence, we now have human rights treaties affirming the rights of women, children, and all men of whatever colour or creed. Principles of universal rights for LGBT people have been the subject of global debate. As the community of rights expands, the picture of the paradigmatic rights-bearer changes.

But these changes are sometimes met with hostility, not just concerning objections to particular rights (e.g., social and economic rights), or particular rights-bearers (e.g., children), but also on grounds relating to the principle and standing of human rights themselves. This process of contestation and expansion, it is claimed, diminishes the potency of all human rights claims and betrays at best confusion on the part of the proponents for these new human rights. If anyone can be a subject of human rights, and anything can be an object, then human rights violations, far from becoming rare and serious and terrible, will become common and relatively trivial. Carried to its conclusion, this worry would lead us to dismiss the very idea of environmental human rights as just another manifestation of the endless proliferation of human rights claims, which dilutes the significance of those core rights that are *really* human rights.

There is not nothing in this worry, but I think it can be substantially resisted. Certainly, we need not be seduced by it into giving up on a moral idea and legal and political framework that has gained remarkable legitimacy since the Universal Declaration of Human Rights (UDHR) in 1948. Human rights do not guarantee a good life, or happiness; instead they denote a set of moral minimums for a decent human life. We might profitably follow Henry Shue (1990) in speaking of 'basic rights' which protect against 'standard threats' to human dignity. These standard threats speak to the universalism of human rights: Though human societies may differ radically, there are features and practices of social and political life which would be a threat to a minimally decent human life in any context. Human rights express the moral claim that no human being, no matter who or where they are, should be subjected to these things.

The protean character of human rights is explained when we consider that as the shape and content of such threats has changed over time, so the shape and content of what are widely held to be humans' fundamental rights has likewise changed. On one level this is purely technical: Changes in technology have had a profound effect on the ways in which humans live and organise themselves politically and economically; we would expect the legal frameworks that we use to demarcate standards of a minimally decent life to similarly change. But the example of the scope of rights as understood in 18th-century France should also alert us to the ways in which our perception of standard threats is shaped by ideology as much as by practicalities. The content of rights is in part shaped by those who we take to be axiomatic of the category 'human'. If you understand propertied white men to be the paradigmatic human being, then you will not consider food shortages to be amongst the 'standard threats' to the dignity of human beings. The Anglo-American revolutionary Thomas Paine was amongst the few natural rights theorists to take seriously the idea of welfare rights. It took the struggles of 19th-century socialist movements and the presence of socialist and communist state representatives on the drafting committee that created the UDHR to deliver a commitment to both civil and political rights as well as social, economic and latterly cultural rights (Ishay 2008; Woods 2014). Even so, the reception of social and economic rights was shaped by the history of their relative absence from texts that were accepted as authoritative accounts of natural rights – hence, the energetic and to some extent ongoing debate as to whether subsistence rights are really human rights (Cranston 1968; Shue 1990; Pogge 2002).

This history is relevant not just to understanding the ways in which contemporary innovations in human rights theory and practice might respond to environmental issues, but also to understanding both the potential and problematic heritage of human rights from an environmental point of view. Human rights express a vision of the paradigmatic human, which develops over time. If that is true, then, if it is the case that the human in human rights theory is one who stands independent of her environment, who is recognised as socially embedded (otherwise we would not have rights at all) but not really as ecologically embedded, then, insofar as human rights represent an authoritative set of global norms, they are in fact seriously troubling from an environmental point of view. Indeed, ecocentric theorists have long pointed to the traditions of thought to which human rights are substantially indebted as having articulated and perpetuated a vision of the human as apart from nature, as valuing nature at best instrumentally, and as ultimately conceiving of non-human nature as utterly disposable (see, *inter alia*, Marshall 1995, Davies et al. 2018).

The environment and/in human rights

What does it mean to say that humans are ecologically embedded beings? We are material, bio-physical beings: we need air, soil, water and shelter in order to survive. For our access to air, soil and water to be sustainable, we also need functioning ecosystem services, like a stable climate and sustainable levels of biodiversity. We are only beginning to fully understand the complexity of ecological systems. In profound ways, our very existence is utterly dependent upon non-human nature.

It is clear that currently dominant patterns of production and consumption of natural resources are unsustainable, given the scale of the human population and both the volume and nature of pollutants being produced. Though some steps are being taken to move towards cleaner modes of energy production and to reduce waste and pollution, it remains the case that the globalised economy wreaks massive and systemic environmental damage on the planet every year. To take only the example of climate change (which is arguably the most pressing environmental issue at a global level, but by no means the only one), there is a substantial body of scientific evidence of anthropogenic climate change generating profound impacts that threaten the human rights of current and future human beings.[3]

As Simon Caney has noted, climate change violates at least three human rights that are widely recognised and codified in international law: the right to life, the right to health, and the right to subsistence (Caney 2010). Climate change causes an increase in the frequency of severe weather events such as storms, flooding, landslides, tornadoes, and also increases the severity of extreme weather such as extreme heat and droughts (IPCC 2014). People have died and will die from these conditions. These phenomena will intensify if the worst predictions of climate change are not mitigated. Insofar as anthropogenic climate change has exacerbated these conditions, it is plausible to speak of these deaths not as natural tragedies, but as human rights violations. Similarly, climate change impacts upon human health. Changes in average temperatures and in patterns of rain are predicted to substantially increase the geographical spread of various tropical diseases, thereby exposing more people to the risk of (potentially severe) ill health. Finally, in disrupting global food supply chains and pushing up prices, climate change impacts upon human rights to subsistence. These human rights impacts will fall disproportionately on persons already burdened by poverty, disease and conditions of insecurity. Residents of low-lying areas, particularly those in Pacific Island States and indigenous groups in Arctic regions, will be especially affected and potentially face their homelands being submerged.

The existence of the human right to health, rights to water and food, as well as rights to self-determination with respect to territory, may be said to affirm the materiality of human beings, and to implicitly recognise the human as an ecologically embedded being. Such rights have certainly opened the door to an extensionist approach to environmental human rights, that is, an approach that takes currently recognised human rights and adapts them for environmental ends, essentially extending the human rights already accepted and affirmed in law rather than arguing for a more fundamental change in the shape of recognition of new rights. This approach has its merits: It is certainly less controversial, and in making use of existing resources has the potential to facilitate urgent environmental protections that cannot wait for the years of campaigning and negotiation that precede the agreement of new human rights laws nationally or internationally.

Yet, in taking human rights as they are currently to be found, the extensionist approach does little to affirm the complexity of human dependence on non-human nature. Breathable air, usable soil and clean water are not simply resources that can be extracted and consumed. They exist within intricate ecological systems on which we ultimately depend, and which we have altered, to our palpable harm. If our rights to the tangible environmental resources are to be secure, our relationship to non-human nature must be fundamentally re-oriented towards one of stewardship, as Aldo Leopold suggested many decades ago, and away from an attitude of appropriation and mastery (Attfield 1999). This relationship potentially suggests a heightened salience for the duties that are logically correlative to claim rights (Jones 1994). Uniquely amongst international human rights agreements, the African Charter of Human and Peoples Rights includes a list of duties. For the most part, however, human rights documents give moral primacy to the legitimate claims of the human subject. Earlier generations of green scholars gave considerable attention to questions of how the relationship between the human and the non-human might be re-thought so as to shift the balance away from a presumption of entitlement, and of how practices of production and consumption, and indeed ways of living, might be rendered genuinely sustainable (Dobson 2000; Hayward 2005). However, this larger question of what a green good life looks like is somewhat neglected by theorists like Caney who come to environmental issues via a concern with human rights first, and who typically advocate the extensionist approach.

Nevertheless, one need not be an ecocentrist to endorse the view that the non-human environment matters beyond its immediate connection to human rights. More generally, environmentalists have long held that a sense of place and a connection to non-human nature is crucial to most humans' well-being. This conviction is evident in research that is unequivocally anthropocentric, such as the Millennium Ecosystem Assessment (MA 2005), which demonstrates the instrumental value of the non-human environment for multiple facets of human well-being. Human rights aim to protect more than bare existence; they aim to protect the necessary and sufficient conditions for a minimally decent life. For many of us, there is a sense in which we are psychologically or spiritually connected to non-human nature. Indeed, for some, the whole paradigm of human rights is deeply flawed insofar as it cannot escape an instrumental valuation of the non-human world. From an ecocentric point of view, the failure to appreciate the intrinsic value of the non-human world is both symptomatic of, and at least partially causally responsible for, a much deeper malaise from which environmental degradation inevitably results (Marshall 1995; Naess 2003).

The closest the human rights framework comes to dealing with this concern is in attempting to protect the particular connection between indigenous peoples and the environments in which they live, which was recognised in the United Nations' Declaration on the Rights of Indigenous Peoples (2007), which is obviously a fairly recent addition to the body of international human rights. Theorists have also drawn on the human rights framework to press for recognising non-human entities as having the same moral standing as is afforded to humans (Redgwell 1996). Animal rights lawyers have argued that some of the protections of human rights law should be afforded to higher apes such as chimpanzees and orangutans (Woods 2016). More fundamentally, there are diverse strands in human rights practice that point to the notion of environmental human rights being an emergent norm, albeit in extensionist and anthropocentric form. In the next section I summarise some of these developments.

Environmental human rights as an emergent norm?

In 1987, the influential Brundlandt report, *Our Common Future*, defined sustainable development as development that 'meets the needs of the present without compromising the ability of future generations to meet their own needs' (Brundtland et al. 1987). Following this formulation, the right to development has importantly been understood as bringing together concerns of human rights and sustainability. This connection between sustainability and rights was affirmed in Agenda 21, the agreement reached at the 1992 Earth Summit in Rio. The first article states: 'Human beings are at the centre of concerns for sustainable development. They are entitled to a healthy and productive life in harmony with nature' (Gearty 2010: 18). Agenda 21 also committed states, intergovernmental organisations and large corporations to 'protecting the resource base and the environment for the benefit of future generations' (Ibid.). This commitment to realising current generations' rights whilst being mindful of justice to future generations and being in harmony with nature was seen in the Millennium Development Goals and reaffirmed in the Sustainable Development Goals (SDGs).

The idea that we cannot allow current development practices to fundamentally compromise the rights of future generations has apparently become an orthodoxy. And yet, it is far from clear that the two demands – that of ensuring current generations' rights to development and that of ensuring environmental sustainability – are in any sense on course to be met. Recent analysis of the SDGs indicates conflict rather than harmony between the policies that are being promoted to advance development rights and those that are being pursued in the name of sustainability (Spaiser et al. 2016). Both the orthodoxy and the policy failures can be observed in other contexts. The national constitutions of over 90 states worldwide make some reference to the environment in relation to the rights of citizens (Hayward 2005; Jeffords and Gellers 2017). Though some states undoubtedly do better than others (the global Environmental Sustainability Index is one useful barometer of this), it remains the case that few if any states today can be said to be fully honouring their environmental obligations.

Nevertheless, the recognition of environmental rights in national constitutions is important. As Richard Hiskes (2009) argues, constitutions (like human rights treaties) express political communities' shared values, and importantly shape the institutions that are bequeathed to future generations. Constitutional recognition of the importance of the non-human environment expresses a relationship between a political community and its physical home. This is partly related to the significance of territory for the modern nation-state: Most would consider the identity of the nation to be in some sense compromised were it sepa-rated from its territory. This connection between territory and community sheds light on the seriousness of the harm that will befall Pacific Island states if, as seems likely, they are forced to leave their homes. But references to environmen-tal goods in national constitutions are not limited to territory. Indeed, a growing number of constitutions affirm some formulation of a right to a safe, clean or healthy environment, as rights theorists from James Nickel to Tim Hayward have argued is the only consistent position for any liberal democratic state (Nickel 1993; Hayward 2005).

Within the United Nations organisations there have been several initiatives affirming the inherent interconnection between human rights and the environ-ment. A 1994 United Nations Environment Programme report highlighted the human rights impacts of environmental harms. In 2009, the United Nations High Commissioner for Human Rights appointed an Independent Expert, John Knox, subsequently a Special Rapporteur, to advise on the links between human rights and the environment, and to promote best practice both amongst UN agencies and national governments.

Knox (2012) has identified emergent environmental norms in global human rights practice, particularly in relation to the use of procedural human rights to protect environmental campaigners and to facilitate informed environmental protest against harmful development practices. Particularly salient in the Euro-pean context has been the 1998 Aarhus Convention, which has been com-mended as a model of good practice for protecting citizens' rights to information about proposed developments and their environmental impacts, for protecting citizens' rights to participate in decision-making processes, and facilitating citi-zens' access to justice in the event of conflicts (Boyle 2008).

Of course, different jurisdictions have differing norms and progress in one area may well be made alongside setbacks elsewhere.[4] Moreover, it is clear that there have been many cases where the invocation of human rights principles has served to frustrate rather than further environmental protection, e.g., in cases of conflict between the demands of human rights such as rights to property, rights to devel-opment, and claims for environmental protection (Pedersen 2010; Gearty 2010). Rights not directly linked to the environment, such as civil and political rights protecting freedom of speech, freedom of association, and rights to due process, have often been more valuable from the point of view of environmental defend-ers than substantive environmental rights (Gearty 2010; Sachs 1995).

Nevertheless, a few landmark cases have been widely noted. One is the Minors Oposa case of 1993, in which the Philippines Ecological Network successfully brought a case against the government of the Philippines in the name of both current children and future generations. The government of the Philippines was found to be violating current and future children's rights to a healthy environ-ment through its sale of logging rights. More recently, in 2015, a Dutch court ruled in favour of holding the government to owe a duty of care to future generations in the *Urgenda* case (Davies et al. 2018). These rulings are held to be significant because of the recognition of future persons as having rights claims that give rise to correlative duties before those persons come into being. Given the intergenerational nature of many environmental problems, and the economic rationality of 'discounting the future', the 'standard threats' to their dignity and rights faced by future generations will have been substantially caused by the actions prior to their birth, in some cases decades prior. That being the case, it is potentially crucial to the well-being of future generations that their rights be recognised now.

The environmental issue that has received the most sustained political, public and media attention in recent years has undoubtedly been climate change. Although there is agreement amongst the IPCC that some impacts of climate change are most likely observable now, the worst effects of climate change will be felt in the latter half of the 21st century, unless substantial mitigation efforts are undertaken now. As such, a significant proportion of the people whose human rights are most at risk from climate change are yet to be born. The Conference of Parties (COP)21 in Paris in December 2015 concluded years of negotiations to reach a global agreement on tackling climate change. In the months around COP21 there were sustained efforts by governments and NGOs to have included in the text of the agreement references to the human rights impacts of climate change, both now and in the future. A cluster of civil society networks, including a global network of environmental and legal scholars, the Global Network for the Study of Human Rights and the Environment (GNHRE)[5] published proposed texts for declarations of climate change and human rights (Davies et al. 2018). These texts drew on the understandings of the human and non-human nature found in the Declaration on the Rights of Indigenous Peoples, as well as canonical texts like the Rio declaration and the Brundtland report. The GNHRE declaration contained several notably ecocentric statements, including amongst its preamble recognition 'that human beings are part of the living Earth system'; article 2, 'All human beings, animals and living systems have the right to a secure, healthy and ecologically sound Earth system,' and article 7, 'All human beings, animals and living systems have the right to fairness, equity and justice in respect of responses to the threat of climate change' (GNHRE 2016). The declaration affirmed a vision of the human as closely connected to her environment, and as belonging to an intergenerational community (Davies et al. 2018).

Developments such as this and the above cases affirming the rights of future generations call to mind the ways in which the protean character of rights presents an opportunity to challenge dominant norms that have become stale or unhelpful. Human rights at one level reflect hegemonic norms, but they also represent a powerful tool of resistance and change. As circumstances change, we are forced to reconsider what might count as a standard threat to a minimally decent life. In so doing, we are prompted to reflect on the nature of the human being herself, and in proposing new rights, human rights scholars and activists implicitly propose to change the way we understand ourselves and our community.

The Paris talks proved an intriguing focal point for debates about the status of future generations' human rights, the merits of the extensionist approach as opposed to proposing a substantive new right, and the challenges of translating the moral claims in human rights theory into a given policy framework. Despite a considerable groundswell of support in favour of explicitly linking human rights and climate change in the COP21 agreement, substantive references to human rights were ultimately not included in the text. Though it was regarded at the time as something of a political triumph that there was any agreement at all, there was also disappointment at the absence of binding (as opposed to voluntary) carbon emissions caps in the agreement, as well as regarding the relative silence on the interconnection of human rights and climate change (Harvey 2016).

It seems, then, that the idea of environmental human rights is a fledgling global norm: The inherent connection between a sustainable environment and development is widely affirmed, as is recognition of the significance of a healthy environment for citizens' constitutional rights. The status of future generations' rights is less certain; for the most part, human rights legal practice is concerned with the rights of present rather than future generations (Knox 2012). At the same time, it remains the case that, as the global population continues to rise, the global economy depends upon unsustainable patterns of production and consumption which will visit potentially devastating harms on future generations. Against this backdrop there has been an explosion of scholarly literature defending the environmental rights of future generations.

Ecologically embedded beings and the community of rights

I have argued that humans are ecologically embedded beings, and that the protean character of human rights offers at least the possibility of challenging the conception of the human that is more readily deduced from human rights texts and generally accepted principles. In this final section, I will consider some implications for both this conceptualisation of the human and the scope of the community of rights.

In existing human rights, we find the materiality of humans recognised insofar as humans are recognised as having rights to health and to subsistence. This signals that we are vulnerable to our environment, but it at best leaves opaque the complexity of our relationship to non-human nature. In order to live a minimally decent life we need access to consumable environmental resources such as air, water and soil, but those tangible environmental resources themselves depend upon less tangible environmental services like a stable climate and a fairly robust level of biodiversity. If humans individually have rights to any environmental resources, we must also collectively have implicit obligations to sustain the underlying ecological systems, since the latter are a precondition for the availability of the former. That being the case, environmental human rights imply an orientation of something akin to stewardship towards non-human nature, rather than one of mastery and appropriation. This line of argument does not defeat the ecocentric critique of human rights as privileging an instrumental valuation of non-human nature, but nor does it preclude accepting the claim that nature has intrinsic value. Human rights need not – probably could not – cover all ethical claims. One can affirm the primacy of human rights as a framework for evaluating contemporary social and political issues whilst accepting their limitations.

Although human rights law only exceptionally recognises the human rights of future generations, a growing body of literature in legal and political thought does affirm the rights of future people, one way or another. There are many interesting points of division in this literature; here I want to pick up only one: What should be the content of the rights of future people? This is a relevant question, as it is not settled simply by accepting the claim that we should extend the scope of the community of rights to include future humans. I noted above that it has often been through the actions and demands of those excluded from a community of rights that their claims to equal treatment have been recognised, and this has led to both an expansion in the community of rights and with it a degree of re-thinking of the paradigmatic subject of rights, which has in turn sometimes affected the content of rights. In this case, however, the content of the rights of future persons is much debated.

Clearly, future generations are not in a position to advocate on their own behalf. By the time they are in a position to do so, it will be too late. Cumulative environmental harms can pass critical, sometimes irreversible thresholds, without actors realising what they have collectively done. Climate change is a classic case of this sort of 'tragedy of the commons'. The question that arises, then, is what sort of rights do future persons have that demand protection now, and how, if these rights were to be recognised, would it affect our understanding of human rights.

Jonas Brännmark (2016) raises an intriguing thought that is closely connected to my acceptance of the protean character of human rights, though he himself does not make that connection. Brännmark takes the future rights of future persons to be rights to a given threshold of environmental quality. Though the threshold model of human rights is held to be problematic by various human rights scholars (Tasioulas 2010), this move need not be controversial in itself given that many human rights in fact function in this way. For example, the right to health is not (and could not be) a right to an absolute standard; rather, it is a right to a socially acceptable threshold, defined principally in terms of access to healthcare. Similarly, one of the earliest and most influential defences of the right to a safe environment defined this right in terms of a threshold – one that would be socially accepted as 'reasonable' for the community (Nickel 1993).

The difficulties that Brännmark sees in this arise if we accept that future generations have human rights claims that can impose duties on us now: (1) We may not be able to judge what an acceptable threshold for a safe or healthy environment will be considered to be 100 years from now. If we again compare environmental rights with health rights, a threshold that might once have been accepted as a reasonable standard of health might well be rejected today. Certainly that is likely to be the case in most wealthy, industrialised countries. However, the thresholds demarcating what is considered to be a reasonable standard of health and access to healthcare from a human rights point of view also varies between countries within a generation. (2) Moreover, even if we do hazard a guess as to what an acceptable standard for future generations might be, we will actually have comparatively little impact on how access to human rights will be distributed within future generations. This is because future generations will have considerable control over how they distribute other goods, such as wealth and political power, which will likely have a significant impact on a given individual's access to their rights in general. Again, if we compare the distribution of rights observable 100 years ago, had we been alive at that time we might have predicted that the remarkable growth of wealth and technology would have been sufficient to end deaths from starvation, malnutrition and readily preventable diseases. We might have thought, if we owed anything to future generations, we had fulfilled that obligation by creating the conditions for the growth in wealth and technology that has come to pass. Brännmark's point is that whatever inheritance we bequeath to future generations, we will have at best very limited ability to shape the ways in which the distribution of power and wealth shapes the actual fulfilment of rights.

This sort of concern is presumably a factor in Richard Hiskes' (2009) vision of intergenerational environmental rights as essentially communitarian rights, rather than universal rights. On Hiskes' account, we owe human rights duties to future generations of our own countries, not to humans in general, for the duties to the latter, he argues, have no motivational purchase for us. We are shaped by our love of our own country, and can be moved to feel an affinity with our own successor generations, but not, Hiskes thinks, with future generations of humanity in general. On the contrary, Brännmark sees future generations as a distinct political group, and intergenerational environmental human rights as a third-generation group right owed to a specific generation. A different view entirely is put forward by the environmental rights sceptic, Wilfred Beckermann (1999), who argues that the most valuable thing that we can bequeath to future generations is not environmental goods at all, but more widespread respect for human rights. Crucial to his reasoning is the environmental impact of conflict: Quite simply, if we could largely eliminate armed conflict and the military-industrial economy, we could take a substantial chunk out of global carbon emissions and resource use.

Far from being competing visions of what is owed to future generations, these apparently different perspectives point in a common direction: What we owe to future generations is a world in which it is at least possible for them to fulfil their future human rights – both in terms of their own rights and in terms of fulfilling their obligations to others. That will be much more readily possible if we bequeath to them an environment that meets a minimum threshold. We cannot know precisely what threshold future generations would choose for themselves, but we can make prudential calculations of what they would not choose – e.g., they would not choose an average rise of global mean temperatures of 2°C, they would not choose rapid rates of species extinction. So we have to work very hard, right now, to substantially mitigate the worst predicted effects of climate change. Insofar as it is true that currently dominant human rights norms do not embrace a conceptualisation of the human as an ecologically embedded being, they make that task a little more difficult. So there is environmental value in thinking seriously, as Beckermann and Hiskes variously suggest, about the political inheritance we bequeath to future generations. It seems likely that human rights will continue to shape peoples' thinking for many years to come – they are not by any means the only game in town, but they have proved an enduringly appealing moral and political concept. If we engage in the project of challenging dominant understandings of human rights so as to fully affirm the human as an ecologically embedded being, then it is feasible to think that there is at least some prospect of improvement in the chances of future generations' rights being protected, not only in the here and now insofar as we extend the scope of the community of rights intergenerationally, but also in the future. Bequeathing a vision of the human in human rights as an ecologically embedded being does not preclude the possibility of this specific notion, or the wider framework of human rights, being rejected by a future generation. Just as the idea of natural rights was largely abandoned by 19th-century thinkers in favour of utilitarianism, so too future thinkers may find the very idea of human rights unhelpful. But, as Brännmark reminds us, we can only work on those factors influencing future rights which it is within our power to affect. As things stand, those factors include both the physical content of the rights of future persons (who will be, regardless of our efforts, ecologically embedded beings) and the conceptual apparatus with which they understand themselves and their rights.

Notes

1 I am grateful to the editors and to contributors to the 2015 Mancept workshop on environmental human rights for helpful feedback and discussion.
2 The answer to this question is yes, insofar as the question misconceives the function of human rights. Human rights protect the conditions for a minimally decent life. Gender

discrimination is an urgent and important wrong insofar as it is a root cause of such harms as female infanticide, FGM, unequal basic education opportunities, unequal provision of healthcare and even basic subsistence.

3 I will largely leave aside here the question of whether future persons can be said to have rights from a philosophical point of view, and will not address the much discussed 'non-identity problem', as I have discussed these at length elsewhere (see Woods 2015, 2016).

4 For a detailed overview, see, inter alia, Gearty 2010; Pedersen 2010; Boyle 2008, Davies et al 2018.

5 Full disclosure: I am a member of this network and was a member of the drafting group for the declaration.

References

Attfield, R. (1999) *The Ethics of the Global Environment*. Edinburgh University Press, Edinburgh.

Beckermann, W. (1999) 'Sustainable Development and Our Obligations to Future Generations' in Dobson, A. ed, *Fairness and Futurity: Essays on Environmental Sustainability and Social Justice*. Oxford University Press, Oxford, 71–92.

Beitz, C.R. (2009) *The Idea of Human Rights*. Oxford University Press, Oxford.

Boyle, A. (2008) 'Human Rights or Environmental Rights? A Reassessment' *Fordham Environmental Law Review*, 18, 471–511.

Brännmark, J. (2016) 'Future Generations as Rights Holders' *Critical Review of International Social and Political Philosophy*, 19, 680–698.

Caney, S. (2010) 'Climate Change, Human Rights, and Moral Thresholds' in Humphreys, S. ed, *Human Rights and Climate Change*. Cambridge University Press, Cambridge, 69–90.

Cranston, M. (1968) 'Human Rights, Real and Supposed' in Raphael, D.D. ed, *Political Theory and the Rights of Man*. Macmillan, London, 43–53.

Davies, K. et al. (2018) 'The Declaration on Human Rights and Climate Change: A New Legal Tool for Global Policy Change' *Journal of Human Rights and the Environment*, Forthcoming.

Dobson, A. (2000) *Green Political Thought* (3rd Edn.). Routledge, London.

Gearty, C. (2010) 'Do Human Rights Help or Hinder Environmental Protection?' *Journal of Human Rights and the Environment*, 1, 7–22.

Glendon, M. (1994) *Rights Talk: The Impoverishment of a Political Discourse*. Free Press, New York, NY.

GNHRE. (2016) Declaration on Human Rights and Climate Change. http://gnhre.org/declaration-human-rights-climate-change/.

Grear, A. (2013) 'Vulnerability, Advanced Global Capitalism and Co-Symptomatic Injustice: Locating the Vulnerable Subject' in Fineman, M.A. and Grear, A. eds, *Vulnerability: Reflections on a New Ethical Foundation for Law and Politics*. Ashgate, Farnham, 41–60.

Harvey, F. (2016) 'Paris Climate Change Agreement Enters Force' *The Guardian*, 4 Nov.

Hayward, T. (2005) *Constitutional Environmental Rights*. Oxford University Press, Oxford.

Hiskes, R. (2009) *The Human Right to a Green Future*. Cambridge University Press, Cambridge.

Hunt, L.A. (2007) *Inventing Human Rights: A History*. Norton, New York, NY.

IPCC. (2014) Climate Change 2014: Synthesis Report. Contribution of the Working Groups I, II, and III to the Fifth Assessment Report of the Intergovernmental Panel on Climate Change. IPCC: Geneva, Switzerland.

Ishay, M.R. (2008) *The History of Human Rights*. University of California Press, Berkeley, CA.

Jeffords, C. and Gellers, J.C. (2017) 'Constitutionalizing Environmental Rights: A Practical Guide' *Journal of Human Rights Practice*, 1.

Jones, P. (1994) *Rights (Issues in Political Theory)*. Macmillan, London.

Knox, J. (2012) Report to the United Nations Human Rights Council of the Independent Expert on the Issue of Human Rights Obligations Relating to the Enjoyment of a Safe, Clean, Healthy and Sustainable Environment. United Nations, A/HRC/22/43.

MA. (2005) Ecosystems and Human Well-Being: A Framework for Assessment. www. millenniumassessment.org/en/Framework.html.

Marshall, P. (1995) *Nature's Web: Rethinking Our Place on Earth*. M. E. Sharpe, London.

Naess, A. (2003) 'The Deep Ecological Movement: Some Philosophical Aspects' in Light, A. and Rolston, H. III eds, *Environmental Ethics: An Anthology*. Blackwell, Oxford, 262–273.

Nickel, J. (1993) 'The Human Right to a Safe Environment: Philosophical Perspectives on Its Scope and Justification' *Yale Journal of International Law*, 18, 281–296.

Pedersen, O. (2010) 'Climate Change and Human Rights: Amicable or Arrested Development?' *Journal of the Environment and Human Rights*, 1, 236–251.

Pogge, T. (2002) *World Poverty and Human Rights*. Polity, Cambridge.

Redgwell, C. (1996) 'Life, the Universe and Everything: A Critique of Anthropocentric Rights' in Boyle, A.E. and Anderson, M.R. eds, *Human Rights Approaches to Environmental Protection*. Clarendon Press, Oxford, 71–88.

Sachs, A. (1995) *Eco-Justice: Linking Human Rights and the Environment*, World Watch Paper 127.

Shue, H. (1990) *Basic Rights: Subsistence, Affluence and US Foreign Policy* (2nd Edn.). Princeton University Press, Princeton, NJ.

Spaiser, V. et al. (2016) 'The Sustainable Development Oxymoron: Quantifying and Modelling the Incompatibility of Sustainable Development Goals' *International Journal of Sustainable Development and World Ecology*, 2016, 1–14.

Stammers, N. (1999) 'Social Movements and the Social Construction of Human Rights' *Human Rights Quarterly*, 21, 980–1008.

Tasioulas, J. (2010) 'Taking Rights Out of Human Rights' *Ethics*, 120, 647–678.

van Kley, D. ed. (1994) *The French Idea of Freedom: The Old Regime and the Declaration of Rights of 1789*. Stanford University Press, Stanford.

Woods, K. (2014) *Human Rights*. Palgrave Macmillan, Basingstoke.

Woods, K. (2015) 'Environmental Human Rights' in Gabrielson, T. et al. eds, *Oxford Handbook for Environmental Political Theory*. Oxford University Press, Oxford, 333–345.

Woods, K. (2016) 'The Rights of Future Humans *Qua* Humans' *Journal of Human Rights*, 15 291–306.

2 Defining the natural in the Anthropocene

What does the right to a 'natural' environment mean now?

Ashley Dodsworth

In January 2014, then British Prime Minister David Cameron announced that his government was 'going all out for shale' (Cameron 2014). This meant that, in order to meet the county's energy needs, the Conservative government would seek to promote hydraulic fracturing, the process in which water and chemicals are pumped underground at high pressure to fracture rocks and release shale gas and which is commonly known as fracking. But fracking is highly controversial and there has been sustained opposition within the UK to the practice. Greenpeace's chief UK scientist Doug Parr for example argued that 'you cannot put a price on the air you breathe, the water you drink or the beauty of the countryside' (Parr, quoted in Mason 2016). Parr's formulation reflected the arguments of anti-fracking activists who protested the decision to over-rule local opposition to fracking in Yorkshire:

> we resolve to continue to fight to remain free from fracking, to protect our communities, our beautiful countryside, our air and water, and to protect the future of the planet . . . it is a war on our human rights to clean air and water.
> (Quotes taken from Parveen and Harvey 2016)

In these arguments there is an implicit understanding of the environment and natural resources as requiring protection from fracking. This idea of defending the environment from human interference is frequently present within environmental protests – the protest movement against building new roads, which became prominent in the 1990s for example, drew upon this conception (see Doherty 1998). The air, the water and the countryside need to be 'left alone', and protected from human activity, and rights language is invoked in order to give strength to these claims and prevent the proposed actions from taking place.

Yet, as Joseph Sax pointed out, there is no right to an untouched environment, for 'surely there can be no precept to leave nature untouched' (Sax 1990, 95). The growing understanding of the Anthropocene age in which we now live gives weight to Sax's point. The present geological epoch has been labelled the

Anthropocene because it has been so shaped and changed by human activity. There is debate surrounding the exact beginning of the Anthropocene as some scholars argue for a date around 8,000–10,000 years ago, whilst others point to 1,500, and some argue that the changes that caused the Anthropocene have occurred since the Second World War (Angus 2015 and see Ruddiman 2005; Steffen, Crutzen and McNeill 2007 for the opposing arguments). That even the latest of these dates is over fifty years ago highlights the breadth of time between the tipping point of human activity, the point at which it marked a new, distinct geological age, and the present. If we are at least fifty years into the Anthropocene, how do we think about 'our beautiful countryside, our air and water'? How do we conceptualise the natural in an age that is defined by human interaction with, if not our destruction of, nature?

This chapter will explore this problem of defining the natural[1] with respect to rights to natural resources. The problem of defining the natural has been raised by Raymond Williams, and discussions of the impact of classification of the Anthropocene epoch for environmental political theory has already begun (as seen in the discussions on the *Inhabiting the Anthropocene* blog) although the implications of this work for the understanding of environmental rights have yet to be explored in detail. Doing so is essential for any understanding of environmental rights and, as we seek to rethink and re-engage with environmental rights, we need to start with the history and context of the subject of such rights. Recognising the history of human interaction with the environment limits the claims that such rights can make, however I will argue that it also shows the necessity of rights to these resources.

In order to make this argument I will first set out this problem, with reference to the insights of Raymond Williams, and with links to Richard White and the debates over the term Capitalocene and the labour theory of property. As a result of this examination, I conclude that it is not possible to speak of a right to *natural* resources. However, this does not mean that such rights are not viable – as the second section will show, most theorists of environmental rights draw upon some form of qualifier in their formulation of such rights. My argument is that the historical context must be recognised, either through adding this term to the qualifiers used or explicitly drawing out what is implicit in the terminology currently used in the literature and the debates surrounding the use of environmental resources. The final section returns to Williams' work to highlight the fact that although recognising the historical fact of human activity upon environmental resources may limit the claims that can be made, it also highlights how important rights are in ensuring the equality of all is recognised within debates over the use of the environment. Problematising the natural reveals that debates over practices such as fracking are not therefore merely debates over whether environmental resources should be used or preserved – instead they are debates over the continuation of use or what type of use is permitted and by whom. Yet a revised understanding of what is natural also reveals how important it is to ensure that there is equal standing in these debates, an equal standing that rights can provide. Revisiting the concept of the natural demonstrates how essential rights to those resources are.

The problem of the natural in the Anthropocene

The geological period that we are living in is termed the Anthropocene in recognition of the extent to which the planet has been marked, influenced and shaped by human activity. As Richard White has pointed out 'long centuries of human labour have left indelible marks on the natural world . . . virtually no place is without evidence of its alteration by human labour' (White 1996, 172). Other commentators have suggested that perhaps the term 'Capitalocene', meaning 'the historical era shaped by relations privileging the endless accumulation of capital' (Moore 2015, 173; see also Malm 2015) might be more appropriate, in recognition of the role that capitalism has played in creating such 'indelible marks'. Using the term Capitalocene also draws attention to the fact that such change is not the equal responsibility of all humanity, but due to the deliberate choices of a minority. This new recognition, of both the extent of human interaction with the natural world and the subsequent point regarding the justification of and responsibility for this, problematises our understanding of natural resources, which in turn creates tensions within the concept of rights to those resources.

This problem was identified by Raymond Williams in his lecture and subsequent essay on *Ideas of Nature*, which examines the development of humanity's understanding of nature. Williams pointed out that humanity has 'mixed our labour with the earth, our forces with its forces too deeply to be able to draw back and separate either out' (Williams 1980, 83). As a result:

> a considerable part of what we call natural landscape has the same kind of history. It is the product of human design and human labour and in admiring it as natural it matters very much whether we suppress that fact of labour or acknowledge it. Some forms of this popular modern idea of nature seem to me to depend on a suppression of the history of human labour . . . [and it may] often confuse us about what nature and the natural are and might be.
>
> (Ibid., 78)

Williams here points out that it is, at the very least, hard to distinguish between what is natural and what is the result of human labour and activity, where the line between human and nature is to be drawn. (He and White also note that this attempt at boundaries implicitly places humans 'outside' of nature, in denial of our ecological embeddedness (a term taken from Kerri Woods – see Woods 2010,

77, 146).) Moore refers to this as the 'one system/two system' problem, wherein scholars of the Anthropocene see humanity as both part of nature and as an outside forcing acting upon it (Moore 2015, 170). This point is sharpened when we consider what is actually meant by labour. Initially labour seems to mean the action of the body, with White noting that growing, harvesting, walking, climbing and other forms of movement through the environment are forms of work (White 1996, 172). However the act of labour goes beyond this. In his discussion of Locke, Daniel Russell extends the understanding of labour further, in a way that is crucial to this argument. Russell notes that labour 'is a directive principle' that turns 'something that might meet a need into something that actually does' (Russell 2004, 309). This identifies labour with human agency, in that it gives shape and direction to natural resources and involves choosing which resources to labour upon and in what way. Thus it

> is not one factor among the many that go into the production of some good, but the very special factor that directs, co-ordinates and organises all the other factors in order to meet goals they cannot meet on their own.
>
> (Ibid., 311)

So it is not the act of drinking in and of itself that classes as labour, but the process of deciding where to drink from, when and how much. Exertion, on White's account, is the mark of labour and Russell's account reminds us that exertion can be both physical and mental. Once the decision-making process is factored into our understanding of labour, then distinguishing between what is 'natural' and what is the result of human activity becomes even more complicated.

This problem, inherent in the discussion of the Anthropocene and the later work on the Capitalocene and explored by Williams and White, relates to the continuing debates surrounding the labour theory of property. This understanding of ownership grows out of Locke's definition of property as the result of combining labour with natural resources (Locke 1980, 19–20). This understanding of property is based explicitly on ownership of natural resources and the way in which human activity can transform them – what is identified in this chapter as a problem is the central appeal for Locke. But there is a key unanswered question here, namely why combining human labour with a natural resource results in the resource belonging to the labourer, or those who hired them, rather than the labour being lost. Robert Nozick illustrates this point with the example of pouring a can of tomato juice into the ocean, pointing out that this action will see the juice lost rather than making the ocean his:

> why isn't mixing what I own with what I don't a way of losing what I own, rather than gaining what I don't? If I own a can of tomato juice and spill it

in the sea so its molecules (made radioactive so I can check) mingle evenly throughout the sea, do I thereby own the sea or have I foolishly dissipated my tomato juice?

(Nozick 1974, 175)

The debate over the labour theory of property is extensive and complex (see for example Cohen 1995 and Wissenburg's contribution to this volume) but it is a useful reference, as the points I am raising in this chapter are the mirror image of this debate. Nozick, Cohen and others examine why combining labour with a natural resource results in a loss of that labour; my question is whether it leads to a loss of the natural – is the sea still a natural resource if I have spilt radioactive tomato juice into it? And what if radioactive juice has been spilt into the ocean for decades?

To illustrate, the labour theory of property, particularly the understanding set out by John Locke, says that if I plant a tree or hire someone to plant it for me (reflecting back to the arguments in favour of the term Capitalocene) in a patch of earth,[2] then I am entitled to exclusively claim the tree and the fruits that result from it are my property. I therefore have a right to the tree and its produce because I have worked upon it and brought about an 'improvement' and increase in the produce of the earth (Locke 1980, 26–27). What I wish to question is do we still see the tree as a natural resource after this activity? On one hand the tree is obviously alive, it grows and responds to its environment, taking in natural resources of its own in the form of water and carbon dioxide and producing waste products, and it completes these processes without human aid. The tree can live on once the original planter has died, indeed it can outlive them for decades if not centuries. On the other, it is the product of human labour and activity which has placed it in this spot and, potentially, helped nurture it through pruning, etc. Furthermore, the choice of human labour has also ensured its survival, as no-one has chopped it down or planted other trees too close to block its light and water and stunt the room for growth. The tree is shaped by human activity, again per-haps decades and even centuries worth of labour, and deciding what is the result of labour is hard to untangle. To return to Williams we have 'mixed our labour with the [tree], our forces with its forces too deeply to be able to draw back and separate either out' (Williams 1980, 83).

Transformation and alternation due to human activity affects almost all natural resources, albeit to a greater or lesser extent. The course of a river, for example, is shaped by damning and building new channels and the make-up of the river itself can be altered by the release of waste products. Oceans can shrink as land is reclaimed from the sea and artificial atolls built, or they can expand as land is deliberately submerged or allowed to sink beneath the waves. The amount of water in the oceans is also affected by human activity as the increasing sea levels due to human-generated climate change show. Even mountains are shaped by human activity, as they are worn away or shaped by people climbing and walking on them, or through blasting for tunnels and passages. A final example will demonstrate this point and the problem that is posed for rights to natural resources. Shari Collins-Chobanian and Richard Hiskes argue for the right to clean soil, as a precursor to the right to food (Collins-Chobanian 2000; Hiskes 2009). In England the make-up of the soil has been shaped by over a millennia of farming, sewage and animal husbandry. The chemical composition of the soil has therefore altered through human activity, as nutrients have been added to the soil through the use of fertilisers and removed through planting and growing crops. The soil has also been dug up and transported, been shaped into ditches, pastures, moats and defensive walls and farmed as small strips or large fields. This activity and its consequences must be factored in to any understanding of 'clean' soil.

This is not then a zero-sum game, in which natural resources are either untouched or destroyed by human activity, but rather a continuum or spectrum, with the boundaries between environmental resources and the products of human activity blurred. Knowledge and awareness of the history of human engagement with 'natural' resources therefore complicates the idea of rights to natural resources. But this does not mean that the right to natural resources is incoherent or unsound. Instead there is a two-part effect – emphasising the need for the *right* to natural resources, whilst complicating the understanding and use of the right to *natural* resources, as the next two sections will demonstrate.

Historical context as an additional qualifier for environmental rights

It is hard to argue for right to natural resources when we cannot be sure where human labour ends and the natural begins. A better formulation would perhaps be a right to environmental resources 'as they currently are', or a right to resources to 'remain in their current state'[3] or rights to resources that are 'safe, clean and historically/contextually informed'. The suggestion of qualifiers to environmental rights reflects the larger literature. For example, Joseph Sax explicitly stated that there is no right to an untouched environment, to prevent trees being felled, rivers dammed or pollution released (Sax 1990, 94–94). Instead he argued that:

> The question is whether the majority can be said to owe to each individual a basic right not to be left to fall below some minimal level of substantial protection against hazard. The question is not free from doubt, but I believe a fundamental right to a substantive entitlement which designates minimum norms should be recognised.
>
> (Ibid., 100)

Later scholars of environmental rights followed Sax's lead and focused on the standard of resources in general. Tim Hayward suggests the right 'of every individual to an environment adequate for their health and well-being' (Hayward 2005, 1) and specifies that this right requires 'the promotion of a certain level of environmental quality' (Ibid., 29). James Nickel defended a 'narrow' conception (Nickel 1993, 284) of a right to a safe environment for 'the environment, or the level of safety from environmental risks should be satisfactory or adequate for health' (Ibid., 285). This is balanced against the recognition that 'the total elimination of risk is impossible' (Ibid., 285). Jan Hancock argues for 'the human right to an environment free from toxic pollution' (Hancock 2003, 107). Hancock's use of the phrase 'toxic pollution', rather than being a tautology, reflects his distinction between naturally occurring hazards and pollution that is created by human activity, with only the latter a violation of environmental rights.

Other works on environmental rights focus on specific resources instead of the generalised approach to the environment as a whole, and these works also use qualifiers. Shari Collins-Chobabianian and Richard Hiskes for example both defend the right to 'clean air, water, and soil' (Collins-Chobanian 2000, 145; Hiskes 2009, 2). This formulation is reflected in the contemporary debates over fracking, with campaigners claiming to be acting in defence of human rights as fracking can threaten access to clean air and water. Qualifiers are therefore already being used in the definition and description of environmental rights – adding awareness of historical context to rights to resources is therefore building on this understanding of how environmental rights work.

As both Nickel and Hayward point out, this looseness of definition that results from the use of qualifiers reflects the definition of other types of rights, such as the right to political participation or education, which are designed to ensure that these rights can be universally applied (Nickel 1993, 285, 295; Hayward 2005, 31). With regard to environmental rights these qualifiers are used in order to reconcile different environmental needs and contexts, reflecting past actions whilst remaining flexible enough to account for future requirements. Using qualifiers such as 'safe', 'clean' or 'free from' allows rights-holders to be involved in the processes whereby these terms are interpreted according to scientific and cultural standards and the community's own relationship with their environment. These terms also reflect the fact that a pristine, untouched environment is not possible, meaning that a right to an untouched environment would not be feasible and furthermore may not be desirable. Again Sax makes this point, noting that an untouched environment would be one without industrialisation and development and so without the benefits that these processes can bring and that rights-holders should be given the necessary information and processes to enable them to make this choice for themselves (Sax 1990, 97–99). This argument is recognising the historical use of environmental resources and the combination of human activity and natural resources that has taken place. What I am arguing is that this recognition needs to be made more explicit and in all formulations of environmental rights.

These qualifications are approaching the problem identified by Williams and White, albeit from the opposite direction. What I am suggesting is that the two concerns need to be brought together, that the historical context of the qualifiers applied to environmental rights must be shown. There is currently an implicit recognition of this in formulations within the literature, such as Sax's point that there is no such thing as a right to an untouched environment. Discussions of rights of indigenous peoples to resources sacred to them, which Hancock and Hayward defend, also suggests an awareness of the larger history of resources and the myriad ways people have interacted with them over time. This needs to be brought to the fore if rights to natural resources are to be of use in the Anthropocene epoch.

For example the definition of resources 'as they currently are/in the form they are presently in' could be used to refer to resources in general. Specific references to historical context could also be added to the qualifiers used, creating a 'right to a safe environment, given its previous use'. Alternatively, the context inherent in the already accepted qualifying terms 'clean', 'adequate' or 'free from' could be explicitly cashed out. A stronger response would be to refer to specific resources, to speak of a right to a lake, or a well in its current condition, with the history of human engagement with that resource noted, rather than a more generalised right to water. As a result the specific context of such resources can be acknowledged more easily. This would also help reframe the debates over the use of the environment. These are not debates over the 'use' vs 'not-use' of a particular environment. Instead they are debates about the 'continuous', 'changed' or 'renewed' use of environmental resources. The debates over building a new road, or beginning the fracking process are not debates over preserving or saving pristine natural resources from being touched by human activity. They are about preventing further use of these resources, or, more specifically, about wanting to use them in a different way. This understanding is often implicit within understandings of environmental rights, as shown by Sax, and environmental protests, as seen in the anti-fracking rhetoric, but it needs to be made more explicit in order to accurately reflect the historical use and labour performed upon 'natural' resources.

The need for rights

The previous section has shown how the recognition of the history of human work upon and within the environment complicates our understanding of 'natural' rights, requiring that the historical context be added to the qualifiers used to define and describe such rights. Yet paradoxically, whilst an awareness of the blurred boundaries surrounding the concept of natural complicates our understanding of rights to these resources, it also shows why such rights are necessary, particularly if we accept the arguments for the Capitalocene. And the reason why rights language remains essential is the equality they ensure for their holders, as this section will show.

Rights are designed to ensure that all have an equal standing[4] from which to make a claim to the world around them. As Marx noted, rights by their 'very nature can consist only in the application of an equal standard' (Marx 2000, 615). To have a right is therefore to count, and to 'count' to the same extent as others, who must acknowledge and fulfil this claim, no matter the disparities in power and status. Rights therefore prevent the individual from being used for the good of all, ensuring that they have a say and a voice in debates that concern them. This idea of equality is particularly central to environmental rights as it reflects how all individuals equally depend upon the environment for survival. While the extent of this reliance may vary, the inherent ecological embeddedness of all human existence is consistent (Woods 2010, 146). The equality of standing and respect implied by rights is therefore necessary to safeguard this most fundamental requirement of (and for) all.

In contrast to the equality that rights discourse is meant to guarantee, recognising the historical uses of resources involves recognising the inequality in this use. Raymond Williams makes this point explicitly: 'if we say only that we have mixed our labour with the earth, our forces with its forces, we are stopping short of the truth that we have done this unequally' (Williams 1980, 84). For when humanity has laboured and acted upon their environment 'what was being moved about and rearranged was not only earth and water but men' (Ibid., 80) and the conquest of nature 'will always include the conquest, the domination or the exploitation of some men by others' (Ibid., 84). Indeed as Williams points out, the act of labouring upon natural resources was historically seen as proof of inequality of ownership, as those who owned environmental resources did not have to labour upon them for their survival, whilst those who did not own resources had to sell their labour to those who did (Ibid., 76). Here Williams anticipates the arguments of scholars such as James W. Moore (Moore 2015) and Andreas Malm (Malm 2015) who develop the term Capitalocene in order to highlight the role of capital in driving environmental transformation and the subsequent destruction of both people and planet. As Malm points out 'the ensuing emissions explosion is the atmospheric legacy of class warfare' (Malm 2015). Capitalocene scholars also draw attention to the unequal responsibility for this change, which is obscured through the use of the universalising term *Anthropocene* that suggests all humanity is equally participant in the transformation of the environment. Yet human activity upon the environment has historically and continues to be carried out under unequal and unfair conditions, with those who performed the labour often denied the results and their activities directed to ends which they themselves did not have a say in.

This point was referenced by Sax, who argued that 'the most tragic images of environmental harm are those involving hapless victims, those who without sufficient knowledge of involvement and without choice had risk and damage imposed upon them' (Sax 1990, 97). Sax and other environmental rights scholars rightly draw attention to the unfair distribution of environmental 'goods' and 'bads' (see Hiskes 2009, 16–21; Woods 2010 and also the larger literature on environmental justice, such as Schlosberg 2007; Walker 2012). This refers to the unequal access that sees some have a greater access to the use of resources, whether in the form of enjoying resources directly, such as walking or swimming (White 1996) or from benefitting from the use of them without sharing the disadvantages, such as having cheap energy without living on top of a fracking site. In contrast others are either unable to access resources directly or have to bear the brunt of pollution or environmental instability, such as those who live by fracking sites or next to a contaminated land site. But a greater explanation is needed to join this recognition – explaining *why* resources are in the condition they are in and through the actions of *whom* is needed to explain and even justify the qualifiers of 'safe' and 'clean'. Hancock comes closest to this in his explanation of the source of 'toxic pollution' and his larger approach to environmental rights, which sets these rights against a capitalist system (Hancock 2003). But this approach needs to be more historically rooted and extended.

Rights provide a solution to this problem, as they provide a way of explaining why past actions are problematic, whilst providing a means of redress that must be acknowledged. If all have a claim to environmental resources, then we have a way to articulate why the past, unequal use of and access to these resources is unfair. And we also have the means through which to ensure that the present use of resources is more equitable. As an example, consider the debate over building a new road or a new housing estate that will involve cutting down a forest. The forest exists due to human activity, either in the form of planting the forest, curating and caring for it, or in the repeated previous decisions *not* to cut it down. To say all have a right to this 'natural' resource is therefore complicated. However in recognising the human labour that has gone into the forest, it becomes clear that this labour was not equally performed – that those who planted or cared for the trees were unlikely to have gained ownership over them and that the previous decisions regarding the use of the forest was unlikely to have been made through full consultation with all affected. Recognising the rights that have been unfulfilled in the course of human activity that have shaped the forest may explain the condition that the resource is in, but it certainly underscores the importance of recognising the rights of all to this resource moving forward in future decisions.

Overall then, while the 'natural resources' or 'environment' part of these rights may be problematic and require contextualisation, this knowledge conversely makes the need for a rights claim stronger.

Conclusion

This chapter has argued that the concept of rights to natural resources is increasingly problematic given our increasing understanding of the effect human activity has had upon the world and the growing recognition of the history of this labour and work. From the work of Raymond Williams and Richard White to the recent discussion of the Anthropocene and Capitalocene, the definition of natural has become contested, as the first section showed. The historical context of resources must therefore be included as a qualifier when formulating rights to resources. That this is not as radical a move as it first seems explains why this problem need not undermine environmental rights entirely. The second section showed that qualifiers are already used to limit environmental rights and provide a more precise definition. Adjectives such as 'safe', 'clean' and 'adequate' are used to reflect the fact that an untouched environment is not possible, a mere pipe dream, and indeed may not even be desirable. The natural is already questioned and defined; what this chapter argues is that historical context needs to be added to this.

Whilst this recognition of the history of human work upon the environment calls into question and destabilises the understanding of the natural, it paradoxically emphasises the need for rights in these disputes. Rights are designed to ensure the equality and equal standing of all, which was not always recognised in the conduct of most labour upon the environment, as Williams again pointed out. There is a long history of human activity upon resources, but it is a history most frequently categorised by inequality and oppression, as the proponents of the term Capitalocene show. Rights however can reflect this difference and provide the means through which to bring about redress and a more equitable future. Rights to natural resources thus emerge as more complicated but more necessary than ever.

One of the key implications of this argument is the need to focus on rights to specific resources. If historical use and context is to be included, and I believe I have shown that it must, then it seems that we cannot speak of generic rights to resources. Forests in Northern Scotland will have a different history to those in Wales, which will differ again from forests in the South of England, and land threatened by fracking in Yorkshire is different from that in other parts of the UK. In the debates surrounding the use of each, the rights involved must be specific, must be the right to this particular resource. In practice there may be little difference, as the rights guarantee the same claims, privileges and liberties.

But the distinction is important. Understanding and practical use of these rights can only be possible when they reflect the resource in question. This is not to suggest that rights must be inherently localised and their holders restricted – and whether or not that would be a useful approach for environmental rights is a question for another day – just that the specific details of the subject of this right must be reflected. Doing so also reflects the differences in environmental resources. To speak of a generalised, universal right to water when referring to water in wells, ponds, oceans, rivers and streams does not pay enough attention to the differences in the form of the resource, differences frequently caused by human activity. The right to *natural* resources will therefore be more specific, and could potentially differ from resource to resource, but they will be more reflective and better able to apply and respond to specific debates over the use of the environment.

It is on this point regarding use that I wish to end. What I have argued in this chapter is that the problem of defining the natural highlights that environmental rights are rights to ensure that a certain type of use is made of the environment and to ensure that all can take part in this debate. This is not a debate over the use or otherwise of resources, between human activity on the one hand and an untouched environment on the other, as White notes. Instead the choice is between continuing use and stopping it, or, more accurately between different kinds of use. To call back to the debate over fracking, debating whether or not to allow fracking to take place is a debate over whether environmental resources should be used to produce energy or as a site for safe housing and living space, about whether the water that is required should be used for industrial processes, or for subsistence requirements, or left in oceans and rivers to provide spiritual and aesthetic enjoyment. We have no right to an untouched, pristine environment. What we do have is a right to participate in the decisions made regarding the natural resources to which we are all entitled and, more importantly, all depend on for our shared survival.

Notes

1 This is a problem linked to language, particularly English – other languages and cultures may have different understanding and terms for environmental resources though my argument regarding the need to recognise historical context will still stand.
2 Locke's argument is underpinned by the concept of the state of nature, in which resources are unowned and available to all. However this concept is not discussed here, due to reasons of space and the central argument that very few resources are untouched and so in a state of nature.
3 This seems to rule out an improvement in resources – rights to water in its current state could perhaps suggest that polluted rivers not be cleaned or that carbon not be taken from the atmosphere. However this objection does not stand as rights represent moral thresholds or minimums (see Caney 2010, 164–165 for an example of this approach),

meaning that the standards they represent are the *least* we are entitled to. Preventing the further degradation of resources is the minimum required, and does not rule out an improvement in their state.

4 Rights have not always been used in this way – indeed the historical context of rights makes very clear that they have been used to exclude with the rights of woman and people of colour, amongst others, systematically denied. This account is not seeking to deny or minimise that fact and the harm that was caused, but instead discuss the ends that rights are meant to secure.

References

Angus, I. (2015) 'When Did the Anthropocene Begin . . . and Why Does It Matter?' *Monthly Review*, 67(4), (http://monthlyreview.org/2015/09/01/when-did-the-anthropocene-beginand-why-does-it-matter/).

Cameron, D. (2014) 'News story: Local councils to receive millions in business rates from shale gas developments', *Announcements* (www.gov.uk/government/news/local-councils-to-receive-millions-in-business-rates-from-shale-gas-developments).

Caney, S. (2010) 'Climate Change, Human Rights and Moral Thresholds', in Gardiner, S.M., Caney, S., Jamieson, D., and Shue, H. eds, *Climate Ethics: Essential Readings*. Oxford University Press, New York, 163–177.

Cohen, G.A. (1995) *Self-Ownership, Freedom and Equality*. Cambridge University Press, Cambridge.

Collins-Chobanian, S. (2000) 'Beyond Sax and Welfare Interests: A Case for Environmental Rights' *Environmental Ethics*, 22, 133–148.

Doherty, B. (1998) 'Opposition to Road-Building' *Parliamentary Affairs*, 51, 370–383.

Hancock, J. (2003) *Environmental Human Rights: Power, Ethics and Law*. Ashgate, Aldershot.

Hayward, T. (2005) *Constitutional Environmental Rights*. Oxford University Press, Oxford.

Hiskes, R.P. (2009) *The Human Right to a Green Future*. Cambridge University Press, Cambridge.

Inhabiting the Anthropocene, ongoing blog series (https://inhabitingtheanthropocene.com).

Locke, J. (1980) *Second Treatise of Government*. Macpherson, C.B. ed. Hackett, Indianapolis.

Malm, A. (2015) 'The Anthropocene Myth' *Jacobin*, (www.jacobinmag.com/2015/03/anthropocene-capitalism-climate-change/).

Marx, K. (2000) 'Critique of the Gotha Programme', in McLellan, D. ed, *Karl Marx: Selected Writings*, Second Edition. Oxford University Press, Oxford, 610–616.

Mason, R. (2016) 'Trying to Bribe Public to Accept Fracking Won't Work, Say Campaigners' *The Guardian* (www.theguardian.com/environment/2016/aug/07/fracking-bribe-public-accept-greenpeace-labour-cash).

Moore, J.W. (2015) *Capitalism in the Web of Life*. Verso, London.

Nickel, J. (1993) 'The Human Right to a Safe Environment' *Yale Journal of International Law*, 18, 281–295.

Nozick, R. (1974) *Anarchy, State and Utopia*. Blackwell, Oxford.

Parveen, N. and Harvey, F. (2016) 'North Yorkshire Council Fracking Declaration a "Declaration of War"' *The Guardian* (www.theguardian.com/environment/2016/may/24/anti-fracking-activists-declare-war-north-yorkshire-ruling-kirby-misperton).

Ruddiman, W.F. (2005) 'How Did Humans First Alter the Global Climate?' *Scientific American*, 292, 46–53.

Russell, D. (2004) 'Locke on Land and Labour', *Philosophical Studies*, 117, 303–325.

Sax, J.L. (1990) 'The Search for Environmental Rights' *Journal of Land Use and Environmental Law*, 6, 93–106.

Schlosberg, D. (2007) *Defining Environmental Justice*. Oxford University Press, New York.

Steffen, W., Crutzen, P.J. and McNeill, J.R. (2007) 'The Anthropocene: Are Humans Now Overwhelming the Great Forces of Nature?' *AMBIO: A Journal of the Human Environment*, 36, 614–621.

Vansintjan, A. (2015) 'The Anthropocene Debate: Why is a Useful Concept Starting to fall apart?' *Uneven Earth* (www.unevenearth.org/2015/06/the-anthropocene-debate/).

Walker, G. (2012) *Environmental Justice*. Routledge, Abington.

White, R. (1996) '"Are You an Environmentalist or Do You Work for a Living?": Work and Nature', in Cronon, W. ed, *Uncommon Ground: Rethinking the Human Place in Nature*. W. W. Norton, New York, 171–185.

Williams, R. (1980) 'The Idea of Nature', in Williams, R., ed, *Problems in Materialism and Culture*. Verso, London, 67–85.

Woods, K. (2010) *Human Rights and Environmental Sustainability*. Edward Elgar, Cheltenham.

3 Reconciliation of nature and society

How far can rights take us?

Ted Benton

Sustainable development: hope and disappointment

First, I will consider the view of our place in nature which has come to shape both elite and popular understanding, and public policy in relation to the rest of nature. More than 20 years ago the green environmental philosopher Robyn Eckersley produced a five-fold typology of such philosophical approaches (Eckersley 1992). The two frames furthest from her preferred ecocentric perspective were 'resource conservation' and 'human welfare' ecologies. Since that time there has risen to dominance a doctrinally pure market fundamentalist ideology according to which the play of market forces, unrestrained by political intervention, will yield optimal results in terms of both want-satisfaction and efficiency in the use of resources. However, widespread experience of what are seen as 'market failures' having to do with the externality to the market of many of the costs and benefits of economic activity has led to the development of the discipline of environmental economics. This retains the basic assumptions of market fundamentalism, and, while recognising market failures, proposes adjustments to market relations as the main way of addressing them. However, even in proposing these adjustments, the perspective cannot avoid recognising a role for state intervention in setting the new boundary conditions under which market exchanges are expected to produce socially or environmentally benign outcomes.

Although at the level of rhetoric the philosophy of unrestrained markets seems to hold sway, in fact some form of accommodation to Eckersley's two categories of resource conservation and human welfare ecology is tacitly accepted. However, in the absence of any over-arching ideological framing, these two sorts of approach are quite indeterminate in their practical implications. Resources needed now might not continue to be, given possible future patterns of want and possible technological advances; not everything that we need from nature is readily interpreted as a 'resource'; and what, indeed, is to be included in the concept of human welfare is a matter for intense controversy.

Fortunately, a more comprehensive ideological framing has been constructed. Historically, this has its roots in the attempts to reconcile two apparently contradictory global demands during the 1970s and 1980s. The first was, crudely, a northern demand which recognised the likelihood of global environmental and hence socio-economic collapse if currently poor countries were to achieve economic parity with currently rich countries. The poor countries were somehow to be persuaded not to degrade their environments and resources in the way that the rich countries had so far done. The second demand was from representatives of the poor countries, as well as those of the poor in the rich countries, that the vast inequalities across the world in peoples' economic and social conditions of life were intolerable and must be addressed by 'development'. In short, undeniable considerations of social and economic justice demanded global economic growth with the probable consequence of mutual ruin. The concept of 'sustainable development', fully articulated in the 1987 Brundtland report (WCED 1987), effected an almost miraculous squaring of the circle: 'development that meets the needs of the present without compromising the ability of future generations to meet their needs'. The international diplomacy, under the auspices of the United Nations, that attempted to put policy content into this aspiration, culminated in the Rio 'Earth Summit' of 1992. This produced a great deal of elaboration of the principles and practices favourable to sustainable development, but only two legally binding agreements: the framework convention on climate change and the convention on biodiversity. These were great achievements, but, with the benefit of hindsight, we can see that they were woefully inadequate by themselves to achieve their aspirations.

Nevertheless, the concept of sustainable development as articulated in that context had profound moral and political significance. First, it insisted on human need-meeting as a universal standard by which to judge social and economic practice and its outcomes. Second, it acknowledged the crucial importance of building into those practices material respect for the naturally given conditions upon which they depend. Third, it proclaimed that the requirements of future generations make a moral claim on the activities of the current generation.

That these challenging claims were radically inconsistent with the prevailing world order was illustrated by the world trading and investment negotiations being conducted simultaneously, but without reference to the Rio process. Starkly put, the concept of sustainable development required normative regulation of international investment to give priority to the meeting the needs of the poor, and to do so in a way that protected the environmental conditions of meeting those needs into the indefinite future. The new trading and investment regime that emerged from the Uruguay round of GATT negotiations aimed to set capital free from regulatory restraints other than those intrinsic to ensuring that only considerations of free exchange and the unhindered pursuit of profit would figure in economic decision-making. The limited role that some nation states and a few supra-national bodies had played in harnessing wealth creation to social and environmental purposes was to be severely restricted and would run the risk of being outlawed as a 'disguised restriction on international trade' (see, e.g. Trebilcock and Howse 1995). The institutionalisation of these prescriptions in the shape of the WTO, IMF, World Bank and related agencies has provided an overwhelmingly powerful bulwark against the implementation of the normative vision of sustainable development. Henceforth poverty would be alleviated as a by-product of the single strategy of unrestrained, globalised capital accumulation. Indeed, poverty was greatly reduced in many previously 'poor' countries, in the sense that large numbers were taken out of poverty. However, it was not reduced in the sense that those millions who were left behind remained poor, and often became still poorer, while a global elite of the super-rich consolidated its power (see, e.g. Stiglitz 2013; Klein 2014, esp. ch 2; Porritt 2005, esp. ch. 5). Meanwhile, the same global process of capital accumulation, unrestrained by recognition of its own dependence on naturally given conditions, produced a multidimensional ecological crisis which it had no means of addressing.

This poses the question: how could the warnings and aspirations of Rio and the demands of sustainable development be so readily swept aside? Part of the answer to this has to do with the power differential between the major global economic institutions and the politically representative organisations of the United Nations. That, of course, leads to further questions about what underlies that differential. One relevant piece of evidence is the growing presence and influence of corporate interests in the subsequent recall conferences of Rio and the associated conferences of the framework convention on climate change and biodiversity convention. Here, I want simply to mention the conceptual transformations of the concept of sustainable development that quite quickly evacuated its normative content and rendered it amenable to the demands of capital.

Key to this was the development of a version of neo-classical economics which attempted to incorporate ecological conditions into economic calculation: to internalise environmental 'externalities', as they are represented in that discipline. This begins with the recognition that economic activity, not to mention human life itself, is dependent upon naturally given conditions in the form of materials, energy sources, pollution sinks, climatic stability and so on, which can be understood functionally through such concepts as 'planetary life-support systems', 'ecosystem services' and so on. The next step is to assign a monetary value to such 'environmental assets', on the basis of cost/benefit calculations of one kind or another. For example, it might be asked what it would cost to replace or compensate for the hypothetical loss of a particular asset and to compare that with the cost of conserving it. This was essentially the method of the well-known Stern Report on the costs and benefits of action to avoid run-away climate change (Stern 2006). A similar logic is currently employed to make the case for conservation of insects which provide 'pollination services': the market value of foods which depend for their quantity or quality on insect pollination is calculated and set against the cost of conservation measures to retain sufficient habitat in agricultural systems.

Once monetary values can be assigned to environmental assets, the way seems to be open to offsetting the tendency for businesses to degrade such assets as clean air, unpolluted waterways and so on as 'free goods', to be exploited without cost. Green taxes, tradable pollution permits and the like can be imposed, converting these assets from free goods to expensive commodities. Taken further as a systematic approach, the values of these immensely varied conditions, processes, materials, living and non-living beings and their interconnections can be totalised and represented as 'natural capital'. It is then possible to speak of the various forms of 'capital' that we rely on for survival and well-being: human-made capital, social capital, human capital and so on (for example, Porritt 2005). A series of new interpretations of 'sustainable development' now come into view, some of them designated 'weak', others 'strong'. Weak sustainability is achieved if total capital is not allowed to deplete over time. That is to say, we are allowed to live off our inherited natural capital so long as we replace it with an equivalent value of human-made capital. Some environmental economists try to set limits to this: sustainability is not consistent with running down 'critical' or 'irreversible' natural capital, for example. A stronger version has the requirement to maintain the value of 'natural capital' across generations, living only on its revenue.

For well-meant but misguided reasons this economistic language has now become the *lingua franca* of the larger organisations in the environmental movement: speaking the language of power and wealth to the powerful and wealthy. There are several reasons for resisting this tempting form of seduction. Interestingly, the approach transgresses one of the major principles of its founding tradition of economic thought: there are no 'objective' values, only the relative values that emerge in the subjective preferences expressed by partners in actual economic exchanges. But, *ex hypothesi*, environmental valuation is designed to assign value to goods which do not figure in market exchanges, and, from the point of view of the conservationists, need to be protected from any such fate.

If, inconsistently, 'objective' value is to be attributed, then on what grounds? Some methods involve questionnaires to access preferences in the absence of actual exchanges, but these produce different outcomes depending on who is asked, how the questions are worded and in any case do not pick up the 'tacit' elements in actual market activity. Alternatively, as in the cases mentioned above of climate change and pollination, hypotheticals are constructed as to the cost of environmental losses compared with the cost of replacing or compensating for them. The problems here are many, but they include the difficulty of incomplete knowledge of consequences of loss of the 'service', and of the technical and social means of repair or replacement over relatively long periods of time. There are unknowns here, both known and unknown unknowns. Relatedly, it is rarely the case that attempts at amelioration of one ecological loss do not impinge on others. Biofuels, for example, might in principle be a carbon-neutral form of energy generation, but taking out the land required to produce them will either impinge on biodiversity or on local food production. Economic cost/benefit analysis is not good at seeing the complex interconnections between different systems of concern. Equally, of course, depending on who is doing the calculation, the matter of *whose* costs and *whose* benefits are at stake, and how to allocate them is unlikely to be 'objective'.

Once subordinated through these devices to the dominant framework of globalising 'free markets', the requirements of 'sustainable development' become conditions for the continued world-wide accumulation of capital. Questions of the socio-economic distributive consequences of 'sustainability' – i.e. questions of social justice – which were central to the Brundtland concept disappear from view, while environmental protection becomes a matter of conserving those aspects of nature which can be shown to provide more economic benefit than could be obtained by degrading or destroying them. While presenting itself as a purely technical framework to guide policy, this new version of sustainability has profound but inexplicit normative assumptions. First, 'sustainability' has become detached from any ethically justifiable or questionable set of purposes. The injunction is to 'carry on' – with what or why is no longer up for debate. The implicit normative assumption, in other words, is that the preservation of the prevailing system of economic relations is an unquestioned good. Second, as just suggested, so long as the conditions for continued economic growth are secured, then matters of social justice in the allocation of the benefits and costs of economic growth simply do not arise: such distributions are value-neutral outcomes of the 'blind' play of market forces. Third, nature figures in economic calculation purely on the basis of its instrumental value. It is of value only in so far as it can be assigned economic value, represented as 'natural capital'.

It is interesting that this framework for thinking about relations between ourselves and between us and the rest of nature has become overwhelmingly dominant among both policy communities and environmental social movements. It is particularly interesting given that its implicit (and occasionally explicit) normative commitments fly in the face of the actual valuations that all of us make in our everyday lives, and exhibit in the life choices we make. My main contention is that these alternative evaluations are key cultural resources that should be recovered, developed and mobilised if the potentially catastrophic consequences of the dominant discourse and the practices it sustains are to be avoided.

Rights: their necessity and insufficiency

The case for rights

So, what are these alternative 'lay' or common sense forms of valuation? Perhaps the most widely shared and most fully articulated philosophically is the morality of rights and justice. In some ways it is a resource for resistance to the economistic paradigm, but it is also surprisingly good at allying itself with it. It is usually universalistic in scope, and often egalitarian, at least in its intentions. In relation to environmental 'bads' it has high potency. The environmental 'externalities' acknowledged by the neo-classical tradition in economics have a history of falling on the lives of socio-economically poor, politically marginalised and often racially delineated sections of the population. Engels's classic 'Condition of the Working Class in England' drew together evidence about the ways in which adulterated foods, poor and overcrowded housing, lack of access to fresh water, lack of sanitation and air pollution affected the lives of working-class families in early to mid-19th-century industrial centres. The injustices of class included not only exploitation, unsafe conditions and insecurity in places of work, but also physically and morally degrading conditions in places of residence and family life. Recognitions of these forms of injustice – together with justified fear of the wider threat of infectious diseases – provoked major public health initiatives which subsequently ameliorated many of those abuses in Britain and many other European countries. However, urban settlements in many other parts of the world continue to share many of the abuses denounced by Engels, and newer, often more insidious environmental threats and costs also affect marginalised and disadvantaged communities even in the most 'developed' countries. Especially in the US a powerful 'environmental justice' movement has protested environmental harms such as poisoning from chemical waste as in the notorious 'Love Canal' episode (Martinez-Alier 2002, Cole & Foster 2001, Mies & Shiva 1993).

The concept of environmental rights has real purchase in such cases, relying on a notion of what conditions are necessary to the living of a satisfactory human life. The liberal rights tradition tends to emphasise freedom of thought and association, freedom from incarceration and inhumane treatment, equality under the law and security in the ownership of property. However, a more socio-economically nuanced version of the liberal tradition also recognises that there is more to having a right than being protected from the abuse of it. Freedom of thought implies universal access to education, equality under the law implies universal access to the necessary resources, while security in ownership of property means something different depending on how much or how little you have. A more ecologically nuanced conception of rights argues the case for the inclusion among those conditions necessary for the living of a satisfactory human life, both negative ones, such as freedom from flooding, toxic air pollutants or hazardous wastes, and positive ones, such as access to green spaces, or availability of accessible and sustainable (!) public transport.

This set of claims, put together as environmental rights claims, can and has provided moral authority and mobilising power. Indeed, the UK government recently (2 November 2016) suffered a legal defeat over its failure to comply with EU legislation on air pollution, which is responsible for some 50,000 premature deaths each year and for many tens of thousands more cases of sublethal suffering. Interestingly, much of the pollution at issue is emitted from diesel vehicles, previously promoted in virtue of their lesser contribution to climate change.

The concept of environmental rights as so far defended remains within the frame of Eckersley's notion of 'human welfare ecology'. It posits a strong link between an appropriate environmental setting and the ability to live a fulfilled human life. Still, it might seem that the concept continues to think of the importance, or value of those conditions as contingent on, the quality of life they confer on the humans who enjoy them. In other words, the position remains anthropocentric, retaining an instrumental, although enlightened, view of the value of non-human nature. I think this is not, or not necessarily, the case, and will return to this later in the argument, but for now it will do just to recall that these thoughts arise from taking the idea of environmental rights beyond defences of the means to satisfy 'basic' or survival needs to a claim for opportunities to realise more fully, or perhaps distinctively, human experiences and responses to nature.

So much for the *content* of rights in relation to nature. The universalism of the discourse of rights points to further questions about the range of subjects who might qualify as bearers of rights. Overwhelmingly the modern philosophy of rights and justice has taken it as given that individual human beings are the paradigm subjects for rights attributions. However, once questions are raised about just which distinctively human characteristics underpin that paradigm status it turns out to be difficult to police the boundary between humans and others. The utilitarian tradition, with its emphasis on pleasure/pain or happiness/suffering as the keys of moral standing, stretches the boundary beyond the human species to all sentient beings. However, the utilitarian calculus gives a contingency to the sorts of treatment of sentient beings that are permissible that sits awkwardly with the main tradition of thinking about rights. Rights are supposed to trump (if I can still use that word) other moral considerations, and are upheld independently of consequences.

In the broadly Kantian tradition, the proposal to take rights beyond the species boundary has been eloquently made by Tom Regan (1988). For Regan, humans have right in virtue of their 'inherent value', and this turns on a set of distinctive attributes: the ability to make autonomous choices, a sense of self-identity through time, capacity to benefit from or be harmed by the actions of others and so on. However, these attributes are shared with other species – most clearly other primates, but also most adult mammals and probably birds, too.

Both evolutionary science and the experience of sharing our lives with members of other species point to the pertinence of these cross-species comparisons. That conceded, it follows that it would be inconsistent and hence unjust to assign inherent value and rights to members of the human species alone. A common objection to this line of reasoning is to argue for a conceptual connection between possession of rights and capacity for moral agency. Since, the argument runs, only humans have moral agency, non-humans cannot properly speaking be bearers of rights. Regan's response is a powerful one. If rights are restricted only to those individuals who have full moral agency, then what is the moral status of those humans who lack that capacity: infants and many groups of psychologically impaired people, such as sufferers from advanced dementia, for example? The options are to deny that such humans are inherently valuable, and so to deny them the status of rights-holders, or to recognise them as vulnerable and dependent beings, and, because of that, especially in need of recognition of their rights to humane treatment. Regan adopts the second option, introducing a category of 'moral patients' who have rights, despite lack of, or impaired, moral agency. If we accept as rights-holders, individual humans who lack full moral agency, then it would be inconsistent to deny that status to animals who share the other attributes that qualify such humans as 'moral patients'.

There are difficulties in Regan's argument, to do with the notion of 'inherent value' and with the comparisons between fully developed non-human animals and damaged or undeveloped humans (this debate now goes under the heading 'the argument from marginal cases'. See e.g. Tanner 2009). Nevertheless, his case for extending rights across the species boundary is a powerful one. Where individuals of a species can be said to be autonomous in pursuit of their needs and interests, they might be protected from harms perpetrated by humans through recognition of their 'negative' rights. That is, restraint on the part of humans from interfering with their autonomous need-meeting and general life activity. However, as the human domain expands, the interests, even survival, of both domesticated varieties and wild species depend increasingly on recognition of a duty of care and of intervention where possible on behalf of vulnerable or threatened individuals, populations and species, to secure the conditions for them to thrive.

Limits of rights 1: inequality

The claims made in these terms for non-human animals to have moral standing, and for this to amount to the attribution of rights to them, have achieved much through their embodiment in animal welfare and rights movements and the practical ethos as well as legislation that they have achieved. Still, however, it is important to indicate some of the limitations of the concept of rights for the achievement of a wider 'settlement' in the relations between humans and the rest of living nature, and to think about other ways in which its achievements might be deepened and extended.

The first and most obvious limitation is that of effectiveness (this and related arguments are made at greater length in Benton 1993, 2006, 2011). Despite near-universal assent to the United Nations Declaration of 1948 and successive deepening of its vision, new forms of slavery have emerged and become widespread, and, short of slavery, large sections of the working population remain *de facto* unprotected from abuses in their working lives, lack free access to health care and are excluded from the law by financial hardship even in those societies with the most historically entrenched legal recognitions of universal rights. In many such regimes it is often the case that the formal recognition of equal rights stands in stark contrast to the inability of many citizens to exercise such rights as are essential to the living of a satisfactory human life. The deepening of social and economic inequalities over recent decades has combined with a coordinated international project to draw back the role of the state in compensating 'left behind' groups and fostering social integration (Devine, Pearmain & Purdy 2009).

If all of this deprives large proportions of the underlying human population from full enjoyment of the rights that their society proclaims, how much more must this be true of the situation of the non-humans whose welfare is dependent on their place in human society? The situation of domestic pets is perhaps the least threatening, and most amenable to the protection of rights. In the case of cats and dogs, their role as pets presupposes 'personality' and the capacity to form emotional bonds. In their case, widespread popular sentiments complement legal requirements regarding their treatment. Even here, however, both neglect and active cruelty, as well as abandonment are not uncommon, and full enforcement of legal requirements is limited by the privacy of the domestic space (also the scene of widespread abuse of vulnerable humans). Still more precarious is the position of domesticated mammals and birds not kept as pets, or companion animals, but for their economic value. The largest category here includes poultry, sheep and cattle bred and managed for food. Some of these have so far resisted incorporation into intensive regimes, but the tendency under modern capitalist agriculture is for them to be kept in close confinement regimes and selectively bred to maximise their 'productivity' and hence profitability. Quite independently of any intentional cruelty or neglectful treatment at the level of individual interactions, they are subjected to systemic abuse of their bodily development and physiological function as well as denial of opportunities to express the psychological and behavioural dispositions of their species. In these cases, active rights and welfare campaigns have imposed restraints on the relevant regimes, but in the absence of wider public scrutiny and democratic accountability the amelioration offered is relatively slight (but no less important for that), and difficult to enforce effectively. This is illustrated by a recent legal case in the UK which inverts the usual hierarchy of rights-holders. A company of contractors has been ordered to compensate trafficked Lithuanian workers who they have used as 'slave labourers' to collect high-welfare organic and free-range eggs (*Guardian* 21/12/16).

Limits of rights 2: unattributable harms

A further feature of the concept of rights as commonly used in political and legal discourse is the identification of the responsible agent who is the actual or potential perpetrator of abuses of the rights of a given subject. Sources of harm to which rights-holders are vulnerable are typically thought of as abusive acts on the part of other individuals, or public bodies – the sovereign power, or state. The difficulty with this, especially in the current period, is that so many of the threats to even the most basic conditions for the well-being of humans and other animals are not readily assignable to any specific agency. Sometimes a specific incident of, say, pollution of a watercourse, can be attributed to release of toxic chemicals from a road accident. However, increases in air pollution from road traffic, loss of wildlife habitat from agricultural intensification, deaths from antibiotic resistant microorganisms, loss of oceanic biodiversity, losses from increased storm and flood damage resulting from climate change – these are all pervasive sources of harm with innumerable sources, more reasonably seen as effects, recognised or not, intended or not, of the dominance of a particular model of civilisation. The German sociologist Ulrich Beck referred to this state of affairs as one of 'organised non-liability' (Beck 1987).

So far the drift of my argument has been to endorse the attempt to extend the protections offered by 'classical' conceptions of rights and justice to include, in the case of humans, defence of those features of their environment that are important to their living a satisfactory human life. The argument also points to the value of including non-human animals within the moral community to whom rights are attributed. The case for animal rights has much to recommend it, and in practice has, along with utilitarian arguments, done much to ameliorate the suffering of large categories of non-humans which have been caught up in human social and economic practices. However, this endorsement of rights-based strategies is subject to some qualifications. One is the unequal *de facto* ability to exercise rights, access to enforcement of them and opportunities to seek remedies in the event of abuses on the part of subordinate groups in profoundly socially and economically unequal societies. This is true of subordinate social groups of human subjects, but is even more pertinent in the case of non-human subjects who depend, as 'moral patients', on vicarious advocacy of their rights claims by human supporters. The second qualification suggested so far has to do with the unattributable, pervasive sources of environmental harms to both humans and non-humans that characterise our current modes of organising social and economic life.

The necessity of rights

Both of these qualifications derive from perceived limitations of the moral (and legal) framework of rights to offer secure protection of the conditions of individual well-being (both human and animal) when adopted in societies such as our own, characterised by (probably) unprecedented levels of inequality, and a dynamic of environmental destruction and degradation that is also unprecedented.

However, to say that the protections offered, and sometimes secured, by rights claims are nevertheless limited in some respects is by no means an argument for abandoning the fight to secure recognition of rights wherever that can be done. Steven Lukes (1985) has argued persuasively that individuals living under even the most benign set of institutions we can imagine would still stand in need of rights. It might be thought that an egalitarian society of abundance might be one in which, in the absence of competition for resources, and without significant differentials of power, citizens would have no interest in harming one another's basic interests and so would spontaneously avoid abusive behaviour. Such social conditions might make the whole apparatus of rights redundant, it seems. However, it should not be just assumed that, if the competitive individualism that intensifies envy, conflict and self-interested dispositions in our own society were removed, people would spontaneously behave in wholly benign and respectful ways to one another. Quite apart from the possibility that some form of 'primary aggression' lurks in the human psyche, as claimed by some psychoanalytic traditions, there are many sources of human personal envy, hostility, disappointment and self-interested dispositions that could not be eliminated by even the most utopian institutional forms. Interestingly, even the deep utopianism of William Morris's *News from Nowhere* (1993) recognises the persistence of sexual jealousy and the suffering of unrequited love. Lukes adds yet another condition which imposes a need for rights. This is lack of complete understanding of one another's needs. Despite wholly benign intentions we may (and probably often do) inflict harm on others through relative ignorance. Rights, such as freedom of expression (and we might add education), can lessen the risk of this in the relations between humans and between them and public authorities, but have less purchase in the case of relations between humans and non-humans whose inner lives are more opaque to us.

These arguments tell powerfully in favour of the continuing necessity for relations to be regulated by the recognition of rights in any feasible future society. At the same time, it is clear that rights are limited in their capacity to secure adequate protections for both humans and animals under contemporary social and economic conditions. This is decidedly not an argument for abandoning the fight to secure recognition of rights wherever that can be done. It is, rather, an argument to the effect that where rights fail to gain sufficient footholds, other moral and cultural resources may need to be called upon as reinforcement. While radical social, economic and ecological transformation can never eliminate the need for recognition of rights, it may still reduce the structural causes of hostile and abusive interactions and so make the demand for enforcement of rights less necessary, or necessary in fewer context of life. It is arguable (and there is empirical evidence in support, here: see, e.g. Wilkinson & Pickett 2009; Layard 2005) that a more egalitarian society, and one in which assets that are important for living a satisfactory life are communally shared would be one in which needs were met more readily and conflicts of interest ameliorated. The apparatus of rights would have less work to do, and might be more effective where it was still needed.

Limits to rights 3: other life forms

So far we have rehearsed some of the limitations of reliance on the assertion of rights as the principal way of restraining the destructive power of current socio-economic processes. These limitations apply both to protection of humans and (some) non-humans. However, there is yet another set of limitations to the effectiveness of rights in their capacity to regulate our relations with the rest of nature. I endorsed the case for extending rights attributions beyond the species boundary, but there are difficulties in relation to how far beyond the species boundary rights can go. So far the most powerful forms of animal advocacy have relied on the claim that other species are similar to ourselves in relevant respects, mostly to do with our capacity to suffer, or to have a sense of ourselves as 'subjects of a life'. If these are the attributes in virtue of which we qualify as bearers of rights, then how far out from close evolutionary relatives of ours do these relevant attributes reach? Mammals, birds and perhaps other vertebrates might qualify. Regan sensibly argues that if in doubt we should be inclusive, but the further out we go beyond the boundaries of our own species, the harder it gets to take seriously the commonalities on which rights attributions rely. Many invertebrates spend most of their lives as little more than feeding automatons, while their adult lives are often brief and with little time or capacity for reflection on identity and the meaning of life. If they possess any inner life at all, it is of necessity quite opaque to us. Beyond the invertebrates are fungi, plants and a huge array of microorganisms. Of course, it is possible to claim that they have rights, and to propose institutional arrangements such that their advocates are able to plead their case (Stone 2010). This, understandably, is an approach that is attractive to radical and environmental lawyers, and where it can gain public support it is a potentially successful one. Again, however, it seems likely that in the absence of the paradigmatic metaphysical underpinnings of rights claims in the subjective lives of persons, and in the absence of any ability on the part of those whose rights are advocated to make the case on their own behalf, the protections on offer will be overridden by more powerful competing claims. Indeed, where rights specific to (some groups of) humans conflict with those of non-humans, then superior power holds sway, as recognised in a poem by John Clare, written between 1812 and 1831:

> Each little tyrant with his little sign
> Shows, where man claims, earth glows no more divine
> On paths to freedom and to childhood dear
> A board sticks up to notice 'no road here'
> And on the tree with ivy overhung
> The hated sign by vulgar taste is hung
> As though the very birds should learn to know
> When they go there they must no further go.
> Thus, with the poor, scared freedom bade good bye
> And much they feel it in the smothered sigh,
> And birds and trees and flowers without a name
> All sighed when lawless law's enclosure came;
>   (from J. Clare, 'The Moors' (or 'The Mores')
>   in Thornton (ed.) 1997:89)

Limits to rights 4: morality and ecosystems

There is another limit to the power of rights advocacy to ameliorate the relations between humans and the rest of nature. This is also to do with scope, and is also implicit in Clare's poem. Where advocacy of rights for non-humans has its most success is in attempts to protect domestic animals of one sort or another from abuse or neglect. What gives these approaches a foothold is that the animals whose fate is at stake are bound up within human social structures, as 'living resources' in agriculture, as quasi-human companions, as experimental subjects, as adjuncts to policing or as subjects for popular entertainment. These animals (including birds) are participants in human societies, standing in definite social relationships to individuals or specific groups of humans, and playing a variety of different parts in social reproduction according to their physical and psychological attributes. It is in virtue of their presence within human societies, along with their mental abilities and vulnerabilities, that it makes sense to include them in the moral community and assign rights to them. Of course, there is something deeply unsettling about this, since so many of the parts played by animals in society rely on a façade of pretence that they are mere objects, 'factors of production', with economic but not moral value. Keith Thomas, at the end of his classic study of changing attitudes to nature in early modern England, explains clearly why this relationship has become so unsettling:

> The early modern period had thus generated feelings which would make
> it increasingly hard for men to come to terms with the uncompromising

methods by which the dominance of their species had been secured. On the one hand they saw an incalculable increase in the comfort and physical well-being or welfare of human beings; on the other they perceived a ruthless exploitation of other forms of animate life. There was thus a growing conflict between the new sensibilities and the material foundations of human society. A mixture of compromise and concealment has so far prevented this conflict from having to be fully resolved. But the issue cannot be completely evaded, and it can be relied upon to recur. It is one of the contradictions upon which modern civilization can be said to rest.

(Thomas 1983:302–303)

So to our second limit of scope. Still the great majority of organisms live, die and interact with one another externally to human society. Let us call these 'wild' animals, plants, etc. Since these do not stand in social relationships to individuals or groups of humans, there is an ecological limit to the plausibility of assigning rights to them, compounding the taxonomic one. Partly this has to do with the way in which ecosystems operate as morality-free zones. Opponents of animal rights often like to score points by reference to the absurdity of blaming a lion or a python for its lack of compassion for its prey. Advocates of animal rights have available the concept of 'moral patient'. Predators are not moral agents and so can have no moral responsibility for what they do, but, like human moral patients, they still have moral standing. Our treatment of them is subject to moral evaluation, while their treatment of their prey is not. But there is an ecological response, too. The patterns of relationship that constitute ecosystems, independently of human interventions in them, are simply ones not governed by moral rules, but by historically evolving contingent networks through which individuals feed, reproduce, excrete, produce and decompose and through their activities contribute to wider processes of cycling of water, nitrogen, carbon, oxygen and so on. Independently of and prior to human interventions, moral categories just have no place here.

Nevertheless, the human social world does impinge upon the functioning of ecosystems, and, through that, on the conditions for survival and flourishing of whole communities of living beings. Increasingly, the condition 'independently of human intervention' loses its sphere of application. The drastic expansion of the domain of human operations, especially over the past century, has incorporated large areas of previously independently functioning ecosystems into narrow functionality for human purposes, simplifying them and disrupting their former role in ecological reproduction (a process referred to by Foster and his associates as a 'metabolic rift' (Foster et al. 2010). Areas which have so far not been fully integrated into these processes of agricultural intensification and industrial production have nevertheless usually been to one degree or another modified by them, through isolation and fragmentation or through the effects of pollution or climate change. The transformations wrought are sufficiently profound for this short stretch of time to be up for serious scientific debate as inaugurating a new geological epoch – the 'Anthropocene' (more plausibly termed the 'Capitalocene' (Moore 2015)).

Given that human survival, let alone flourishing, is at stake in this state of affairs, there are clearly powerful prudential considerations pointing to the urgency of taking ameliorative action. However, enlightened self-interest has so far had surprisingly little success in mobilising the sorts of collective action that would be needed. As we have seen, internationally coordinated popular pressure gave rise to several important agreements at the Earth Summit of 1992, and yielded the initially subversive concept of sustainable development. Despite that hopeful beginning, some 25 years later biodiversity loss has accelerated, and greenhouse gas emissions continue to rise. The recent Paris agreements, widely welcomed, but still far from what would be needed to avoid the risk of catastrophic runaway climate change, now appear to be doomed by the accession of a climate change–denying US administration.

Other grounds for hope?

So, if the combination of scientific evidence and collective self-interest cannot halt the march to disaster, what might the alternatives be? At the wider strategic level, of course, linkages between well understood and justified outrages at the violence and grotesque inequalities endemic in the current world system and the associated crisis-ridden relations between it and the rest of nature need to be made where they are not already apparent. However, at root, this is a cognitive matter. Understanding alone may not be enough to motivate deep change. The language of rights and justice does have a part to play, especially in contrasting the status of those who benefit from the system of rule with that of those, the great majority, who suffer its social, economic and ecological costs.

As we have seen, however, there are limits to what can be done with rights and justice, while the economistic appeal to 'natural capital' is likely to take us in the wrong direction. So what cultural resources do we have to complement these approaches in challenging the prevailing order of things? A good place to start is with reflection on our everyday experiences of nature. The spread of pet-keeping can be interpreted in many ways, but at least one important strand is a widely shared desire to reach out for mutually respectful relations across the species barrier. The enormous popularity of televised wildlife programmes evidences a viewing public enthralled by images of the intimate and often quite alien lives of other species. Increasingly owners of private gardens have an eye to the wildlife that can flourish there, and often provide winter feed for birds and plant bee-friendly flowers, install 'bug hotels' and so on. Pastimes such as rambling, mountain walking, outdoor painting and sketching, the very large memberships of voluntary wildlife and conservation societies and so on all attest to powerful and widely held feeling for nature, despite long periods of urbanisation. Many thousands across the world demonstrate to protect the polar regions or tropical moist forests from exploitation and destruction, without ever thinking they might visit or experience these wonders. People articulate these feelings in many ways, some of which have rather different roots from the 'extensionist' strategies of both animal rights and welfare. Often what is valued is the recognition of something strange and radically 'other' in the lives of the species which fascinate us, or in the workings of an ecosystem such as the deep ocean, Arctic ice cap or apparently barren desert. Ethical traditions that emphasise valuing of difference and respect for the 'other' are important in challenging racialist and xenophobic responses to the effects of capitalist globalisation referred to above, but they also have their place in fostering moral sentiments of care and responsibility for the myriad species that are not sufficiently similar to ourselves to sustain plausible defence in terms of rights. Clare, again:

> E'n here my simple feelings nurse
> A love for every simple weed.
> And e'n this little 'shepherd's purse'
> Grieves me to cut it up – Indeed
> I feel at times a love and joy
> For every weed and every thing.
> A feeling kindred from a boy.
> A feeling brought with every Spring.
> (from J. Clare, 'The Flitting',
> in Thornton (ed.) 1997:75)

The legacy of romanticism in philosophy and the arts gives us a great wealth of metaphysical, aesthetic and moral reinforcements to proclaim a radically different 'settlement' of our relations to nature. The emotional intensity of encounters with awesome and overpowering aspects of the natural world cuts against the prevailing mundane use of economic calculation in the use or conservation of 'natural capital', as if nature were an inert and submissive resource, to be controlled and regulated at human whim. More broadly one can consider the great works of art, literature and music inspired by nature. For example the American composer John Adams, writing of his 2003 orchestral piece, *The Dharma at Big Sur*:

> I wanted to express the moment, the so-called 'shock of recognition', when one reaches the edge of the continental land mass . . . Rather than gently yielding ground to the water the Western shelf drops off violently, often from dizzying heights, as it does at Big Sur, the stretch of coastal precipice

midway between Santa Cruz and Santa Barbara. Here the current pounds and smashes the littoral in a slow, lazy rhythm of terrifying power. For a newcomer the first exposure produces a visceral effect of great emotional complexity.

(Adams 2006)

Certainly Adams writes of the powerful emotional and aesthetic dimensions of his experience of the Big Sur, but these effects can only be understood as responses to a nature which exists independently and is active in shaping his consciousness – without respect and even awe for the natural phenomena he describes, there could be no such deep emotional responses. To interpret this relationship between a thinking and feeling human and his surroundings as an instrumental one in which the object is valued in virtue of its contribution to the subject's well-being, or valued emotional state would be to radically misunderstand it.

Adams's response to Big Sur is rooted in the 'otherness' of the natural processes he describes, but the sculptor Henry Moore has a quite different take on his inspiration from nature:

[I]t is forms that I have come across in the natural world – from pebbles or tree trunks to a whole valley – which have often shown me how to interpret the human body. My work is a marriage of man and landscape, which is why I prefer to have it displayed out of doors with the sky, clouds and trees. And I believe that something of the same synthesis of man and nature makes up the character of us all.

(Moore 1980)

This deep sense of unity between humans and the rest of nature is another source of resistance to the interpretation of human fulfilment or inspiration in the presence of nature as instrumental and anthropocentric. It seems that, contra Eckersley, reflection on the more fully uplifting experiences of nature points to the inseparability of those experiences from a recognition of those aspects of nature as of value in themselves, independently of their ability to arouse those experiences in us. We are 'taken out of ourselves' in identifying ourselves as linked to a greater totality, or in reaching out to a reality beyond ourselves. In his early philosophical musings, Marx gave expression to this understanding of humans as part of, and not set against, the rest of nature, but he also recognised the work of human imagination that was required for us to grasp the significance of our place in nature, and to develop the cognitive, moral and aesthetic means to give sense and meaning to one's experiences – or to gain 'spiritual nourishment' as he puts it:

Just as plants, animal, stones, the air, light etc., constitute a part of human consciousness in the realm of theory, partly as objects of natural science, partly as objects of art – his spiritual inorganic nature, spiritual nourishment which he must first prepare to make it palatable and digestible – so too in the realm of practice they constitute a part of human life and human activity . . . Nature is man's inorganic body – nature, that is, in so far as it is not itself the human body. Man lives on nature – means that nature is his body, with which he must remain in continuous intercourse if he is not to die. That man's physical and spiritual life is linked to nature means simply that nature is linked to itself, for man is a part of nature.

(Marx [1844] 1959:70–71)

The evolutionary view developed by Wallace and Darwin a little later than this, put new scientific content into that view of the unity of humans and the rest of nature: for all their immense diversity the other species with which we coexist on the planet are our more or less close or distant relatives, as well as being intertwined with us in relations of interdependency. There can be few more beautiful expressions of this than that offered by Darwin at the end of his *Origin of Species*:

It is interesting to contemplate an entangled bank, clothed with many plants of many kinds, with birds singing on the bushes, with various insects flitting about, and with worms crawling through the damp earth, and to reflect that these elaborately constructed forms, so different from each other, and dependent on each other in so complex a manner, have all been produced by laws acting around us . . . There is grandeur in this view of life, with its several powers, having been originally breathed into a few forms or into one; and that, while this planet has gone cycling on according to the fixed law of gravity, from so simple a beginning endless forms most beautiful and most wonderful have been, and are being, evolved.

(Darwin [1859] 1968:459–460)

Drawing upon and making politically effective these diverse strands of personal and popular feeling for nature may provide inspiration for change, beyond the more limited, but still necessary, demands of rights and justice.

References

Adams, J. 2006 'Cover notes' *Dharma at the Big Sur*. New York, Nonesuch Records.
Beck, U. 1987 *Risk Society*. London etc., Sage.
Benton, T. 1993 *Natural Relations*. London, Verso.
Benton, T. 2006 'Do we need rights? If so, what sort?' In L. Morris (ed.) *Rights*. London & New York, Routledge, 21–36.
Benton, T. 2011 'Wild law: Why rights – and could we do without them?' *Environmental Law and Management* 23(6):327–332.

Cole, L. & Foster, S. R. 2001 *From the Ground Up: Environmental Racism and the Rise of the Environmental Justice Movement*. New York, New York University.

Darwin, C. [1859] 1968 *The Origin of Species*. Harmondsworth, Penguin.

Devine, P., Pearmain, A. & Purdy, D. (eds.) 2009 *Feelbad Britain*. London, Lawrence & Wishart.

Eckersley, R. 1992 *Environmentalism and Political Theory*. London, UCL.

Foster, J. B., Clark, B. & York, R. 2010 *The Ecological Rift*. New York, Monthly Review.

Klein, N. 2014 *This Changes Everything*. London, Allen Lane.

Layard, R. 2005 *Happiness*. London, Penguin.

Lukes, S. 1985 *Marxism and Morality*. Oxford, Oxford University.

Martinez-Alier, J. 2002 *The Environmentalism of the Poor*. Cheltenham, Edward Elgar.

Marx, K. [1844] 1959 *Economic and Philosophical Manuscripts of 1844*. Moscow, Progress.

Mies, M. & Shiva, V. 1993 *Ecofeminism*. London & New Jersey, Zed.

Moore, H. 1980 *Preface to M. Shoard: The Theft of the Countryside*. London, Temple Smith.

Moore, J. W. 2015 *Capitalism in the Web of Life*. London & New York, Verso.

Morris, W. 1993 *News from Nowhere and Other Writings*. (ed.) C. Wilmer. London, Penguin.

Porritt, J. 2005 *Capitalism as If the World Matters*. London, Earthscan.

Regan, T. 1988 *The Case for Animal Rights*. Berkeley, CA, University of California.

Stern, N. 2006 *The Stern Review on the Economics of Climate Change*. Cambridge, Cambridge University.

Stiglitz, J. F. 2013 *The Price of Inequality*. London, Penguin.

Stone, C. D. 2010 *Should Trees Have Standing?* Oxford, Oxford University.

Tanner, J. 2009 'The argument from marginal cases and the slippery slope objection', *Environmental Values* 18(1):51–66.

Thomas, K. 1983 *Man and the Natural World*. London, Allen Lane/Penguin.

Thornton, R. K. R. (ed.) 1997 *John Clare*. London, Everyman.

Trebilcock, M. J. & Howse, R. 1995 *The Regulation of International Trade*. London & New York, Routledge.

WCED. 1987 *Our Common Future*. Oxford, Oxford University.

Wilkinson, R. G. & Pickett, K. 2009 *The Spirit Level: Why More Equal Societies Almost Always do Better*. London, Allen Lane.

4 The foundation of rights to nature

Marcel Wissenburg

Introduction

Environmental human rights are rights to nature. More precisely, environmental human rights are rights to (the fair distribution of, or fair access to) natural resources and/or rights to (the fair distribution of, or fair protection against) nature-related burdens. While certainly not completely *reducible* to ownership rights, environmental human rights do have an origin in what is called original acquisition and original ownership – fair access to environmental goods and resources ideally starts with fair acquisition.[1]

For the record, we should distinguish clearly between *private* ownership and *original* ownership. In environmentalist literature, academic and other, private ownership is often seen as a contributory cause to environmental and social degradation (see e.g. Bromley 1991; Hettinger 1998a), and private property is in turn associated with liberal political philosophy and/or liberalism, libertarianism and neo-liberalism as ideologies. There are two types of responses to charges of this kind. One is the classic liberal and libertarian reply that privatization properly understood is the most effective response to environmental collective action problems (see e.g., Machan 1998; Epstein 2009; Schmidtz 2012; Tomasi 2012). Another is one I develop here: that one major cause for this alleged incompatibility problem (Wissenburg 2006) lies not in any specific political ideology nor in private property as such but in its *origins* – in original acquisition.

In this chapter, I shall develop two archetypes of original ownership, both rooted in the natural law tradition (cf. Richard Epstein's (2009) dichotomy). One is orthodox, characteristic of right-libertarianism (a classic example being Nozick 1974) as well as classical liberalism. The other is more lenient, and characteristic of both the left-libertarianism of Steiner (1994, 2009) and Vallentyne (2007) and of social liberalism of the Rawlsian kind. The orthodox tradition presumes original non-ownership of nature, whereas the lenient tradition assumes that nature is a common asset prior to original acquisition. This typology of course does not do justice to the richness of nature ownership theories; there is, for example, an important further distinction to be made between collective owner-ship by humanity and collective ownership by a people or a 'cooperative venture for mutual benefit' (Rawls 1999a, 73). However, this simple dichotomy suffices to demonstrate that, probably against intuition, if one is interested in protecting nature against human (over-)exploitation, then the best way to think of original ownership is in terms of the orthodox notion of non-ownership. While the com-mon asset tradition ultimately weighs only the *relative* strength of communities' claims to nature, the orthodox tradition requires *intrinsically* good reasons: it can, at least in principle, impose limits on original acquisition and make room for the *non*-appropriation of nature, for *non*-consumption and *non*-destruction. By impli-cation, an orthodox conception of original non-ownership is a necessary condi-tion for any legitimate theory of environmental human rights, precisely because it is a safeguard against short-sightedness.

Assumptions

In what follows I shall, for the sake of simplicity, make a number of assumptions about the meaning of terms like 'property', 'ownership' and 'environmentalism' which I should clarify first.

For one, I assume that property and ownership exist ultimately only in the mind (although of course they do shape and are reproduced through physical reality). Ownership is a claim to the recognition of a convention. Even moral realist and natural rights–based conceptions of ownership are conventional in the one sense that matters here: they have to be believed in to effect ownership practices. No conception of property or ownership is authoritative: some are just more widely shared than others, or more influential; some are specific for a par-ticular society, and some may even define that society (cf. Freeman 2002).

Cross-culturally (Munzer 1990; cf. Widerquist 2010), property *can* always be understood (even though this may not be part of a culture's self-image) as a set or bundle of 'rights' or permissions,[2] things one 'may do' according to legal or popu-lar convention (cf. Hohfeld 1919; Honoré 1961; Becker 1977; cf. also Waldron 1988; Carter 1989; Tomasi 2012). Lawrence Becker (1977, 20) counted 2047 sets of rights that could be described as conceptions of property, but argued that on a conventional understanding of property, some rights at least must always be part of the set, such as the right to the capital accrued from a good (cf. 'ecosystem services'); the rights to destroy, transfer or consume; and the right (veto power) to exclude others from the enjoyment of the good owned. By implication, rights that are not part of such sets function as *limits* (Cohen 1978; cf. also Macpherson 1978; and Nozick 1974, who talks of side-constraints), i.e., limits on acquisition, use, transfer and expropriation or taxation. I shall use ownership and property as (for our purposes) synonymous, though it must be stressed that many prefer to reserve the term ownership for 'full' ownership, characterized by a very specific bundle of property rights, each of which would be necessary, and only altogether sufficient, to deserve that name (cf. Epstein 2009; Gaus 2012).

I further assume that anything can be owned, even the self and the human genome (cf. Steiner 1994; Bergström 2000). Without prejudice, merely for the sake of simplicity, I assume that only humans can own.[3] None of this means that only humans have value or that only humans assign (something equivalent to) value. I distinguish four basic types of owners:

(1) *Individual* or private ownership – while one could argue (e.g., Macpherson 1978a) that any ownership theory ultimately attributes ownership to individuals in some way or other, what distinguishes individual ownership is that it is direct, unmediated, not given in trust by or to a 'larger whole'.

(2) *Corporate* or cooperative ownership is the combined administration and execution of individual ownership rights of the members of a corporation or cooperative venture; owners retain a right of veto and of exit. State ownership is a form of corporate ownership (cf. Macpherson 1978a; Bromley 1991): here the state is the corporation holding goods in trust from the citizens.

(3) *Common* property (cf. Macpherson 1978a; Bromley 1991) on the other hand implies that ownership rights are held indivisibly rather than in the names of individuals; group members are trustees for the group, rather than the other way around. Common ownership can again be divided (on no other basis than that it is appropriate in the present context) into four sub-types:

   (3a) *ad hoc* common ownership, by a group defined and delineated by its property;

   (3b) *embedded* common ownership, where the common property is not a necessary but a contingent feature of the group;

   (3c) *collective* ownership, where the owning group is a nation, state, people, or perhaps tribe, i.e., a delineated group that defines not just itself but also its constituent sub-groups; and finally

   (3d) *universal* ownership where, in line with e.g., cosmopolitan political philosophies, no one is excluded from membership of the one all-embracing group.

Finally, there is (4) *non-ownership*, a category on which, in the past, few words have been wasted. It was usually taken as a primitive term requiring no further explanation.

Becker (1977; also Bromley 1991), pointing back to Pufendorf, distinguishes two ways in which nature is 'unowned' prior to original acquisition: as 'positive common property', a joint ownership where all own a well-defined share (in my terms: corporate or collective ownership) and 'negative common property': the good is owned by no one, and is equally available to all. Here, nature seems free for grabs, and all that seems required to create legitimate property is 'to show how taking possession of something creates any of the rights of property' (Becker 1977, 25).

Last, I shall make two assumptions about nature, environment and their protection, starting with a distinction between (political) environmentalism and ecologism. While environmentalism can be used as a generic term, it will from here on be used exclusively to denote a distinct attitude towards policies on nature, an attitude opposed to ecologism (cf. Dobson 2007; Wissenburg 1998).

Ideal-typically, environmentalism perceives nature as surrounding (environing) society, as an object or objects relative to (human) subjects, and as resources for those subjects. It is linked to what is called in environmental ethics 'shallow ecology' (cf. Devall and Sessions 1985). Standard conceptions of sustainability like Brundtland's are quite representative of this approach. Viewing nature as resources, thus taking what is basically a consumerist attitude, does not imply that destroying nature is morally neutral or even desirable: recycling, winning back lost resources, treading as lightly as possible, consuming nature only with one's eyes (as a source of recreation, inspiration, relaxation, etc.) are all compatible with environmentalism. The logic of environmentalism dictates that nature always be managed in such a way that, within the bounds of human demand, it produces the widest and largest possible supply of resources. This in turn implies that replacing nature by artifice (plastic trees, a park, tame horses, GM crops, etc.) is *prima facie* obligatory whenever artifice offers a Pareto-optimal advantage. From that perspective, even enjoying nature as a spiritual experience is a form of consumption (Wissenburg 1998); it may not be as destructive as other forms of consumption but still uses nature as a means to an end, theoretically exchangeable for an artificial, more effective and efficient alternative.

(Political) ecologism, on the other hand, conceives of humans and nature as one and indivisible: an autarchic ecosystem. Its associates in environmental ethics are eco-centrism and 'deep ecology'. Without denying that humans use parts of their surroundings as resources (and that those surroundings use us as resources), ecologism does not reduce nature to the status of object but assigns it an independent moral status, often (problematically) termed intrinsic value. Ecologists will, because of that independent value, reject any change to or use of nature that objectifies it and makes it less 'natural'. Ecologists will define the role of humans as that of guardians *of* nature, while environmentalists will see them as stewards *for* the rest of humanity, present and future.

My second nature-related assumption is that X is more nature-friendly or 'greener' the more X approaches ecologism. In itself, this is merely a matter of definition – no value judgment to the effect that being green (in any sense) would be morally better is presumed. If there is a ground to call ecologism rather than environmentalism nature-friendly, it is merely that environmentalism is not interested in nature *per se.*

Two theories of original ownership

Legitimate original acquisition is (cf. note 1) a near-necessary condition for any kind of legitimate transfer including redistribution to address environmental human rights claims or to correct historic injustice. If the origins of environmental goods are dubious, then their transfer and possession will also always be morally tainted, no matter how noble the intentions behind the transfer. I shall reduce the countless types of 'original ownership' or ownership before original acquisition to two, illustrated by four strands of political theory incorporating one of these two types (cf. Epstein 2009 for a similar dichotomy). The first type of original acquisition I call orthodox: it assumes that nature was literally unowned before its appropriation by individuals; there were no subjects to whom any (moral, or of course legal) ownership rights were assigned or attributed before the moment of original acquisition. (Non-ownership is, however, not the same as the total absence of subjects of rights: we shall see below that it is important to further distinguish between non-ownership as being a trustee or *steward* for a 'silent' owner – say, God – and non-ownership as *guardianship* of the non-owned good – say, nature.) The orthodox view of original acquisition is typical of (many representatives of) right-libertarianism and classical liberalism – two schools of thought that are difficult to distinguish at the best of times (the main difference, in political practice, seems to lie in the degree of admissible market regulation; cf. Machan 1998; Tomasi 2012). Fortunately, for our purposes the differences are irrelevant – what is relevant is that authors in both schools use or presume the idea of original acquisition.

I call the second type of original acquisition lenient not because it is in any way permissive or vague but because it does not draw a strict line between 'before' and 'after' original acquisition. On the lenient view, nature is a common asset prior to privatization. Again, two political theories can illustrate the common asset tradition: left-libertarianism and social liberalism. I distinguish social liberalism and left-libertarianism by their appreciation of desert based on the use of individual talent.[4] While social liberals are inclined to perceive the initial distribution of talents (including ambition and effort) as undeserved and its results as (therefore) questionable, left-libertarians perceive the decision to employ one's talents as irreducibly authentic, autonomous and definitive of the human as an individual being – which would generate a valid claim to the fruits of one's labour.[5] Left-libertarianism distinguishes itself from right-libertarianism by embracing the common asset idea (Steiner 2009; Vallentyne et al. 2005), which makes it possible to argue that acts of original acquisition (privatization) impose costs in terms of e.g., lost opportunities and freedoms on others, costs which call for compensation and thereby for the creation of a limited redistributive cooperative scheme.

Orthodox theories of original acquisition are (too) easily reduced to shades of the common asset tradition, in part because most liberal and libertarian academic literature focuses on (not) *limiting* private property rights, i.e., on grounding or refuting private claims to exclusive decision-making power over use and transfer and against seizure. Implicitly, limiting often looks like attributing property rights to a prior common owner, a group other than a corporation (see above), thereby making (some) individual property rights derivative. That in turn makes the classic question of legitimate original acquisition appear redundant, the focus being on determining collectively what you may do with property, rather than establishing where and how you got it in the first place.

Locke and the roots of original acquisition theories

While massively quoted and paraphrased by advocates of orthodox original acquisition, John Locke is neither a libertarian (that would be anachronistic) nor a proponent of the orthodox view – but he is indubitably its father.[6] He would be the ideal-typical representative of the original non-ownership tradition if it were not for the presence of God. In Locke's (1924) work, there *is* a party prior to original acquisition, even a party granting rights, a party in whom rights originate. One might argue that God does not Himself hold rights since He is above and beyond rights. A fair representation of Locke's classical liberalism would see him as defending nature's being unowned in at best one very particular sense: while humans are stewards for God, it is questionable whether the term ownership can be applied at all to Locke's God, since (for instance) it is unclear with what substance God mixed His labour, against whom He claims a right, or in which place He was before He created 'space'. Still, humans remain stewards even after original acquisition: just like the English relative to their king (cf. Widerquist 2010), humans are eternal tenants. They manage a part of humanity's collective stewardship but do not own it in the fullest possible sense: rights to capital and interest are limited by the presumed intentions of the overlord. God has given nature to humanity 'in common' (cf. Trachtenberg 2014), and while only individuals can take natural resources out of the state of nature and turn them into private property, that freedom is limited by the provision that enough and as good be left in common. In other words, on Locke's view humans:

(1) do not have all the rights one would associate with the most extensive conception of property (full ownership) – which is a disturbing piece of information for those who see in Locke the founding father of possessive liberalism and modern (neo-)liberal conceptions of unfettered ownership;

(2) can have a set of property rights (rights to interest, capital, etc.) consisting of only those natural rights that are consistent with a similar set for others and with God's intentions with His creation;
(3) can obtain these rights only if the famous four conditions for original acquisition have been met (need, no waste, enough and as good, mixed labour).

It is worth mentioning that Locke's account of original acquisition does not define the natural rights tradition. There is, of course, also Hobbes (1968), for whom nature may be a gift from God to all of humanity, but with no moral or theological strings attached (at least not in the context of his *political* philosophy): anyone who, in the state of nature, takes possession of a good in the pursuit of his survival has a legitimate claim to it; and anyone taking it from another for the same goal has an equally valid claim – if not more valid since the previous possessor has vacated or relinquished it, *nolens volens*. Before original acquisition, all of nature was then effectively 'free for all'. Of course, once a sovereign has been created and positive law instituted, the free for all ends: the sovereign becomes the first original owner of all the land and everything it produces, and the first also to own rather than possess.

Two further versions of original ownership under natural law can be found in the works of Hugo Grotius and Adam Smith. According to John Salter (2010), Grotius too understood nature as common property in the sense of 'free for all': God gave the human race 'a general right over things of a lower order', as 'common and undivided possessions of all men, as if all possessed a common inheritance' (Grotius in Salter 2010, 9). Property rights originate in physical possession, replaced (*pace* Locke), later in history and in 'polite' society, by a series of conventions that more precisely delineate property rights, though not because of the threat of a Hobbesian war of all against all (Salter 2001). That would, after all, imply that there is scarcity in the state of nature, which in turn implies that God did not give humanity everything it needed, which would be both blasphemous and, since all things come from God, logically inconsistent. The convention of property may be an answer to scarcity, but scarcity can only have emerged after the Fall, when vanity began to rear its ugly head and when men began to 'refine' life (Salter 2010, 18).

Adam Smith accepted most of Grotius's theory – without the references to God, though. Scarcity did make it necessary to let the convention of property replace simple original acquisition through possession, but Smith understood scarcity in quite modern terms as the inevitable product of population growth in a finite world, where more intensive use of resources (through agriculture, technology, etc.) can temporarily alleviate pressure but obviously offer no permanent solution (Salter 2010).

So the natural rights tradition has to be read carefully: it does not unequivocally assume that nature was no one's property before individuals acquired parts of it. It is perhaps possible, in a case like Hobbes's, to read it as if nature was unowned prior to original acquisition by the sovereign – but in other cases nature is clearly gifted to humanity (or a people) in common and held in common. Even in the fairly complex case of John Locke, nature is initially freely available to each and every individual, but whatever is thereby privatized was previously common good – perhaps held by tenants rather than owners, yet the operative word remains 'common': the community held, though did not execute, rights normally considered consistent with the concept of ownership.

Orthodox non-ownership

Libertarianism, or at least that strand of proprietarian right-libertarianism associated with names like Nozick, Gauthier, Rothbard and Narveson, claims to be the modern heir of the classical natural rights theory of original acquisition, and interprets the latter as a theory of original non-ownership.

In Nozick's classic formulation of right-libertarianism, ideal-typical for the libertarian version of non-ownership, there is no God or owner before original acquisition; nature is free for all. In Nozick's own words, 'Locke views property rights in an unowned object as originating through someone's mixing his labour with it' (Nozick 1974, 174). Humans become *private* owners by mixing their labour, leaving ample room for the creation of *corporate* ownership but none for *collective* ownership. In Nozick's streamlined version of Locke, original acquisition is only limited by 'the' Lockean proviso that enough and as good of a natural resource be left for others, with the amendment that 'otherwise' proper compensation should be provided. There are of course, technically speaking, four Lockean provisos (see above); therefore there are further legitimate grounds to regulate original acquisition, but the core message is clear: original acquisition in the orthodox tradition really is an act of privatization of a piece of previously *unowned* good.

Nozick's position represents orthodoxy among right-libertarians. Murray Rothbard directly quotes Locke as saying that ownership originates in a self-owning individual mixing his labour with the soil, and that soil is 'unused and uncontrolled by anyone, and hence *unowned*' (Rothbard 2002, 31). David Gauthier, while allowing for even collective ownership by families (and presumably tribes; Gauthier 1986, 214), and while stressing that full compensation is due whenever the Lockean proviso is violated, still sees ownership as originating in individual acquisition of previously unowned resources, a process 'by which we may move from a Hobbesian state of nature, in which there are no exclusive rights whatsoever but only liberties, to the initial position for social interaction' (Gauthier 1986, 208). Other (sometimes implicit) representatives of the non-ownership tradition include Machan (1998); Schmidtz (2012) and Tomasi (2012).

Jan Narveson's ideas on nature and original acquisition (1998, 2001), less 'theory-laden' than Nozick's or Rothbard's, illustrate quite adequately how 'free for all' may be confused with 'free for grabs' (in settings other than Hardin's classic text) – and why right-libertarianism and non-ownership have a rather bad name with environmentalists like Bromley. As Narveson (1998) says, nature is wilderness, and wilderness is

> unoccupied bits of nature, land or sea or whatever . . . by definition not owned. Note that it is not only not owned by you or me, but also it is not owned by some nebulous group called "Mankind"; nor is it owned by some alleged god who is supposed to have manufactured it, for some mysterious reasons of his own. Nature, so far as people in general know about it, is just there.

Ownership is created by (Hobbesian) possession and (Lockean) mixing of labour – Narveson isn't clear on whether 'and' means 'or': people come to own nature 'by just being on it and working on it, in the first instance' (Narveson 1998).

Ownership, original or after transfer, implies for Narveson unfettered rights to (Honoré's term) capital: 'to own it, in general, is to have the right to use it as you please' (Narveson 1998). Your particular faith, sensitivities or convictions cannot limit my property rights – I may tear down my house even if it is some hero's birth place, or even if it would harm '"ecological integrity" or some such thing that we ordinary folk do not understand' (Narveson 1998). The only valid source of limits to property rights, Narveson argues, lies in the answer to this question: 'in what aspect or regard is something about the nonhuman environment such that we may therefore impose some or other requirements on people?' Note also that 'making things understandable' requires human ears listening to human voices; as Hettinger (1998b) observes,

> Professor Narveson . . . believes that only humans count morally and that what happens to nonhumans (including animals, plants, species, and ecosystems) is morally irrelevant, unless some human cares about it. On his view, concern for nonhuman nature for its own sake is an idiosyncratic aesthetic or religious preference that society has no right to impose on those who disagree . . . , a mere matter of taste.

Note, however, that although Narveson rejects e.g., mental health, aesthetics, spiritual wellbeing and the like as valid grounds for infringements on property (for him, only bodily harm works), this does not have to be the final word within libertarianism. There may be good arguments to broaden the set of true harms, or indeed broaden the circle of the harmed itself – Nozick, unlike Narveson, was quite willing to consider animals' interests morally relevant, arguably even in a fuller sense than animal welfare campaigners like Peter Singer. What matters here is not how one specific right-libertarian justifies the set of rights defining property or the choice of subjects to whom (rights against) property can be assigned – what matters is that (a) even right-libertarians *can* allow limits on property rights, and that (b) this is a wholly different question than 'who owns nature, *originally?*' An unpopular position on the limits of property cannot be held against arguments on original acquisition.

Contrary then to popular opinions such as Bromley's (1991), free for all is definitely not the same as free for grabs, or in more formal words: initial non-ownership does not *necessarily* mean (a) the absolute freedom to claim ownership to any unowned X and the concurrent right to have that claim respected;or (b) the absolute freedom to take any unowned X out of the state of nature. Original acquisition of previously unowned nature, taking goods in a free for all, *still* has to be justified. This is the kind of question Hale (2008) hinted at: you do not necessarily take what belongs to *another* but you do take *what is not yours*. And it is the latter act that needs to be justified for original acquisition to be legitimate.

The common asset tradition

Proponents of the lenient tradition are fairly silent on original acquisition and on the justification of private property. A virulent right-libertarian like Narveson would probably say that this is because they do not care about, even reject, individual rights including those to property, and the more dispassionate Nozick would merely argue that social liberalism and left-libertarianism create irresolvable contradictions by both heralding individual rights and (in ignoring or qualifying rights springing from original acquisition) limiting them for an alleged common good. The truth of the matter is that, while such paradoxes and contradictions may exist, the lenient tradition does presuppose, respect and embrace the institution of private property – it merely argues for different definitions of the sets of rights to capital and profit, it argues for more room (and broader sets of rights) for corporate ownership, and it focuses on the property rights of corporations rather than those of individuals only.[7] In other words, the agenda of the common asset tradition is dominated by issues to do with criteria for proper and improper transfer – and by a series of unfortunate accidents, the agenda is even further dominated by questions of criteria for the transfer of material goods already held in corporate ownership (cf. also Munzer 1990). And still, it is not all that difficult to unearth the underlying social liberal and left-libertarian position on original acquisition and previous ownership.

Rawls's *A Theory of Justice* (1999a), and even more so *Political Liberalism* (1993), follow and in part define the social liberal agenda, which is concerned with social goods and/or already owned goods. Here, private property is a convention, more precisely and in line with *A Theory of Justice* and *Political Liberalism*, the sets of rights making up 'ownership' and the assignment of ownership are conventional, and the convention is a historically and locally interpreted application of the Two Principles (cf. Rawls 1999a, 171ff.). Thus, ownership within a just (social liberal) society is typically a mixture of private and corporate ownership rights, with possibly other forms of ownership derived from these. But how did we come to own goods in the first place? For an insight into the real origins of property, we need the *Law of Peoples* (Rawls 1999b), where it turns out that at least in principle, all peoples always already have what they need to exist – Grotius nods approvingly in the background. It is only under exceptional circumstances that societies grow into 'burdened societies', and only some of those become burdened due to (my phrase) 'natural poverty', i.e., environmental factors: 'Burdened societies . . . lack the political and cultural traditions, the human capital and know-how, and, often, the material and technological resources needed to be well-ordered' (Rawls 1999b, 106). Even then, the environmental side of the equation is more often than not the result of political mismanagement – referring to Amartya Sen's famous work on famine, Rawls ultimately blames the demand side of society (presumably population growth rather than vanity – now Adam Smith smiles). As a consequence, no burdened society can lay claim to the resources of another. In conclusion:

(a) nature as a global pool of resources is always already the property of particular peoples;
(b) nature is not the corporate property of humanity – since claims to others' shares are excluded;
(c) nature was, before its original acquisition by a (metaphorical) people, a common asset, more precisely, the universal common property of humanity: each people has an allotted share independent of approval by others.

While most other social liberal theories of justice are far less developed than Rawls's, they all seem to presuppose something similar to Rawls's model: prior to any conventions on corporate and individual ownership, nature was a common asset, and each one's just share was already determined from the outset by prioritizing the urgency of individual human rights (right-claims). Perhaps cosmopolitanism should be seen as the ultimate example of the common asset tradition: cutting out the middle man (the state, making corporate ownership truly instrumental to the realization of individual rights), it seeks to assign all of nature and all that is made of nature to all of humanity in one single formula of justice (cf. e.g. Risse 2013).

Left-libertarianism (Steiner 1994, 2009; Vallentyne 2007; Vallentyne et al. 2005; see also Newman 2011, n5) differs profoundly from social liberalism in the justification it gives for 'expropriation' of private property, for the creation of corporate property and for legitimate redistribution. It embraces desert (through effort, ambition, labour, etc.) as the foundation of private ownership, but it also sees grounds for compensation to those deprived from benefits they might otherwise have had (or already enjoyed; cf. Davidson 2014) when resources are taken out of nature through legitimate original acquisition. Hillel Steiner has even applied this argument to the value of the genetic endowments of children, for which, he argues, parents should be taxed (Steiner 2009). In deviation from right-libertarianism, this results in the creation of a treasury chest out of which a program of (re)distributive justice can be financed.

A necessary assumption for such a redistributive scheme to be legitimate is that those who do not 'originally acquire' a piece of nature have a collective, shared, indivisible and equal claim to benefits they never realized. While a right-libertarian would immediately find fault with the idea of desert based on merely potential effort, what is more interesting for us is that we cannot make sense of this collective claim without assuming, further, that nature before original acquisition is some group's common property – and I shall carefully avoid the question which group; the keyword here is *common*. Nature is not free for all, either free for grabs or freely available under conditions; it is instead a common asset, and whoever expropriates part of it cannot (legitimately) do so unless both the resource *and* any as yet unrealized profit have been replaced by a somehow proper equivalent – i.e., in left-libertarianism, original acquisition seems possible only when it is *as if* nothing changes for the rest of us. If some sort of assumption of prior common ownership were not made, if we assumed that initially *nobody* possessed or owned nature (cf. Bergström 2000), no grounds for compensation, particularly for missed profit, would exist.

Original ownership and the protection of nature

No modern political theory is complete without the inclusion of an environmental dimension, no environmental political theory and no theory of environmental human rights is complete without an account of legitimate original acquisition, and no account of original acquisition is complete without an answer to the question who would 'own' nature before ownership exists. We have discussed two accounts of original acquisition and prior 'ownership'; it is time to determine, as promised, which one is greenest.

Social liberal and left-libertarian theories assume a kind of common ownership (collective or universal, even) and focus on grounds for allowing or tolerating appropriation by individuals. They differ by the types and the severity of the limits posed on individual appropriation – among others, the amount of resource X that may be appropriated, the reasons and purposes, the methods, and finally the price or compensation required. Yet for all their diversity, common asset theories are very similar at a fundamental level. *In extremis*, they are all environmentalist:

they are anthropocentric (cf. Hayward 1997) in viewing nature as resources, as consumer goods, and they aim to maximize efficiency in exploiting nature. At least in principle, they do not seem to be one bit 'greener' (as in: nature-friendly) than extreme, Narvesonian right-libertarianism.

Anthropocentrism can be cured (up to a point) by either extending the community or extending the kinds of 'use' made of nature – though in many cases at a high price in terms of moral appeal: only a consistently cosmopolitan theory can avoid the danger of ranking the interests of the pet dog over those of the starving foreigner. The common asset tradition's lack of intrinsic interest in nature however cannot be cured; it is in fact what defines the tradition: it is all about human (or other) *subjects* versus *objects* in the form of natural (or other) resources.[8]

Orthodox theories reveal a slightly different appreciation of nature – still the attitude of a consumer, but a far more careful, frugal consumer, one who has to justify each and every act of acquisition based on needs, both immediate and future use, rather than rights – which includes immediate preference satisfaction. It is because of this that orthodox theories offer room to understand humans as guardians *of* nature next to or instead of as stewards *for* someone else.

The orthodox theory of initial non-ownership or 'free for all' is not the same as Garrett Hardin's amoral commons: free for all does not mean free for grabs. Original acquisition has to be justified. Although some libertarians require very little in the way of justification, that is not a given. As the continued debate (particularly in environmental political theory; cf. Trachtenberg 2014) on the Lockean proviso and Nozick's amendments illustrates, we cannot in advance exclude the possibility that libertarianism becomes a very demanding theory on the point of legitimate original acquisition. And no matter how flexible some libertarians may be, the orthodox tradition as such always requires proof for the legitimacy of acquisition, proof that relates to the good itself, while in the lenient tradition, original acquisition must be accounted for in relation to the claims of other subjects. At the very least then, orthodox non-ownership puts the onus of proof for the moral legitimacy of original acquisition and use of nature on the would-be user. Let me first discuss the latter aspect: the reason to appropriate nature, the Lockean 'need'.

What gives right-libertarianism its bad name is its association with a very radical, comprehensive interpretation of the set of rights that would include the most extensive freedom to destroy one's property no matter how offensive that act or the chosen means and methods. But *jus ad rem*, a right to a thing however broad, is not *jus in re*, absolute and perfect dominion over a thing: whatever property may mean, the set of property rights defining the conception of property for society A can be assigned (be legitimate) if and only if certain provisos, conditions on original acquisition, are met first. If those provisos are strong enough, the set of rights defining property according to right-libertarianism may well turn out to be less extensive than traditionally thought.

For example, Hettinger (1998a) rejected the libertarian conception of property among others because of Narveson's unyielding anthropocentrism, which would not allow us

> to see why the right to destroy should not be included as part of land ownership or the ownership of biodiversity on the land. Destroying a toaster that humans made is one thing, destroying land that we inherited is something quite different.

Yet this may well be a peculiarity of Narveson's. John Hadley (2005; cf. Wissenburg 1998; Sheard 2007 for a similar argument on behalf of future generations) argued extensively that an unconditional right to destroy cannot be part of the rights one has to the capital of an object X (which in turn is a subset of the set of ownership rights), as it permanently excludes others with potentially valid claims. With that unconditional right gone, even right-libertarians would be obliged to interpret original acquisition as taking up a strong and positive duty to sustainable resource management – an attitude at least as green as anything one might expect from the common asset tradition. There really is room for a green rethinking of private property.

In fact, the right-libertarian insistence on the irreducibly personal nature of property may well offer more protection against the destruction of a good (since only my personal reasons are relevant) than the lenient tradition, where the common good or the good of others can overrule my veto on the use (destruction) of my good. The intuitive perception of right-libertarian ownership rights as absolute, universal, complete and perfect, and therefore harmful to nature, is misguided.

Whether or not right-libertarian property rights are, on balance and after careful reconsideration of their justification, stronger or more extensive than lenient conceptions of property is a moot point – and in so far as it isn't yet, it should be. The fact is that there are no grounds of principle why an orthodox conception of original acquisition would be less ecology-friendly. It all depends on the quality of the arguments for the inclusion of each single imaginable constituent right (to use, let, rent, destroy, consume, etc.) in a unified and unifying conception of property.

The choice for non-ownership over the common asset theory will, then, not only affect whether 'taking from nature' must be justified, the way in which it is justified, the conditions under which it is justified and the degree to which it is justified – it will also affect the subsequent chain of events after original acquisition, i.e., the composition of the set of rights that make up ownership, the conditions under which interference (taxation, appropriation, redistribution) can be legitimate, and (if required) the recipients and form of proper compensation.

Let us return now to the phase preceding ownership and the execution of legitimate ownership rights – to original acquisition itself. It is here that we see the real difference between 'lenient' schools and the orthodox tradition. The former, representing the common asset tradition, do not really acknowledge a thing like 'original acquisition', since they ascribe ownership as always already in the hands of a community. As a consequence, what has to be justified in regard to property rights is *who* will use a good and *how* it is to be used – but *that* its use is justified (*that* 'this land is ours to do with as we please') seems to be beyond question.

As an illustration, consider how Hettinger (1998a) describes the question of attributing 'ownership' to biodiversity in the common asset tradition:

> Is biodiversity, most of which is found in poor, developing countries of the southern hemisphere, a commons belonging to all of humanity or do these countries of origin have national sovereignty over these biological resources? I have suggested that individual landowners may possess and use the biodiversity found on their land, but with restrictions. Their ownership is a kind of trusteeship involving duties to preserve the renewable natural resources of the land. The ecological services the land provides (flood control, wildlife habitat, climate stability, maintenance of biodiversity and so on) are not something over which the landowner is sovereign. To prohibit the landowner from destroying these capacities of the land is not to take any rights away from him, for these common goods of the land are held in public trust. This is the kind of land ownership that is compatible with a land ethic. In a similar way, biodiversity around the globe is a common heritage, not just of humanity, but of all life, both present and future. All communities of the world have legitimate interests in what a country does with the biological resources found within its territory.

While the Hettinger quote shows that the common asset tradition need not be irreversibly anthropocentric, it also shows that it starts out from the assumption that there is by definition always a valid claim to every bit of nature; what matters is the strength of one community's claim relative to the other's. Thus, the common asset tradition's attitude towards nature remains environmentalist.

The advantage of the orthodox non-ownership tradition is that it does not make such assumptions. Instead, it assumes that original acquisition, the creation of property *as such*, requires justification, and justification of a particular kind: no claim to property can be valid unless intrinsically good reasons are offered, rather than comparatively better reasons. Ultimately, the common asset tradition espouses a stewardship ethic. In its ancestor, the natural law tradition, the acquiring party addresses his or her claim to a political community (or possibly humanity as a whole) that acts as the *steward* for a third party 'beyond' the ownership discourse, God. It is this third party that sets the rules – promoting the same environmentalist attitude that is also inherent to the common asset tradition, yet adding an extra hurdle to jump to prevent a too short-sighted attribution of environmental human rights to humans here and now, at the expense of the non-human world and the future.

Under orthodox non-ownership, on the other hand, there is no 'initial' stewardship. Here, any claim to the legitimacy of original acquisition should not be directed to other claimants and not be decided by relative strength, or directed to a higher authority and assessed by conformity to a metaphysical or mystical, by definition arbitrary, truth. Instead, acquisition (and the collection of rights making up ownership) has to be proven to be legitimate in itself. Metaphorically, one could say that this makes any collective not a steward for a pre-owner but a guardian of the object of ownership itself, a guardian for nature.

Conclusion

All things considered, it seems that the most orthodox legitimization of private property is *initially* and *in theory* 'better for nature' and more conducive to a restrained, responsible and morally defensible use of natural resources than left-libertarian, social liberal or other common asset theories. The former offers room for non-appropriation, non-consumption and non-destruction where the latter do not. Non-ownership 'always already' offers a more balanced theory of environmental human rights, one less easily allowing the sacrifice of the important to the urgent, the interests of the future to those of the present. Two questions remain, both expressing doubt as to whether all this was not just a purely academic exercise.

First, is there no way in which the common asset tradition can be repaired and in the end offer nature the same protection and consideration promised by the non-ownership tradition? Of course it can: the steward (the collective or common owner) can decide that it is in the best interest of humanity not to privatize and consume this particular bit of nature for the time being. But amending the common asset theory that way will always be like a rule-utilitarian offering protection for human rights: both types of protection remain contingent and come with no guarantees.

Secondly, is it realistic to expect the orthodox tradition, more specifically right-libertarians, to embrace the idea that acquisition should be justified in such a way that its impact on nature is taken into account? Considering the attitude of authors like Narveson, for whom belief in the intrinsic value of nature expresses a 'special interest' and a personal faith that should not be imposed on others, this seems unlikely. Yet younger generations of libertarians have argued for two directions forward. One is that it is as yet unclear if (the protection of) nature actually is a special interest and if it is so different from a 'special interest' in freedom or autonomy (cf. Sagoff 1992). The other is that while some libertarians may believe that any 'need' (as in the need to privatize a piece of nature and turn it into a resource) is legitimate as long as the prospective owner believes in it, no matter how silly – it is at the same time (cf. e.g., DiZerega 1996; Scriven 1997) possible to argue that, as a matter of individual moral duty and responsibility, anyone considering original acquisition *should* give due consideration to the effects on or interests of nature.

Notes

1 For many philosophers and legal scholars, legitimate original acquisition is a near-necessary condition for legitimate ownership, thereby also for legitimate individual transfer and collective (re)distribution – 'near-'necessary because sometimes (for example, in cases of historic injustice) tracing back property rights to the original owner(s) is impossible, and correction is achieved by other means (for example via Robert Nozick's (1974) principle of rectification). For others, illegitimate acquisition throws a diminishing and ultimately disappearing shadow over the legitimacy of all subsequent (non-corrective) transactions; if (say) enough time has passed, possession becomes ten tenths of the law. I presume here that the second position is logically inconsistent. That is not to say that this question is irrelevant; it is in fact crucial for the defence of redistribution in support of environmental human rights and/or reparation of historic injustice.
2 This logically includes for example obligations: an obligation to X is a permission to X and the absence of the permission to not-X. For standard definitions of related conceptions, see Hohfeld (1919).
3 Two remarks are in order here. First: on an interest conception of rights (as opposed to a will-based conception; see Raz 1986), animals can have rights, including ownership rights (cf. Hadley 2015). Secondly: if we allow for the possibility of animal ownership rights, then we must accept that there may also be animal environmental rights parallel to environmental human rights (possibly contradicting each other, or perhaps with the latter as a special case of the former); not doing so might be construed as speciesism and human chauvinism (cf. Hayward 1997).
4 This is not the place to develop a comprehensive typology of the various schools and strands of libertarianism and liberalism; in the *present context*, it suffices to distinguish (social) liberalism and (left-)libertarianism on this one point only.
5 See e.g., Locke (1924); Nozick (1974) and Narveson (2001); note that there are subtle and less subtle differences between these authors, and that there is no guarantee that my formulation of the labour theory is beyond reproach.
6 Both Locke's position and that of his contemporary 'real' orthodox defenders of original non-ownership have a very long genealogy, and deep roots in Roman law (Epstein 2009; cf. Salter 2001; Trachtenberg 2014).
7 In this chapter I will silently pass over the interesting but distracting question whether it is genuinely impossible for some so-called ecosystem services, the 'production flow' rather than 'stock' of nature (Walshe 2014), to be privatized, hence that they must needs be common property.
8 There is a further problem with the common asset tradition (which will be ignored here): it is often unclear to whom the term 'common' refers, who (in left-libertarianism) forms the group that is deprived of its collective resources: humanity or other, far more exclusive 'cooperative ventures for mutual benefit'.

References

Becker, L.C. (1977) *Property rights: Philosophical foundations*. Routledge, London.
Bergström, L. (2000) The concept of ownership (www.dropbox.com/s/ww7bbjsusfduomz/Ownership.pdf?dl=0) Accessed 25 January 2017.

Bromley, D.W. (1991) *Environment and property: Property rights and public policy*. Basil Blackwell, Oxford.

Carter, A.B. (1989) *The philosophical foundations of property rights*. Harvester Wheatsheaf, New York.

Cohen, M. (1978) "Property and sovereignty" in Macpherson, C. B. ed., *Property: Mainstream and critical positions*. University of Toronto Press, Toronto, 155–75.

Davidson, M.D. (2014) "Rights to ecosystem services" *Environmental Values* 23, 465–83.

Devall, B. and Sessions, G. (1985) *Deep ecology: Living as if nature mattered*. Gibbs M. Smith, Salt Lake City.

DiZerega, G. (1996) "Deep ecology and liberalism" *Review of Politics* 58, 699–734.

Dobson, A. (2007) *Green political thought*. Fourth edition. Routledge, Abingdon.

Epstein, R.A. (2009) "Property rights, state of nature theories, and environmental protection" *New York University Journal of Law and Liberty* 4 (www.law.nyu.edu/sites/default/files/ECM_PRO_061926.pdf) Accessed 21 January 2017.

Gaus, G. (2012) "Property and ownership" in Estlund, L. D. ed., *Oxford handbook of political philosophy*. Oxford University Press, Oxford, 93–112.

Gauthier, D. (1986) *Morals by agreement*. Clarendon Press, Oxford.

Freeman, S. (2002) "Illiberal libertarians: Why libertarianism is not a liberal view" *Philosophy and Public Affairs* 30, 105–51.

Hadley, J. (2005) "Excluding destruction: Towards an environmentally sustainable libertarian property rights regime" *Philosophy in the Contemporary World* 12, 22–9.

Hadley, J. (2015) *Animal property rights: A theory of habitat rights for wild animals*. Lexington Books, Lanham.

Hale, B. (2008) "Private property and environmental ethics: Some new directions" *Metaphilosophy* 39, 402–21.

Hayward, T. (1997) "Anthropocentrism: A misunderstood problem" *Environmental Values* 6, 49–63.

Hettinger, N. (1998a) Who owns nature? A debate (www.bioethics.iastate.edu/forum/hettinger.html) Accessed 25 January 2017.

Hettinger, N. (1998b) A reply to Jan Narveson (www.bioethics.iastate.edu/forum/hettingerreply.html) Accessed 25 January 2017.

Hobbes, T. (1968) (original 1651) *Leviathan*. Penguin, Harmondsworth.

Hohfeld, W.N. (1919) *Fundamental legal conceptions*. Yale University Press, New Haven.

Honoré, A.M. (1961) "Ownership" in Guest, A. G. ed. *Oxford essays in jurisprudence*. Clarendon Press, Oxford, 101–47.

Locke, J. (1924) (original 1689) *Two treatises of government*. Dent, London.

Machan, T. (1998) *Classical individualism: The supreme importance of each human being*. Routledge, London.

Macpherson, C.B. (1978) "The meaning of property" in Macpherson, C. B. ed., *Property: Mainstream and critical positions*. University of Toronto Press, Toronto, 1–13.

Munzer, S.R. (1990) *A theory of property*. Cambridge University Press, Cambridge.

Narveson, J. (1998) Who owns nature? A debate (www.bioethics.iastate.edu/forum/narveson.html) Accessed 21 January 2017.

Narveson, J. (2001) *The libertarian idea*. Broadview Press, Peterborough.

Newman, S. (2011) "The libertarian impulse" *Journal of Political Ideologies* 16, 239–44.

Nozick, R. (1974) *Anarchy, state, and utopia*. Basic Books, New York.

Rawls, J.B. (1993) *Political liberalism*. Columbia University Press, New York.

Rawls, J.B. (1999a) *A theory of justice*. Revised edition. Harvard University Press, Harvard.

Rawls, J.B. (1999b) *The law of peoples*. Harvard University Press, Harvard.

Raz, J. (1986) *The morality of freedom*. Oxford University Press, Oxford.

Risse, M. (2013) *On global justice*. Princeton University Press, Princeton.

Rothbard, M.N. (2002) *The ethics of liberty*. New York Universities Press, New York.

Sagoff, M. (1992) "Free-market versus libertarian environmentalism" *Critical Review* 6, 211–30.

Salter, J. (2001) "Hugo Grotius: Property and consent" *Political Theory* 29, 537–55.

Salter, J. (2010) "Adam Smith and the Grotian theory of property" *British Journal of Politics and International Relations* 12, 3–21.

Schmidtz, D. (2012) "The institution of property" in Schmitz, D. and Willot, E. eds., *Environmental ethics: What really matters, what really works*. Oxford University Press, Oxford, 406–20.

Scriven, T. (1997) *Wrongness, wisdom and wilderness: Towards a libertarian theory of ethics and the environment*. State University of New York Press, Albany.

Sheard, M. (2007) "Sustainability and property rights in environmental resources" *Environmental Ethics* 29, 389–401.

Steiner, H. (1994) *An essay on rights*. Blackwell, Oxford.

Steiner, H. (2009) "Left libertarianism and the ownership of natural resources" *Public Reason* 1, 1–8.

Tomasi, J. (2012) *Free market fairness*. Princeton University Press, Princeton.

Trachtenberg, Z. (2014) "John Locke: 'This habitable Earth of ours'" in Cannavò, P. F. and Lane, J. H. eds., *Engaging nature*. MIT Press, Cambridge, MA, 99–116.

Vallentyne, P. (2007) "Libertarianism and the state" *Social Philosophy and Policy* 24, 187–205.

Vallentyne, P., Steiner, H. and Otsuka, M. (2005) "Why left-libertarianism is not incoherent, indeterminate, or irrelevant: A reply to Fried" *Philosophy and Public Affairs* 33, 201–15.

Waldron, J. (1988) *The right to private property*. Blackwell, Oxford.

Walshe, G. (2014) "Green libertarianism" *Ethical Theory and Moral Practice* 17, 955–70.

Widerquist, K. (2010) "A dilemma for libertarianism" *Politics, Philosophy and Economics* 8, 43–72.

Wissenburg, M. (1998) *Green liberalism: The free and the green society*. Routledge, London.

Wissenburg, M. (2006) "Ecological neutrality and liberal survivalism: How (not) to discuss the compatibility of liberalism and ecologism" *Analyse & Kritik* 26, 125–45.

5 Rights to natural resources and human rights

Petra Gümplová

Exclusive authority over natural resources is one of the most prized rights attached to sovereignty, according to current international law. It implies a set of powers, prerogatives, and immunities, the most consequential of which is the right to legislate and adjudicate property rights over natural resources, including nationalization of foreign property, permission/power to decide on terms of foreign investment or extraction contracts, and control of the sales of natural resources. Allocated to states and their people in the process of decolonization and the post-war transformation of international law, the sovereign right to natural resources was meant to correct – and indeed corrected – the injustice of colonial dispossession of natural resources. Simultaneously, it was meant to secure economic benefits arising from the exploitation of natural resources for the people of developing and newly independent states. The principle that states have an exclusive right to use natural resources occurring on their territories so that they can fully realize the right to self-determination and provide well-being and development to their people lies at the foundation of the new system of the distribution of rights to natural resources.[1]

Yet many countries have failed to use their natural endowments for national development and the well-being of the people. Often, natural resources have been used for the private benefits of ruling elites and oligarchs, to sustain repression, authoritarianism, military rule, and even to wage an unjust war (Ross 2004). In current conditions of growing scarcity and high demand – and hence very high economic value of many natural resources – the right over natural resources can easily be turned into an ability to accumulate private wealth and sustain unjust rule. The case of Equatorial Guinea described by Leif Wenar has become notorious: its president Teodoro Obiang, who came to power unconstitutionally, is continuously able to sell the country's oil and use the revenue to sustain absolute repression of his people, and the lavish lifestyle of his family. Yet millions of gallons of Equatorial Guinea's oil keep arriving in the United States and other countries with unquestioned legal title to these resources – a title which is anchored in the fact of Obiang's sheer might and violent coercion (Wenar 2008, 7–8).

In this and many similar cases, the recognition of the right to natural resources seems to follow the old rule of international law – the so-called principle of "effectiveness" – according to which an entity is recognized as a sovereign state and hence entitled to all the powers, rights, privileges, and immunities ascribed to states by international law if it has an effective control over the population and the territory. The principle of effectiveness, however, is no longer a valid principle (Buchanan 2004, 6). According to current international law, the capacity to sustain control over a population and a territory by means of military force and repression is not considered adequate basis for the recognition of the political entity's exercise of power as legitimate. Today, no new state is internationally recognized as legitimate which came into being through aggressive war and violation of territorial integrity. No foreign occupation can deprive peoples of their right to self-determination and sovereignty. No government can be recognized as legitimate if it institutionalizes apartheid or engages in ethnic cleansing and genocide (Cassese 2001, 12–13).

These and other rules and principles – human rights, the right to self-determination, the prohibition of the use of force to name the most important ones – suggest there are conditions and minimal requirements of justice on which it is possible to assess, as Buchanan has put it, whether or not a given state is a member in good standing of the international community and, consequently, whether it can legitimately exercise all prerogatives and immunities which are attached to that status (Buchanan 2004, 261–269).

That a highly repressive and corrupt dictatorship which came to power unconstitutionally cannot be recognized to have a legitimate right to usurp benefits from the use of natural resources, and especially not use them to oppress its own people in radical ways, is precisely the case in point. Illegitimate power cannot vest rights to natural resources. There are conditions and requirements for a legitimate exercise of the right to natural resources. Yet/In spite of this, sovereign rights to natural resources have not been explicitly linked to some basic justice and legitimacy requirements, neither in theory nor in practice. With the exception of Leif Wenar's critique of the international trade with "stolen" natural resources (Wenar 2008, 2) and Pogge's proposal that states shall not have full property rights to natural resources on their territories (Pogge 2001, 66), political theory and the philosophy of justice have not fostered a discourse about the permissible scope of existing sovereign rights to natural resources, about the conditions of legitimacy of their exercise, and about the most important limits on them.

Such an account cannot be more urgent, morally and practically. Repressive dictatorships using natural resources to perpetrate domestic injustice are just one variant of an obviously illegitimate exercise of resource rights. There are other potentially harmful effects of the use of the right to natural resources, for example when corrupt and illegitimate governments strike bad and inequitable extraction deals which cause immense and permanent environmental harms and bring no economic benefits for the country's people, or when such governments transfer unlimited rights to natural resources to other states or entities, or when they destroy ecosystems with global environmental value or deplete parts of global commons.

From the critical international political theory perspective I seek to explore, the most important task is to clearly define conditions of legitimacy of the exercise of sovereign rights to natural resources. What is required, in other words, is an account of the conditions that must exist in a state for it to be recognized as an entity which can exercise legitimate rights to natural resources. When these conditions are not met, states and governments acting on their behalf are exercising their resource rights illegitimately.[2] To provide foundations for such an account of legitimacy is the focus of this chapter. The key argument I will defend is that international legal human rights should become the core of a much needed framework for thinking about the conditions of legitimacy of the exercise of resource rights.

Co-originality of human rights and rights to natural resources

Human rights as referred to in this analysis are international legal human rights, not moral human rights which are assumed to be enjoyed by individuals solely by virtue of their humanity and independent of institutions (Tasioulas 2012). As my main task is to clarify the positive rights of states to natural resources, I focus on international legal human rights. There is a twofold reason why human rights *qua* international law are the key for a systematic normative account of legitimacy of the exercise of rights to natural resources. First, human rights are historically co-original with the current system of sovereign rights to natural resources, that is, in addition to being mutually founded, they are also both mutually necessary in realization. Both systems of international legal rights are an outcome of the same process of the profound transformation and the development of international law in the post-WWII period and reflect its aim to redefine and reinforce justice, domestic and international. The notion of justice which connects them is an internationally recognized conception of domestic justice for territorially defined sovereign political units emphasizing principles of collective self-determination, individual rights, and national welfare and development.

Second, regardless of their co-originality with rights to natural resources, human rights have legally transformed the scope of sovereign prerogatives and have become *the* accepted and prominent international standard of legitimacy of state power. When human rights are recognized and conceptualized as such – as I will argue they ought to – it is a matter of consistency to apply their legitimating function to an account of sovereign rights to natural resources. Both accounts of human rights are necessary for a full conception of legitimate exercise of resource rights. While the latter account yields a general account of legitimacy of states and enables us to define conditions under which a sovereign state is legitimate or ceases to be legitimate under current international law, the first account allows us to specify legitimacy conditions positively, pointing to specific human rights which matter prominently for a legitimate exercise of resource rights. Let me first focus on the history and the origin of international legal human rights and show that rights to natural resources are inextricably intertwined with international human rights.

The right to self-determination, human rights and the collective ownership of natural resources

Introduced after World War II, from the outset international legal human rights have been central to the attempt to create an international regime that not only provides more effective safeguards of world peace but also articulates a new set of rights of every individual vis-à-vis their states. As Beitz reminds us, the modern practice of human rights has emerged as a response to the widespread perception, amid the ruins of World War II and the horrors of the Holocaust, of the need to remedy a major fault of the international order which concerned the vulnerability of individuals to mistreatment inflicted on them by their own states – and which was due in part to the virtually unlimited internal sovereignty that the norms of the international order conferred on all states. Consequently, the creation of international human rights was aimed, first and foremost, at remedying this flaw of international order based on an unlimited state sovereignty (Beitz 2011, 128–129).

The initial phase of the development of the international legal human rights regime, as human rights scholars and historians agree, was shaped by the politics of state executives and diplomats involved in the founding of the United Nations and dominated by attempts to mitigate the limits on state power implied in international human rights. The risk that internal treatment of one's own citizens could come under international scrutiny and that international human rights could become genuine limitations to state prerogatives ensured that they were made rather toothless at the outset. The Universal Declaration of Human Rights (UDHR) adopted by the UN's General Assembly on December 10, 1948 did not create binding international human rights law.

With the goal of establishing mechanisms for enforcing the UDHR, the UN Commission on Human Rights proceeded to draft two covenants which would complete and reinforce the declaratory UDHR and give human rights binding force in international law. The work of the Commission was derailed by Cold War conflicts. Progress began again in the early 1960s as the process of decolonization unfolded. Newly independent states and independence seeking groups asserted the importance of human rights via their claims and appeals to the right to self-determination. It was this process of decolonization which returned human rights to the UN agenda (Schrijver 1997; Reus-Smit 2013; Jensen 2016).

It is at this historical juncture where the establishment of the system of sovereign rights to natural resources originated, as an outcome of the struggle for independence and the collective liberation from colonial powers. The majority of emerging and newly independent states (together with already independent developing states) claimed national ownership of natural resources. They sought to end the practice of colonial and contractual dispossession of natural resources on their territories and they wanted to secure economic benefits arising from the exploitation of natural resources for themselves and their populations. They saw their claims to national ownership of natural resources as inherently implied in the newly invoked right to collective self-determination. Claiming the right to political self-determination together with sovereignty over natural resources reflected a widely shared insight that national ownership of natural resources facilitates and reinforces both economic development and political independence (Schrijver 2013).

The national ownership of, or the sovereignty over, natural resources has thus been inextricably linked to and justified by the collective right to self-determination. It needs to be emphasized here that in order to play the central role in what has arguably been the most profound political realignment of the international order in modern history, self-determination had to be reinvented from an ethno-nationalist political principle into a legal right (Cassese 1995, 11–34). The reinvented right to self-determination recognized that "all peoples" with a political identity, not only ethnic groups or minorities, have the right to self-determination, especially if they had been subject to unjust oppression and colonization. The reinvention also involved acknowledgement of the view that political independence and national ownership of natural resources are two inextricably connected and mutually reinforcing facets of this right.

The reinvention of the right to self-determination and its normative foundations so that it could become the key justificatory principle of decolonization occurred in the context of the negotiation about human rights covenants in the Commission on Human Rights. As a result of intense negotiations, the right of self-determination together with the provision about sovereignty over natural resources were included in both human rights covenants.[3] As Reus-Smit argued, the reinvented right to self-determination was thus grafted on to emergent human rights norms and asserted as necessary for the satisfaction of human rights, with postcolonial states having played a prominent role in this assertion (Reus-Smit 2013, 188). Reflecting on the controversies surrounding the inclusion of the right of self-determination and its basic constituent – the right of permanent sovereignty over natural resources – the Commission on Human Rights called for the establishment of a special General Assembly commission on sovereignty and natural resources. A new commission was established and as a result of its work, a General Assembly Resolution entitled *Declaration on Permanent Sovereignty over Natural Resources* was adopted in 1962. This resolution confirmed and reinforced the notion of a sovereign territorial right to natural resources and reaffirmed its link to the right to self-determination.[4]

There is thus an inextricable historical connection between the right to self-determination, sovereign territorial rights to natural resources, and human rights. However, the anti-colonial reinvention of the right to collective self-determination revitalized concern with human rights, which, at the same time, helped to redefine self-determination's normative foundations. The right to self-determination was named as the very first of all human rights – a threshold right, so to speak – in human rights covenants. At the same time, the right to self-determination included national ownership of natural resources as it was seen by the majority of actors as an economic implication of this quintessential and fundamental political right.

Interpreting this connection, it can be argued that the right to self-determination, sovereign territorial rights to natural resources, and human rights together represent a coherent and internationally recognized notion of justice for the plurality of territorially situated self-determining collectives. This notion involves equal formal rights of collective self-determination, non-intervention, territorial integrity, and sovereign equality for politically self-determining groups which is underpinned by values of political independence, territorial control, national social, economic and cultural development and collective well-being, and individual rights. Territorial ownership of natural resources is an inherent element of this notion of justice because it is a condition *sine qua non* of collective political self-determination – both because in the absence of control over natural resources political independence is incomplete and because economic development, for which natural resources are instrumental, significantly reinforces independence. Human rights are similarly inseparable from the right to self-determination. While the right to self-determination is the condition of possibility of the exercise of human rights and the manifestation of their totality, human rights specify the internal content of collective self-determination. National ownership of natural resources and the requirement to use them for national development can also help to fulfil demands implied in social and economic human rights.

What follows from this historical connection and the close moral affinity is that human rights ought to count in a normative account of rights to natural resources, especially in determining the permissible scope of the right to self-determination and, by extension, of the right to natural resources. However, the kind of implication human rights have for the account of rights to natural resources based on this reconstruction of historical affinity is limited to a definition of the moral purpose and permissible scope of rights to natural resources. The co-originality account I have just presented yields the following notion: to the extent to which human rights define the content of the right to collective self-determination, rights to natural resources ought to be instrumental in providing a self-determining collective with resources for the protection and fulfilment of human rights.

A full legitimacy account can be achieved when we further investigate the development and growth of the international system of human rights and their being at the very core of the process of moral transformation of state sovereignty and becoming an international standard of legitimacy of state power. To show that a notion of limited state sovereignty – and hence sovereignty subject to legitimacy criteria – is at the heart of the system of state rights to natural resources, let me now present a conception of human rights which focuses on the sovereignty-limiting function of human rights and their being a valid and accepted international standard of the political legitimacy of state power. Human rights transform sovereignty by legalizing a set of limits on sovereign powers, prerogatives, and immunities, thus serving as the vantage point for the evaluation of political legitimacy of states. These same conditions of legitimacy then need to be applied to resource rights.

Human rights: limited sovereignty and international standard of legitimacy

Current practice of human rights involves a vast, complex, and multi-level legal, political, and institutional system.[5] It has been shown that human rights have become a significant force in world politics (Teitel 2011; Sikkink 2011). It has been demonstrated how human rights have had a profound impact on domestic politics and domestic constitutional change (Sikkink and Risse 1999; Simmons 2009). Since the 1970s, human rights have been used by resistance and social movements and civil society groups to claim rights against their own governments and demand constitutionalization of human rights (Cohen 2012). Recently, international issues – global trade, finance, access to pharmaceuticals, climate change, migration (including environmental migration) – are being framed as issues of human rights (Risse 2013).

The conception of human rights I propose to use and which will serve the purpose of plausibly reconfiguring rights to natural resources is in fact nothing more than an interpretive account of international legal human rights which emphasizes its sovereignty-limiting function and interprets human rights as an international standard of political legitimacy of states. I will rely on Allen Buchanan's recent interpretation of human rights, because unlike other philosophical conceptions focused on moral human rights,[6] he provides an interpretive account of human rights as international legal norms relevant in the practice, their key sovereignty-limiting function, and their being the prominent international standard of legitimacy of state power (Buchanan 2004, 2013).

Sovereignty-limiting function of human rights

Human rights are rights belonging to all human beings regardless of their nationality, residence, national or ethnic origin, religion, or any other status or membership. They are guaranteed by international law and its various sources, most importantly by human rights treaties. What human rights we have can be simply determined by consulting official lists of human rights in international law documents, particularly the International Bill of Human Rights, which includes UDHR and both international human rights covenants. They include security rights (protection of people against murder, genocide, torture, rape), due process rights (protection against abuses of a legal system), liberty rights (protection of freedom in areas of belief, expression, association, assembly, movement), political rights (liberty to participate in politics through communication, assembling, voting, protesting, serving in public office, etc.), equality rights (guarantee equal citizenship, equality before the law, non-discrimination), social welfare rights (require provision of education to all children and protection against severe poverty – right to education, right to health), and economic liberties (right to own property, equality of making contracts, freedom from slavery and servitude, right to form and join unions, rights against discrimination in the workplace and all spheres of trade and commerce, equal pay) (Buchanan 2013, 168).

The key characteristic of international legal human rights, Buchanan suggests, is that they involve a robust commitment to the equal basic moral status of all individuals on the one hand, and to their well-being on the other (Buchanan 2013, 32). While the status egalitarian function of human rights follows from their prohibiting various forms and practices of discrimination, the well-being function of human rights follows from their protecting people from harms and abuses inflicted by their own states and, even more so, from the requirement that all states provide their citizens the goods and services characteristic of the modern welfare state – health care and education, protection against unemployment, medical insurance, etc. Human rights, then, are international legal norms that not only help to protect all people everywhere from severe harms perpetrated by states, but also prescribe states to fulfil a relatively expansive range of functions via a set of legal, political, social, and economic institutions.

Therefore, as an international legal system, human rights have one major function, which is to redefine the permissible scope of sovereign power and to impose rather stringent limits on what can rightfully be claimed as a sovereign right or prerogative. Indeed, this sovereignty-limiting function has been part of the system of human rights from the very beginning. The basic idea of the system of international legal human rights since its inception in the immediate aftermath of WWII has been to develop a regime of international law whose primary function is to provide a universal standard for regulating the behaviour of states toward those under their jurisdiction and at the same time subject states and their treatment of their people to scrutiny by an emerging international community (Cohen 2012, 165–166; Beitz 2011, 128–129).

By prescribing a set of individual rights to all human beings, human rights impose duties and obligations on states, thus circumscribing the permissible scope of sovereign power and providing a set of substantive limits on its *internal* exercise. I agree with Buchanan that this is the key innovation and function of international human rights law, namely to limit sovereignty in its internal exercise, within the state's own jurisdiction, and for the sake of individuals themselves, with the aim of affirming equal moral status of all individuals and to help to ensure that all have the opportunity to achieve a certain level of well-being by providing necessary resources and institutions (Buchanan 2013, 23). In any case, sovereignty can no longer be understood as a political fact of absolute, unlimited, and impermeable state power standing above international law. The supremacy claim involved in the concept and the institution of sovereignty – a claim to supremacy of the political authority and its exclusive jurisdiction over a population within a territory – now means that the political authority has a limited scope and that there are limits on what it can legally claim to belong to its prerogative.[7] The states can no longer claim sovereign rights to violate human rights.

This sovereignty-limiting function is legally normative in character. Human rights impose international legal obligations on states and on their behaviour.[8] To a much lesser extent, Buchanan concedes, human rights limit state sovereignty as a matter of effective constraints, i.e. what states can actually do. States are surely able and capable to do what they are prohibited from doing by international human rights law – and there are, sadly, too many cases of gross human rights violations in many parts of the world. The lack of effective constraints has to do with the procedural weakness of the international legal system. Implementation and enforcement are left to states in their own territories. The international community lacks the authority to enforce human rights and to stop gross and systematic violations, except in cases of crimes against humanity, such as genocide (Buchanan 2013, 23).

Human rights as an international standard of political legitimacy

Before I move further, let me emphasize that the sovereignty-limiting notion of human rights I have just presented is nothing more and nothing less than a descriptive, interpretive claim about human rights as an international legal system. It is derived from the fact emphasized by Buchanan that in the current system, legal duties that correspond to individual international legal rights are ascribed primarily or exclusively to states. Moreover, a particular state has human rights duties solely towards its own nationals and individuals who are under its territorial jurisdiction. When a state is unable or unwilling to fulfil these duties, other states may have some sort of responsibility to achieve their fulfilment, but this responsibility does not currently rise to the level of a fully-fledged legal duty. However, this is neither an essentialist claim that human rights can or ought to limit only states, nor a normative claim that aims of human rights are best achieved or fulfilled by limiting states' powers and prerogatives. The international human rights system could be different – better – if primary duties to fulfil human rights were assigned not only to states but also to international organizations and global corporations. Indeed, there are good reasons to hope that the system is moving in the direction of these changes, especially corporations' increasing respect for human rights (Buchanan 2013, 24–25).

The point I wish to argue for next is: by circumscribing the permissible scope of sovereign authority and by providing a set of limits on sovereign rights and prerogatives, human rights also provide an international standard of legitimacy of state power. Human rights, as I argued, limit the internal exercise of sovereign authority vis-à-vis the citizens subjected to it. Now I argue that whether, and to what extent, states respect those limits determines their international legitimacy. Respect for human rights, in other words, accrues international legitimacy to state power in international arena. Such an international legitimacy standard is important and urgent because being a sovereign state means being ascribed a unique set of rights and immunities granted by international law. Most obviously, states are supreme and exclusive agents in the making, application, and enforcement of laws within their territorial jurisdiction. Furthermore, states can be party to agreements, treaties, and alliances, they are entitled to non-intervention in their domestic affairs and have international support in preserving their territorial integrity in the face of various threats. Not less significantly, as Buchanan reminds us, states can also participate in the process of international law making and its adjudication. Equally important – and usually missing from most international law theories' lists – is sovereignty over natural resources.

Whether a sovereign entity can exercise these powers is a moral issue and does need to be subject to legitimacy concerns. As a result of these sovereign rights, privileges, and immunities states can sell off natural resources, borrow money, make long-term foreign investment contracts, and more. These rights support and enhance a state's ability to wield political power and coerce. Their exercise can have long-term devastating consequences for the people: the borrowing privilege can burden future generations with a huge debt, terms of bad foreign investment deals have to be complied with in the future, and selling natural resources can impoverish a nation or sustain authoritarianism and civil conflict. Given these profound and potentially devastating consequences the exercise of sovereign rights can have; we need to specify conditions under which they can be legitimately exercised. We urgently need a legitimacy criterion which tells us when states are morally justified in exercising the full bundle of powers, liberties, immunities, and prerogatives that constitute sovereignty. For reasons alluded to at the beginning, this is especially the case of rights to natural resources – their exercise significantly enhances the ability to wield and maintain power and perpetrate potential injustice. On a more profound level, natural resources play a key role in the sustenance and improvement of human life. Since they are beneficial for humans and since they are also scarce, and can be depletable and unevenly distributed across the world and hence subject to conflicting claims, the scope of rights to natural resources has to be clearly defined.

Legitimacy, as it is commonly and generally understood, determines when a political institution or entity is justified in exercising political power. More specifically, it is possible to argue that legitimacy turns the exercise of political power into a legitimate exercise of political authority. An attempt to rule without legitimacy is an exercise of sheer, unjustified power. A conception of political legitimacy then determines what the conditions of the justification of the exercise of political power are, or when and under what conditions is the use of political power a legitimate authority (Raz 1986). The importance of such a conception can be established by making a reverse claim – a conception of political legitimacy is important because we want to know when political institutions are *not* justified in exercising power, i.e. when they are not legitimate authorities.

Clearly, states are the most prominent candidates for a legitimacy account. States are dominant and prevalent forms of political organization and the institutionalization of political power. Their capacity to wield political power is greater than the capacity of any other institution. An account of political legitimacy of power exercised by a state is pertinent; and attempts to provide it have been central to modern political thought. Until very recently, accounts of political legitimacy of a state's power were accounts focused exclusively on the issue of *internal* legitimacy, that is, on the conditions under which the exercise of political power within a political entity's own borders is morally justified to this entity's own citizens. States, however, can also be subject to an *international* legitimacy concern. They may or may not be recognized as legitimate by other states, international organizations, and other entities; and recognizing them as legitimate essentially means, as Buchanan has put it, that they can or cannot be recognized as members in good standing of the international system, with all the rights, powers, and immunities that go with such a status (Buchanan 2004, 261).

The account of international political legitimacy of states I suggest is as follows. The international legitimacy account of states determines conditions of moral justifiability in achieving supremacy in the making, application, and enforcement of laws within a territorial jurisdiction, having this supremacy recognized by other states or international entities, and being authorized to exercise a full bundle of sovereign rights, prerogatives, and immunities protected by international law. Human rights, as I have shown, prescribe a set of legal duties to states, thus playing the most prominent role in limiting sovereign power and circumscribing the scope of what belongs to sovereign prerogative. Hence, a state is internationally legitimate if it protects the human rights of its citizens and provides this protection through processes, policies, and actions that themselves respect the most basic human rights. If a state meets the human rights standards, it ought to be regarded as a member of international society entitled to a free exercise of a full set of powers, rights, and immunities that come with this status.

Why must the criterion of legitimacy of states be derived from human rights? Traditional accounts of (internal) legitimacy in political theory identified consent, public reason, or democratic approval as sources of legitimacy. These are however unfit for an account of international legitimacy of states. Neither the consent of the governed, nor public reason or democracy can provide a unified, universal standard for conferring legitimacy on the plurality of states in international realm. Human rights have the unique capacity of being able to supply this universal international standard of the treatment of citizens by a state and hence the standard for international concern and a threshold for a possible remedial action by the international community. This capacity of human rights follows from their legal universality and their being valid and binding on almost all states in the world, with a near universal agreement on their substance and no systematic attempts to dismiss them or to replace them.[9] Moreover, there is what Donnelly has called an "overlapping political consensus" on the conception of justice human rights embody.[10] A distinct advantage of human rights, from this perspective, is that they allow us to identify a minimal standard of justice which cuts across the traditional spectrum of democratic and undemocratic regimes. Furthermore, as Buchanan noted, human rights enable that the justice requirements for international legitimacy can become more demanding over time (Buchanan 2004, 269). Not least importantly, human rights are a dominant moral currency in the practice – they are central to advocacy, critique, and mobilization against injustice.

Given the emphasis on indivisibility and interdependence of human rights, I suggest we accept that a more specific or applied account of international legitimacy of states based on human rights can only be a negative one: it can only specify conditions under which a given state ceases to be legitimate and cannot therefore legitimately exercise powers granted to it by international law, including the right to natural resources. Correspondingly, we can determine that a state is *illegitimate* when human rights are systematically and grossly violated. There are several options of how to specify the minimal threshold. One option is to identify the most urgent human rights using the notion of *jus cogens* – higher, non-derogable norms of international law to which some human rights count. They include the right to life, right not to be subjected to torture or inhuman or degrading treatment, right to be free from slavery, and the right not to be subjected to retroactive criminal law (Klein 2008). Another would be to say that a state is illegitimate when it violates those most fundamental human rights whose violation provides a legal ground for international community's intervention (Raz 2010). Currently, however, there exists a very narrow range of human rights whose violation (inconsistently) suspends sovereignty immunity.[11] In both cases, illegitimacy is defined by the violation of the most profound human rights.

It can be objected that this is a rather minimalist outcome. However, recognizing that there *is* a plausible distinction between international legitimacy of a state power and lack of thereof is an important achievement. It is, as I have suggested throughout this chapter, also practically urgent. In fact, human rights are already being used as a standard in international practice. They have been increasingly applied as a condition for various types of international engagement. Serious human rights infringements inform the politics of military and humanitarian intervention and the politics of economic sanctions and development aid/ assistance. A shared assumption is that the state which does not comply with these most basic required standards of human rights does not retain the right to non-intervention and to other sovereign rights or entitlements.

To summarize, human rights are binding international legal norms ascribed to all human beings. Under current international law, states are the primary holders of obligations and duties to protect and to fulfil human rights. Human rights lay down legal obligations for states and their governments to refrain from certain acts and to act in certain ways. By doing so, human rights have assumed a prominent sovereignty-limiting function which is legally normative in character. Due to their international legal universality and inalienability, but also due to growing political consensus on their embodying a universal conception of justice and protecting individuals against universalized threats and risks of today's globalized world, human rights represent *the* set of norms which redefine and circumscribe the permissible scope of sovereign authority in its domestic sphere. Precisely because of this feature, human rights provide the most fitting and unique standard of international legitimacy of states.

Legitimacy of the exercise of rights to natural resources

The key claim I have tried to support by the above analysis is that human rights are prominently relevant and directly consequential for a normative reinterpretation of rights to natural resources, especially for an account of conditions of their legitimate exercise. In this concluding section I will outline ways to arrive at a more specific notion of international political legitimacy of state power relying on the human rights standard and applied to the issue of resource rights.

There is a blueprint for such an applied account. Leif Wenar has offered a specification of what rights matter prominently and how the failure to protect them results in the illegitimate practice of the exercise of resource rights. Attempting to tackle the causes of the resource curse, Wenar has critically observed that international commodity trade wrongfully allows illegitimate and corrupt governments (essentially anyone who can simply maintain the coercive control over the territory) to sell natural resources. Rules which allow those who have no right to sell natural resources and which also recognize legal titles to acquired stolen goods are defective rules of international trade because they massively violate property rights of many peoples, often the poorest nations in the world. Invoking moral principles of ownership and sale (rightful possession, valid sale, good faith purchase, valid title to a good, etc.) and showing how they are violated by existing institutions and practices is the core of Wenar's analysis.[12]

Following the property rights approach, Wenar attempted to specify conditions which must be obtained in a country if the people, the ultimate collective owners of a country's natural resources according to current international law, can be said to be meaningfully authorizing their governments to sell natural resources and when, by extension, buyers can acquire legal title to purchased goods. According to Wenar, the key to a valid authorization of the sale of natural resources is people's consent. Consent to government's sales of natural resources requires that citizens have information about what their government is doing and can influence the decisions without severe costs or risk. In concrete political terms, being able to consent requires that citizens have at least minimal civil liberties and political rights – freedom of expression, association, right to participate in politics through communication, assembling, voting, protesting, serving in public office, and the guarantee of equality before the law. The key point is that when these basic civil and political rights are not guaranteed, the government has no right to sell natural resources and the purchaser cannot obtain valid title to them (Wenar 2008, 20–21).

Wenar further proposes what in his view is a feasible reform based on enforcing property rights. It involves setting up a mechanism which indicates who is not a rightful seller of natural resources and punishes those who pursue commercial transactions with such a seller. The proposal relies on globally respected monitoring of compliance with civil liberties and political rights by Freedom House, an NGO providing reports on democracy, political freedom, and human rights. Country ratings provided by Freedom House are based on accepted criteria of what constitutes most important civil liberties and political rights; and the systematic monitoring of the compliance makes it possible for states and international institutions to rely on them. Countries which receive a rating of 6 or 7 from Freedom House are countries with very restricted or no political rights.[13] Citizens of these countries cannot have sufficient information about resource sales, or sufficient opportunity to dissent from those sales, or sufficient freedom from political manipulation. As Wenar suggests, a Freedom House rating of 7 should therefore be a decisive indication that such a regime cannot legitimately sell resources from that country. It also puts all potential buyers on notice that the regime within that country lacks valid title to the resources they offer to sell (Wenar 2008, 24). I consider Wenar's proposal plausible and methodologically instrumental for a further development of a full account of legitimate exercise of rights to natural resources. However, Wenar's conception of legitimacy of the exercise of resource rights focused on political rights and civil liberties needs to be systematized and expanded. Most importantly, a broader set of human rights needs to be taken into account and guaranteed so that the exercise of a full bundle of powers and immunities associated with rights to natural resources can be considered fully legitimate. Moreover, the legitimacy account can also be enhanced by putting an emphasis on substantive values which ought to be realized through the exercise of resource rights.

Rights to natural resources involve a bundle of rights, prerogatives, and immunities, such as the right to legislate, adjudicate, and enforce property rights in the region, including rules of taxation, the right to determine who can, and under what conditions, access, extract, manage, and sell resources, or who has the power to enter into treaties that transfer some of the powers to another entity. They also include the right to nationalize foreign investment (Schrijver 1997, 263). Using those powers, governments make a whole range of decisions about natural resources concerning what to do with natural resources, how and to whom to allocate exploration and extraction licenses, what are the terms of investment contracts, rules of taxation, standards for environmental impact assessment, revenue distribution, and government spending. The whole range of these governmental decisions, not merely government's sale of natural resources, ought to matter for a legitimacy account.

Political rights and civil liberties can no longer be considered as sufficient for citizens' ability to express consent or participate in decision making. A strong commitment to moral equality of persons as recognized by contemporary liberal theory and practice requires equal participation and recognition of all if consent is to be considered the key legitimizing resource for decision making. Equal participation and recognition require a broader set of rights making it possible for people to actually be able to express their consent. When people are severely discriminated against, misrecognized, or denied access to basic goods, they can hardly be able to participate as equals and hence considered capable of expressing their consent. A long history of struggles of indigenous groups for the protection and control over their territories and natural resources and continuous injustice perpetrated by states and corporations is precisely the case in point. Structural discrimination, long-standing misrecognition, poverty, illiteracy, lack of access to health care and education, lack of economic and symbolic resources such as the ability to seek legal remedies for wrongdoing significantly undermine indigenous groups' ability to use their civil and political rights.

Therefore, the compliance with basic security rights, equality and non-discrimination rights, due process rights, and social and economic rights which guarantee substantive equality, participatory parity, and recognition is no less important if the decisions are to be made in legitimate way. It is precisely this broad notion of equal moral status and well-being which is involved in human rights. Therefore, human rights in their totality must inform the notion of legitimacy of the exercise of rights to natural resources. When systemic and pervasive violations of all human rights occur, a given state cannot be said to legitimately exercise powers granted to it by international law, including the right to natural resources. Accepting Wenar's suggestion that we rely on globally accepted public standards of compliance with human rights, we can then argue that global monitoring, ratings and indexes which indicate the level of compliance with basic security rights, the degree of governments' transparency and accountability, press and civil society freedom, and the rule of law need to be combined.[14]

Lastly, legitimate exercise of rights to natural resources also bears on substantive values that are realized through the exercise of these rights. In the first part of my analysis I linked human rights historically to rights to natural resources and showed that they belong to an internationally accepted conception of domestic justice for the plurality of territorially situated self-determining collectives, centred around principles of collective self-determination and human rights. The analysis yielded the following conclusion: to the extent to which human rights define the content and limits on the right to collective self-determination which justifies right to natural resources, rights to natural resources ought to be not only exercised in accordance with human rights, but they also ought to be prominently instrumental in providing self-determining collectives resources for the protection and fulfilment of human rights, especially social and welfare rights.

Social and welfare rights thus have another specific role in the legitimacy account I argue for. They indicate that the exercise of resource rights is linked to a set of legitimate purposes and aims. These aims and purposes are inextricably connected to individual social and economic rights (right to social security; right to adequate standard of living and the continuous improvement of living conditions including food, clothing, and housing; right to be free from hunger and hence provide food security and distribution; right to the enjoyment of the highest attainable standard of physical and mental health; and the right to education, and protection against severe poverty).[15] These rights matter prominently for the justification of why states have exclusive sovereign rights to natural resources in the first place – to have access and control over natural resources necessary for a sustainable development and for the fulfilment of domestic social justice demands. Rather than directly obliging states to refrain from abuses but rather prescribe certain actions aimed at the promotion of public good and realization of certain social goals and outcomes benefiting citizens of a given country.

The argument I have made in this chapter is that human rights have to assume a central role in the normative account of the rights of states to natural resources, especially concerning conditions of their legitimate exercise. Because of their historical and moral affinity with rights to natural resources and because of their becoming the internationally accepted standard of legitimacy of state power, human rights in their totality represent a set of conditions which a state must meet for it to be recognized internationally as a state which exercises its rights to natural resources legitimately. Human rights circumscribe a permissible scope of rights to natural resources; and they also determine a set of substantive goals which are to be achieved by allocating these rights to sovereign states. Human rights, in other words, represent key international standards of legitimate natural resource governance. States which systematically and pervasively violate all-important categories of human rights – security rights, civil liberties and political rights, due process rights, equality rights, and social and economic rights – cannot be considered to have international legitimacy for their exercise of sovereignty over natural resources. Seeking effective mechanisms of responding to such illegitimate uses – e.g. international monitoring of resource governance, reforming trade rules, reinforcing consumer ethics – has to become a focus of human rights practice.

Notes

1 The Resolution on Permanent Sovereignty recognizes in its very first article that "the right of peoples and nations to permanent sovereignty over their natural wealth and resources must be exercised in the interest of their national development and of the well-being of the people of the State concerned." Permanent Sovereignty over Natural Resources, GA Resolution 1803, 17 GAOR, Supp. 17, U. N. doc. A/5217. www.un.org/ga/search/view_doc.asp?symbol=A/RES/1803%28XVII%29

2 I borrow Wenar's explicit formulation here. My argument, however, is different. Wenar focuses in particular on the conditions under which it is possible for the people of a given country to authorize resource sales. Correspondingly, Wenar emphasizes civil liberties and political rights, not human rights as such.

3 Covenant on Economic, Social and Cultural Rights, Annex to General Assembly Resolution 2200 (XXI), December 16, 1966; and International Covenant on Civil and Political Rights, Annex to General Assembly Resolution 2200 (XXI), December 16, 1966. The Covenants entered into force on January 3 and March 23, 1976, respectively. Available from www.ohchr.org/EN/ProfessionalInterest/Pages/Core Instruments.aspx.

4 The document recognizes that permanent sovereignty over natural wealth and resources is "a basic constituent of the right to self-determination" and that it is an inalienable right of all states, peoples, and nations to freely and fully dispose of their natural wealth and resources within their territorial boundaries in accordance with their national interests and have full control over their use for the benefit of its citizens.

   Permanent Sovereignty over Natural Resources, GA Resolution 1803, 17 GAOR, Supp. 17, U. N. doc. A/5217 at p. 15. www.un.org/ga/search/view_doc.asp?symbol=A/RES/1803%28XVII%29.

5 It consists of the UN human rights system (UN treaty system, agencies, courts, monitoring and reporting bodies), regional human rights systems (regional conventions and treaties, monitoring bodies and courts), the International Criminal Court and NGOs. The practice involves norm-making (drafting and ratification of treaties and

declarations on global, regional, and state levels; creating, amending, harmonizing domestic constitutions with human rights norms), monitoring of the compliance with treaties, responding to international scrutiny and criticism, decisions of international and regional courts, advocacy work of NGOs and individual actors.

6 According to most philosophical conceptions (e.g. Nickel 2007; Griffin 2008; Wellman 2010; Tasioulas 2012) human rights are the most important among *moral* rights, articulating especially valuable interests and particularly weighty moral concerns that all human beings have irrespective of any personal merit, accomplishment, or associative relationship they have entered into. An essential problem of these approaches is that they are unable to justify all existing international legal human rights; make sense of their content, scope, and the function they play in our world; and are useless for the assessment of the human rights practice by international law institutions (Buchanan 2013, 9–14).

7 I use the term sovereignty similarly as Jean L. Cohen: sovereignty involves a claim to supremacy of the political authority and its exclusive jurisdiction over a population within a territory. It means essentially that there are no equal powers within the polity with independent claims to jurisdiction or political rule. The correlative of domestic supremacy is external independence. Internal supremacy and external autonomy are two sides of the same coin and yet are different: external sovereignty is a legal principle according to which all sovereign entities have an equal entitlement to the same general rights and are subject to the same general obligations under valid international law (Cohen 2012, 26–27, 199–201).

8 Legal validity of some of human rights norms does not even depend on state consent. Most essential human rights, e.g. right not be subjected to torture, slavery, or genocide are considered to be *jus cogens* norms of international law – fundamental principles and norms accepted by international community from which no derogation is possible.

9 Six core international human rights treaties (both covenants, conventions on racial discrimination, women's rights, torture, and the rights of the child) had, in early 2012 on average 172 parties, which represents a very high 88% ratification rate. Substantial majority of states in every regional, religious, or political grouping are parties to most of these treaties. Furthermore, there are no systematic patterns of deviation or attempts to dismiss those essential human rights (Donnelly 2013, 94–100).

10 Human rights embody a conception of justice centred around the notion of moral equality of all human beings, not a comprehensive religious, philosophical, and moral doctrine. This makes it possible for all cultures, regions, and leading worldviews to participate in an "overlapping consensus" on internationally recognized human rights. Such a consensus, although partial rather than complete, and political rather than moral or religious, according to Donnelly, is real and important (Donnelly 2013, 96–97).

11 It is now generally accepted that when a state commits genocide and thus violates the most fundamental human rights of its citizens, a multilateral armed intervention is legally permitted and the Security Council suspends the immunity of such a state against intervention.

12 According to Wenar, a fundamental moral and legal principle governing the sale of property is that in order to complete a valid sale a vendor must have the right to sell. If the goods are stolen, no title can be passed to any buyer (Wenar 2008, 17).

13 Countries and territories with a rating of 6 have very restricted political rights. They are ruled by one-party or military dictatorships, religious hierarchies, or autocrats. They may allow a few political rights, such as some representation or autonomy for minority groups, and a few are traditional monarchies that tolerate political discussion and accept public petitions. Countries and territories with a rating of 7 have few or no political rights because of severe government oppression, sometimes in combination

with civil war. They may also lack an authoritative and functioning central government and suffer from extreme violence or rule by regional warlords. https://freedom house.org/report/freedom-world-2016/methodology

14 There are several respected and recognized indicators which can be relied upon. Genocide Watch monitors countries at risk of genocide and publishes alerts which alert the global public not only to actual cases of genocide underway but where it is imminent. Transparency International monitors corruption and the abuse of public and governmental power for private gain. Its Corruption Perception Index measures the levels of the public sector's corruption in every country. World Justice Project measures the extent to which countries adhere to the rule of law.

15 See Articles 11–13 in International Covenant on Economic, Social and Cultural Rights. www.ohchr.org/EN/ProfessionalInterest/Pages/CESCR.aspx.

References

Beitz C. R. (2011) *The Idea of Human Rights*. Oxford University Press, New York.

Buchanan A. (2004) *Justice, Legitimacy, and Self-Determination: The Moral Foundations for International Law*. Oxford University Press, New York.

Buchanan A. (2013) *The Heart of Human Rights*. Oxford University Press, New York.

Cassese A. (1995) *Self-Determination of Peoples: A Legal Reappraisal*. Cambridge University Press, Cambridge.

Cassese A. (2001) *International Law*. Oxford University Press, New York.

Cohen J. L. (2012) *Globalization and Sovereignty: Rethinking Legality, Legitimacy, and Constitutionalism*. Cambridge University Press, New York.

Donnelly J. (2013) *Universal Human Rights in Theory and Practice*. Cornell University Press, Ithaca.

Griffin J. (2008) *On Human Rights*. Oxford University Press, New York.

Jensen S. L. B. (2016) *The Making of International Human Rights: The 1960s, Decolonisation, and the Reconstruction of Global Values*. Cambridge University Press, New York.

Klein E. (2008) "Hierarchy of Human Rights" *Israel Law Review 41*, 477–488.

Nickel J. (2007) *Making Sense of Human Rights*. Blackwell, Malden.

Pogge T. (2001) "Eradicating Systemic Poverty: a brief for a global resource dividend" *Journal of Human Development 2*(1), 59–77.

Raz J. (1986) *The Morality of Freedom*. Oxford University Press, Oxford.

Raz J. (2010) "Human Rights without Foundations" in Tasioulas J. and Besson S. eds., *The Philosophy of International Law*. Oxford University Press, Oxford, 328–330.

Risse M. (2013) *On Global Justice*. Princeton University Press, Princeton.

Ross M. L. (2004) "How Do Natural Resources Influence Civil War? Evidence from Thirteen Cases" *International Organization 58*, 35–67.

Schrijver N. (1997) *Sovereignty over Natural Resources*. Cambridge University Press, Cambridge.

Schrijver N. (2013) "Self-Determination of Peoples and Sovereignty over Natural Wealth and Resources" in *Realizing the Right to Development*. United Nations Publication, New York, 95–102.

Sikkink K. (2011) *The Justice Cascade: How Human Rights Are Changing World Politics*. Norton, New York.

Sikkink K. and Risse T. (1999) *The Power of Human Rights: International Norms and Domestic Change*. Cambridge University Press, Cambridge.

Simmons B. A. (2009) *Mobilizing for Human Rights: International Law and Domestic Politics*. Cambridge University Press, Cambridge.

Reus-Smit C. (2013) *Individual Rights and the Making of the International System*. Cambridge University Press, Cambridge.

Tasioulas J. (2012) "On the Nature of Human Rights" in Ernst G. and Heilinger J. C. eds., *The Philosophy of Human Rights: Contemporary Controversies*. Walter de Gruyter, Berlin, 17–59.

Teitel R. (2011) *Humanity's Law*. Oxford University Press, New York.

Wellman C. (2010) *The Moral Dimension of Human Rights*. Oxford University Press, Oxford.

Wenar L. (2008) "Property Rights and the Resource Curse" *Philosophy & Public Affairs* 36(1), 2–32.

6 Making sense of the human right to landscape

Markku Oksanen and Anne Kumpula

Introduction

Imagine that one day you wake up and immediately notice that the world around you is not similar to the world you experienced in the previous evening: what surrounds you and what is the source of sensory experiences have altered radically. Most people, depending on their conditions of living and the functioning of senses, may consider this as deterioration of the quality of life and thus if done intentionally, it would constitute a case of harming. The landscapes to which people are biophysically, culturally and emotionally attached arguably belong to the constitutive goods of human life. This is most explicit in the case of exceptional landscapes attributed as sacred or spiritual (see Pungetti, Oviedo & Hooke 2012), but the everyday *milieu*, or the backyard, does not pale in comparison. Because the landscapes are dependent on humans, who collectively can manage and alter them within some, albeit varying, limits, landscape is a political concept so much so that its value for humans has been expressed in the language of human rights. The idea of the human right to landscape does not seem, however, to measure up the more established rights, such rights that are qualified as 'human', 'fundamental' or 'basic'. If so, what kind of right can and should the right to landscape then be?

A natural way of approaching the question is to concentrate on 'landscape'. Landscape is just one of many concepts that refer to the perceptible reality in rather a comprehensive manner. Yet, it has a unique place in environmental debates. Historically, the notion of landscape is often considered to be of early modern origin, distinctively used in the context of painting and gardening. "Landscape came to mean a prospect seen from a specific standpoint" as the famous landscape researcher Yi-Fu Tuan (1990, 133) puts it with a reference to these practices. Others claim its history is longer; in German language, it has been traced back to the ninth century, connoting the shape of elements as affected by humans and outlining political districts (see Kühne 2015, 43–44; Raivo 2002, 90). In the 19th century, 'landscape' and their imageries became embraced with the construction of nation-states so as to refer to the territorial building blocks and sources of national identity and pride (Raivo 2002). Towards the end of the 20th century, the value of landscapes was adopted by local communities and ethnic minorities and it became, as we will see later in this chapter, a part of identity politics. Over the decades, landscapes have begun to denote material, experiential and narrative linkages between generations past, present and future. In this sense, landscapes are a dimension of sustainability, something that the present generation wants to pass on to the next, perhaps even conceiving of this as a duty.

These ideas are detectable in the definition of landscape in the European Landscape Convention, steered by the Council of Europe and agreed upon in Florence in 2000 (hence also known as the Florence Convention). It is the first international treaty to deal directly with the protection, management and planning of important natural and cultural landscapes. According to the Convention, "'landscape' means an area, as perceived by people, whose character is the result of the action and interaction of natural and/or human factors" (Art. 1(a)). In this chapter, this definition is assumed. Since the focus on landscapes is on humans, we have a largely, though not necessarily, human-centred approach to nature conservation at hand and, moreover, the linkages to human rights thinking are evident. However, the Convention mentions the notion of rights only once. The Preamble states that, "The landscape is a key element of individual and social well-being and its protection, management and planning entail rights and responsibilities for everyone." No specific right is defined any further in the Convention.

One could think that the Convention text reflects minimalism regarding human rights, the doctrine according to which only bodily security is to be protected by human rights against intentional cruelty and acts of torture, rape, beating and killing (see Ignatieff 2001, 173). If we endorse minimalism, the right to landscape can be easily disregarded since decisions about the familiar landscapes appear merely as matters of (dis)comfort or are routinely abided "background harms" (like the street noise). As easy as it is to disregard landscapes and soundscape, one should remember that continuous noise is a method of torture and forced displacement and an ineradicable source of sorrow to many people.[1] The purpose of this chapter is to examine why the human right to landscape is not only a fascinating idea but also an actual regime since some elements of it are part and parcel of both *de lege lata* and *de lege ferenda*, that is, the law as it is and the law as it should be.

The Convention also contradicts another traditional element of human rights violations that are acts of the government. The Convention, however, considers the protection of landscape as providing responsibilities "for everyone" but, fundamentally, these responsibilities delimit the right to use one's property. Thus, we have a rather traditional conflict between norms at hand – addressing this conflict is the main theme of this article.

Instead of conducting the analysis in a highly abstract and polity-blind manner, we will approach the theme in terms of actual policies in one country.[2] We will focus on Finland to identify to what kinds of controversies involve landscape protection. Land is invariably a property object that belongs to someone, both to natural and legal persons, but non-owners also have valid interests in land use. Thus, it is of particular interest to consider what it means that an area is in landscape protection policies both (a) from the perspective of landownership and (b) from the perspective of the public and their rights that are not reducible to property rights or some other established right. We will not address any particular legal case in Finland since at present, strictly considered, there are no cases to be addressed.[3] Also the public political debate about national programmes has been moderate there, but certain types of activities are prone to trigger conflicts, although their focus is not solely the landscape.

As for political theory, we will take up questions about the nature and acceptability of the policies that aim to protect cultural landscapes. The implementation clearly involves some regulation of land use over large areas and regulation tends to restrict the number of options open to landowners and to regional planners. Potentially an important way to justify this regulation occurs through the rights discourse – more specifically, in terms of the human right to landscape. We claim that this debate about rights to landscape should be approached via procedural rather than substantial rights because landscape is such an elusive concept, although substantial rights issues do emerge in the context of landscape conservation, both directly and indirectly. Thus the main question is about the ideal political and social processes where the landscape policies are formulated (cf. Finn Arler's considerations about 'landscape democracy', in Arler 2011; Arler & Mellqvist 2015).

A brief outline of things to come: This chapter continues with sketching Finnish landscape programmes and policies. This is followed by an attempt to formulate the key idea of landscape in environmental policies. Thirdly, we take a look at regulation of activities which affect landscape through four examples. Fourthly, we consider methods of landscape policies. The fifth section, before the concluding remarks, pays attention to the multicultural aspects of landscapes policies.

Policing landscapes

Currently, the cultural values in rural, urban and natural landscapes are protected by different legal instruments in most European countries. The European Landscape Convention, with 38 ratified parties, bolsters its significance for national policies and legislation. At the same time, it is rather obvious that the new convention has the potential to bring about new controversies.

Finland has specific aims and ideals concerning cultural landscapes and their protection that are pursued through legislation and government policies. It is a liberal democracy and a member of the European Union but has Nordic customary laws such as free access to private property (excluding homes and some other spaces). Despite examining a single country, two things should be kept in mind: First, in the Finnish debate and the policies adopted by the country, there are many recognisable issues that have been central to green political theory debates, such as divergences between cosmopolitan, nationalistic and provincial, or place-based, views and the considerations of the relative weight of rights in cases of their conflicts. Second, a significant part of the relevant and closely linked regulation on cultural landscape is based on international treaties; to understand how they govern policy making in one country helps to understand the nature of the problem. If human rights thinking also covers landscape policies, it delimits national sovereignty in this respect (see Corrigan in this book); on the other side, those human rights that contradict the specific right to landscape can leave open how sovereign states can implement landscape policies within the human rights framework. Therefore, the legislation and the selection of areas are effectually, if not ultimately, national affairs.

Distinctive to Finland is the recognition of the value of "national heritage" in the Constitution: everyone has responsibility to protect and to maintain cultural heritage in the living environment. This wording has been understood to embrace the valuable characteristics of the cultural landscape including areas of wilderness and biodiversity. The flagship programme commenced in 1992, when the country celebrated its 75th anniversary of independence. Three years later, 27 areas became designated as "national landscapes" (*kansallismaisema*) of Finland. The designated areas are spread around the country. According to the website of environmental administration, these landscapes "have great symbolic value and widely recognised significance in cultural and historical terms, or in the popular image of nature."[4] Despite the nationalist emphasis, the programme is not without multicultural aspects.[5] The same decision included a plan to compile an inventory of "nationally valuable landscapes" (*valtakunnallisesti arvokkaat maisema-alueet*). The new inventory was carried out over 2010–14. As a result, 183 areas became listed under this heading. Again, the website of environmental administration informs us that these new landscapes "represent the cultural landscapes of our country, and their value is based on culturally significant natural diversity, cultivated agricultural landscape and traditional architecture."[6] The latter process is yet to be finalised in the form of governmental decision. Thus, the landscape protection in Finland is to expand significantly, should this process be completed.

The selection processes were mainly conducted by experts and consultancies. Neither the local communities nor the landscape connoisseurs, "people with a special relationship to a landscape," as Arler and Mellqvist (2015, 245) use the term, had a special role in the inventory processes or in the management of these areas. However, strategic environmental assessment was carried out and both the public and the authorities were informed and consulted on the draft programme and the programme was finalised according to the Act of the Assessment of the Effects of Certain Plans and Programmes on the Environment. Although the process was, in all likelihood, lawful, its democratic nature, or the lack of it, opens questions when it is compared to Arler and Mellqvist's more inclusive landscape democracy or to the Swiss system where landscape planning is subject to direct democratic approval at federal, cantonal and municipal levels (see Schuler & Dessemontet 2013).

Finland does not have particular legislation on the protection of landscapes. The implementation of both of these aforementioned inventories occurs through regional land-use plans (zoning) where valuable landscapes must be marked. In practice, this means the following: The national landscapes have special status in the planning process and they "must be taken into account in land use planning".[7] The nationally valuable landscapes, however, lack an explicit role in land use planning but they are of monetary value and therefore "any changes to them are kept to a minimum."[8] At the time of writing (autumn 2016), the political pressure, under the right-wing/centre coalition government, towards land-use deregulation and towards neoliberal legislation might emphasise the role of developers and other land users in the formation of landscape policies. An unintended consequence of deregulation could be that the implementation of landscape policies is settled in the courtrooms instead of political and administrational fora. Should this happen, it would make landscape policies more dependent on the traditional definitions of property relations than is currently the case.

Considering other relevant legislation, there are two important laws that govern landscape use as a form of nature conservation, Nature Conservation Act and Wilderness Act in the northern parts of Finland (Kokko & Oksanen 2016). (Moreover, the legislation on the indigenous Sámi people is relevant and will be covered later in this chapter.) According to the former legislation, landscape conservation areas can be founded to preserve and manage a natural or cultural landscape of outstanding beauty, historical interest or other special value. An area can be of national and local interest alike. The decision establishing the area can contain provisions necessary for preserving the characteristic features of a landscape. However, the Nature Conservation Act also specifies that these provisions should not constitute a significant inconvenience to the property owner. Additionally, landscape protection can be lifted or derogations granted if its protection prevents the implementation of a project or plan of major public interest.

The normative landscape of land use and estate ownership

The landscapes that are highly valued nowadays result from, to a varying extent, human actions. Different institutional settings make people behave differently, generate different outcomes from their actions and therefore produce, often inadvertently, different (cultural) landscapes. This account is a simplification – since it ignores many other relevant human elements such as larger socio-economic context, values and worldviews and technological capacity – but it brings to the fore what lawyers, economists and social scientists tend to emphasise in environmental debates. In the context of landscapes, this was nicely captured by R.W. Emerson in his classic essay "Nature" (Chapter 1, originally published 1836):

> The charming landscape which I saw this morning, is indubitably made up of some twenty or thirty farms. Miller owns this field, Locke that, and Manning the woodland beyond. But none of them owns the landscape. There is a property in the horizon which no man has but he whose eye can integrate all the parts, that is, the poet. This is the best part of these men's farms, yet to this their warranty-deeds give no title.[9]

As he outlines, there are two obvious points of departure for attempting to make sense of the institutional dimensions in the production of different landscapes: the system of exclusive ownership and the common interest in non-exclusive goods. The impact the landowners' decisions and actions have in the surroundings is often best detectible outside of their properties, looked at jointly as landscapes. It is in the public interest to create or protect landscape of a certain kind, and therefore the idea of the public interest – as interpreted by appropriate public agencies – provides the foundation of regulation on private properties.

Although the ownership of an estate can be private, the uses of property do not necessarily take place in the privacy of one's property but the non-owners may be affected through the changes in the landscapes; the owner cannot prevent others from having sensory experiences and then attaching significance to the place. A visitor should respect the property rights and can either admire or disapprove of the way the owner uses the property. But should the owner listen to, and take into account, visitors' and spectators' opinions? If our answer is positive, then a question follows up whether this obligation is based on the non-owners' right to landscape. Should these rights and duties be converted into governmental landscape policies and programmes and monitored by the state administration? Considering the nature of liberal-democratic societies, the presence of the state is crucial. It is the function of the state and its governmental agencies to enforce property relations and the appropriate uses of property, including its use as a part of a landscape. These different viewpoints, evaluations and relevant rights are schematised in Table 6.1.

Table 6.1 Rights, presence and perspectives concerning landscape

Relation to landscape	Evaluative perception	Form of presence	Rights/duties
Owner	Pride/Negligence	Labourer/Idle	Property rights/ Respect for the right to landscape
Non-owner	Admiration/Disapproval	Visitor/Spectator	Respect for property/ The right to landscape
State administration	Obedience/Disobedience Disobedience to the law, "bureaucratic gaze"	Regulator	Inspection and law enforcement

With regard to the alleged right to landscape, the key issue is when and how the interests of non-owners – the interests of the visitors and spectators – are to be taken into account in the eyes of the law. Most of the actions of owners belong to the private sphere in the sense that solely the owner can make the decision and disregard the possible protests from others. However, the owners do not have an unrestricted liberty to use their properties and there are well-established limitations. The key point here is to define the relevance of these limitations with regard to landscapes and their protection and to separate them from pure landscape-based regulation.

The most notable limitation comes from the Roman law: "*sic tuo utere, ut alienum non laedas*", which says that one must use property so that it does no harm or causes no unreasonable injury to adjacent properties. It can also be seen to imply an injunction not to harm the people who live on the neighbouring estates, independently of their status as owners or non-owners. In regard to landscapes, this limitation does not seem remarkable although it could be applicable to some cases in which one form of land use virtually undermines other forms of land use. A case in point is the building of a noisy and polluting mineral processing plant next to a holiday village for senior citizens since it is in the interest of the holiday village owners to have impeccable scenery around it. The purpose of public planning is to prevent these conflicts from emerging or to settle the encounter of different forms of land use: industrial plants are sited in one place and holiday villages are located elsewhere. For the public deliberation on planning, the crucial point is, however, that an industrial plant is a potential health risk, but it can be an aesthetic inconvenience too. The aesthetic aspect is of secondary importance though; the purpose of landscape conventions and policies are to increase the awareness of valued landscapes.

To carve the core idea of landscape, let us set aside the environmental health aspects and the lost business opportunities. At the core are the visual and other sensory experiences and the meanings assigned to the sources of these experiences. Consider the construction as a visual nuisance in the landscape. In what sense could people be harmed or injured when their landscape has been altered and is thus producing new visual experiences? One may think that changes in the visual landscape do not harm anyone although landscapes may lose those qualities to which people are emotionally attached and they may suffer non-fatal welfare losses. Thus, landscape is a matter of (dis)comfort, and nothing more or less. In Finland, for example, the losses followed from the changes of landscape can be compensated – through legal processes – only with strict conditions and the monetary compensations are extremely rare. Despite this, organised societies have both formal and informal regulations about how the neighbourhoods and thus the landscapes ought to look. For example, the smoothness of the lawn may be regulated informally whereas the use of the courtyard as a storage for rusting vehicles might be a matter of formal regulation.

To say it more precisely, formal regulation is put in force by public authorities with the warrants that law provides them; informal regulation lacks this basis. Informal regulation is merely a form of social control exercised by neighbours and communities by various social means, such as private discussions and community meetings or, in worse cases, social exclusion or even illicit interference. Neighbourhoods vary in this respect and some are more tolerable than others. Legally, the informal regulation is not proper regulation; moreover, the legally recognised rights may function as a protective shield against those who want to exercise it. At the same time, property rights can also counteract public regulation of harmless use of property. Whether harmful or not, most societies regulate construction and land use for aesthetic and cultural reasons.[10] Also the aforementioned national programmes fall into this category.

What we encounter here is the problem of defining stakeholders and their engagement. Landscapes are both in common and private interest and their protection should be neither undemocratic nor undermining basic rights that are constitutive to democracy. Who should have a say in scaling landscapes and defining policies concerning them and who should or can be excluded from these actions? Are there people who might have a veto or whose opinion matters more? Good procedures are both exclusive and inclusive in the sense that they determine whose interests can be taken into account and whose interests weigh most. The weighing of conflicting interest is not, however, as simple as in the ordinary neighbourhood conflicts, or civil cases, due to the importance of cultural and natural values. In principle, the communities living in or near to these landscapes should be central to sustaining them, and landscape connoisseurs can be the voice of these communities in some part of policy making. This issue will be fleshed out later, in the section on arguments for the right to landscape. Before that we will take a look at four different cases.

Rights and changing landscapes

One may think that the right to landscape implicitly aims to preserve the land-scape as it exists, so that a stable right involves a request for stability or perma-nency in landscape. Such a request is, however, unfeasible: landscapes change and are changed, slowly or rapidly, with or without humans. Therefore, the idea that the human right to landscape invariably implies the right holder having a justified claim for halting these changes, particularly those which are human-induced, is unfeasible, too: some such requests are sound and/or justified, while others are not, and it is a matter of public decision-making to recognise them and to settle them. The possible right to landscape in this respect differs from those environmental rights that contain a clear element of constancy and stability that could be of more substantial quality. Consider, for example, that there were rights to good environ-ment (protecting against environmental pollution and against climate change through carbon emissions). Through these rights, it is expressed that it is not in human interest to allow health-threatening changes. Of course, the environmental conditions vary all the time but some changes are not even experienced, let alone accounted for, in the same way as the changes in landscapes. A mass death of fish in the river is a visible impact of pollution but without proper investigation of the causes, it lacks a proper account and is a mere landscape change. This is not how-ever, a satisfactory state of affairs and in modern societies an explanation for the change is wanted. In the process of producing such an account, the change in land-scape converts into change in the quality of water that can be labelled as pollution. Two things follow: First, it could be claimed that polluting the environment is not activity that aims at changing the landscape and that whatever changes pollution causes, they become pollution-based landscape changes when a scientifically sound account of the alteration mechanism has been provided. This also provides a crite-rion for distinguishing "the right against pollution" from "the right to landscape". The second implication is that, in the light of the Roman law and the liberal harm principle, "the right against pollution" is more important than "the right to land-scape". Nevertheless, the existence of pure experience-based regulation points to the core idea of landscape and indicates that landscapes and their alteration matter to people independently of linkages to health impairments.

Meguelonne Déjant-Pons, the Executive Secretary of the European Landscape Convention, has suggested that a right to the landscape could be developed by means of combining two established rights, the right to the environment and the right to cultural heritage, and expanding their meanings so that it can be under-stood as a new dimension of these rights (Déjant-Pons 2011, 52–55). Prerequisite for this dynamic reading of these rights is that the right to the environment is not defined too narrowly, only as the right to a healthy physical environment (Rixecker 2011). These ideas resonate with the analysis we make above.

To illustrate the nature of landscape-based regulation in Finland, let us focus on four types of activities. The regulation of these activities is not limited to the aforementioned national landscape programmes, but extends everywhere. Building standards, tree felling, soil extraction or windmill construction change the landscapes and the soundscapes in the mind of anyone capable of having sensory experiences. What they express, however, is that the value of landscapes can be inferior to other values they might have and benefits they might generate. In particular, the right to property – or the land and its resources as property – is an overriding norm that entitles one to transform the landscape sometimes in a rather dramatic sense. It also sets a framework for applying participatory approaches and empowering the public. There are many restrictions on property use to be acknowledged, as we have already seen and will see below.

Building standards

In the areas that are planned in detail, the building standards are tight; in the area without any plan, there is less regulation but the general building standards are still applicable. The building regulation can be very thorough covering such details as the colour of the exterior wall and roof or the quality of the building materials. If one wants to deviate from the colour norms regarding exterior walls and paint the house yellow although only red and green are permitted in the area, one may ask why one cannot do so. It is clear that a yellow house among greens and reds makes it conspicuous. Therefore, it alters the visual composition of the built landscape and is thus classified as harmful by the planners and, presumably, the lawmakers at the local and national levels. It is hard to imagine any other basis than the aesthetic nuisance for this kind of control. Moreover, these building standards create the landscape by legal means. But the built landscape covers only a part of the concept of landscape that we assumed at the beginning of this chapter.

Tree felling

The forest landscape is a typical Finnish landscape and most Finns prefer to have a forested area nearby their homes, although people, of course, are not against forestry and the felling of trees. The close-to-home forests are accessible for anyone. Most forests are, however, places for exercising commercial forestry that implies the possibility of clear cuts here and there. The Forest Act, renewed in 2013, sets policies on forest management and thus indirectly affects the landscape. The forest-use decisions are mainly up to the owners, who can cut down the trees without any consultations with the neighbourhood, who can lose the shelter and the landscape the forest has given. The owner even has the right to change the forestry land use for other purposes than forestry. Here there is little space for landscape considerations and local conflicts have sparked quite frequently.

Soil extraction

Our third type of activity is more related to the peculiar natural history in the north and the formation of esker landscapes after the ice age. In the current Finnish legislation, the Land Extraction Act (1981) is essential to the understanding about regulation based on the notion of landscape. (Despite striking similarities, extraction should be kept legally separate from mining subject to Mining Act.) In fact, an intention behind the act was to protect the esker landscape as a part of the cultural heritage. There are plenty of legal cases in which the notion of landscape plays an important role, and in the last resort the Supreme Administrative Court has to decide whether to allow extractive activities and if so, on what terms they are permitted. There are different factors the court must take into account, such as the aesthetic value of the scenery and the significance of the scenic value. Besides these factors, the impact on water economy, land use planning, property rights, neighbouring areas and the overall economic costs and benefits have to be paid attention to. To have the full picture of the situation, site visits are commonplace in court decision, but the law does not provide guidelines for juries as to how the place should be experienced and from which perspective. The esker landscapes are, naturally, different when looked at from the top or from the lowest point.

Windmills

The fourth case is common to all countries where there are modern, high-rise windmill turbines. Although the public attitudes to the renewable sources of energy and local energy production can be positive, "not in my backyard" movements against windmills tend to pop up. The construction of windmills is private business often taking place on private land but when erected, the structures are perceived afar. Many people experience windmill turbines both as visual nuisances and as spoiling the soundscapes so much so that they might claim having health losses from them.[11] Particularly for the owners of second homes in these areas, the tendency not to endure the turbines is high, while the threshold to express this discontent is low, since their expectations for countryside living presumably differ from those of the permanent residents. If – let us speculate here – it is so that permanent residents are in favour of windmills and the second home owners are against them, it seems fair as a starting point that political processes give more emphasis on permanent residents and allow them to benefit from local power production, the returns from land rent and the employment opportunities. In judicial processes, however, the landowners and residents have to be treated equally regardless of their status as permanent or temporary residents. Whether such a non-discriminatory treatment of persons with different relationships to the area is morally acceptable is an apposite question, then.

All of these cases raise questions about regulation that is enforced in the name of intangible and non-fungible landscape goods. It is interesting to contrast the type of activities where conflicts are common with state-led programmes where there is less tension. Since the launch of the 1992 programme in Finland, there has been little indication of the emergence of a major landscape controversy. For instance, in the 1992 committee report *Maisemanhoito* (*Landscape management*), collectively written by officials from various ministries and other governmental agencies, the outcome was rather unanimous. According to the report, the management of landscape should be a part of the larger set of agricultural policies. Instead of forcing landowners to comply with management protocols, the main idea was to encourage them to continue pertinent activities. It recommended that economic support should be made available if needed. Elsewhere in the report, it is pointed out that taking care of the landscape does not require "unreasonable sacrifices but is easily carried out as long as motivation exists and the knowledge and skills have not been lost." So, the management depends on routine activities (Ympäristöministeriö 1992, 82).

The committee consensus seems to reflect political unanimity at large. Moreover, conspicuous to Finland has been that the general debate on this matter is virtually non-existent. This quietness is somewhat puzzling when compared to other large regulatory programmes. In conservation politics, the debate over biodiversity protection on privately owned lands has been exceptionally heated following EU membership in 1995 and the EU-led policies (see e.g. Hiedanpää 2002). In the parliament (*eduskunta*), since 2011 only one written question from a member of the parliament to the government has been made on landscape protection programmes. In it, the opposition MP expressed her worry about increasing interference and costs for the landowners (Maijala 2014).

The programme on cultural landscape is one of many other environmental programmes and policies that have circumscribed the idea of landownership or added new responsibilities to the owners. Most of them, we reckon, are widely accepted and obeyed but there are exceptions. Theoretically, there are two kinds of general problems: one on settling the disputes over land-use regulation policies, the other concerning competing understandings about landscapes in a multi-ethnic society.

How to reconcile human rights with landscape protection?

Human rights do not constitute a harmonious whole but represent a way to conceptualise human disagreements and conflicts, and to settle them. This is also the case in landscape protection: on one side, there are property rights; on the other, there are rights to landscape. Both of them can be attributed as human rights. In this part, we examine two ways of reconciling human rights with the demands of landscape conservation. First, we mull over the possibility that either of these rights overrides the other. Second, we assess voluntary arrangements and assigning title-based responsibilities.

The landscape belongs to the public sphere but the private ownership of land and non-fungible property is, in many cases, private in the sense of emphasising exclusivity. A conflict ensues and it has two straight solutions:

1) to privatise the (common) landscape or
2) to "commonise" the private property

The first option means that exclusivity of ownership is enforced to the extreme. This option is not, however, feasible since landscapes are not easily hidden from the public gaze. One may even say that landscape is by nature common and to talk about private landscapes is not intelligible even though perspectives vary and access to some perspectives can be limited. (Modern technology such as earth observation satellites and drones with high-density cameras can make it more difficult for owners to block access to a landscape.) The second option does not enjoy high support in many countries and thus is not politically achievable because of the intensification of regulation.

Yet, there are trends in both directions. On one hand, the idea of the human right to landscape has elements that come close to the second option, if the right to landscape is interpreted to override the right to property, thus entitling the external interference in the use of property. On the other hand, the privatisation of landscape means its commodification occurs, for example, in tourism and in some cases it requires the exclusion of non-paying visitors from a landscape spot. At first sight, this can also be in accordance with the human rights thinking because the right to property is standardly considered so important. In real life, however, the problems related to ownership of appreciated landscapes are far more complicated.

As a compromise for the conflict between public regulation and the right to dispose of one's property, a voluntary approach has been suggested in biodiversity conservation and, more largely, in supporting the functioning of the ecosystem services. The situation regarding cultural landscapes seems somewhat different from the conventional nature conservation that emphasises the natural values of, and the lack of human impact in, the protected areas. Some elements in cultural landscape may be protected by law (e.g. trees and buildings), other aspects depend on the continuation of human activities that are not forced by law but even supported, directly or indirectly, through public funding. It follows that the maintenance of cultural landscapes requires cooperation between landowners and the public authorities, and the political processes that produce landscape protection programmes must have the support of civil society.

In nature conservation, the perennial issue concerns the expansion of the monetisation of environmental goods. Accordingly, the voluntary approach to the conservation of cultural landscape might be founded on the idea of Payments for Ecosystem Services (PES) or Landscape Value Trade (see Grammatikopoulou, Pouta & Salmiovirta 2013). It requires that those who benefit from the conservation and thus from regulation of the private land use should pay for the services the landowner provides. The beneficiaries can be anybody such as the governments, nongovernmental organisations or other collective actors and individuals with roles of a different kind. In that sense it is possible to suggest that people or communities that benefit directly from the neighbouring landscape should pay to keep the area undisturbed. But this, again, raises questions about the feasibility of the arrangement.

If a landscape is understood as scenery, is it possible to collect payments from those who visit the area? Or should it be considered that the beneficiary is the people, on behalf of whom the government compensates individual landowners their dues? In some cases, the former is possible but requires that access to a place can be restricted only to those who pay. In the Finnish context, this option is limited to very few places, such as privately owned gardens, because of the customary law everyman's rights that can restrict landowners from requiring an entry fee. Moreover, it might well be the case that constraints on land use in the name of cultural landscape protection and the best places to experience it outside occur to different landowners. Namely, the owner of the real estate with the best landscape benefits twice without his or her own contribution: First, the economic value of the property with a view is usually higher than the value of the property with "no view". And second, if the owner could even have opportunity to collect the entry fee, the owner benefits from it without having to do virtually anything. That leaves us with the latter option, governmental compensation.

Though the landowners might be willing to adopt the voluntary approaches, there are critical voices. Paraphrasing Ruth Grant's (2012, 120) question in her book on the ethics of incentives: What does a "pay for maintaining the cultural character of a landscape" programme communicate? It assumes that the activity is not worth doing for its own sake. It communicates materialistic values – only money and the things that money can buy count in life (cf. on outdoor advertising, Sandel 2012, 185). This seems to be in stark contrast with the ethos of the traditional production of cultural landscapes that is not incentivised with *direct* monetary compensation.

The Finnish report *Maisemanhoito* hints toward this latter understanding about voluntariness. It was based on ideas of the virtuous or model citizens and money plays a lesser role. For example, with regard to houses, it states as follows: "The maintenance, repair and renovation of the building stock is a manifestation of cultural sense of the owner" (Ympäristöministeriö 1992, 84). The tone of the message regarding of the cultural landscape is quite similar: "When it comes to the management of cultural landscape, in general it is best to do as thus far. The land-owners in general know themselves best the appropriate methods of managing" (Ibid. 86). In other words, the good owner is one who cares for the landscape values of the land. Whether or not these duties are or should be legally enforced might be suspect for those who defend an unqualified conception of ownership. There are, however, many voices emphasising that ownership is and should be understood as qualified (see Oksanen, forthcoming). Accordingly, ownership duties in regard to socially valued landscape can be deemed as justified.

Identifying cultural and collective dimensions of landscapes

In the previous sections, the idea of harming others was first understood to materialise through land ownership: Only neighbouring landowners had interests, in landscapes and other things, which merit consideration. In the environmental context, the focus on neighbour relations is too restricted. The harm a noisy and polluting factory causes extends to non-owning people who are affected. They can be harmed and their health can be compromised; this provides one reason for the regulation of industrial emissions. In other words, there can be a human right to a good environment implying a claim for the protection of an area to stay healthy and suitable for living. Land-use limits and bans are less often related to the landscapes and how they look. But without these experiential dimensions, environmental regulation is incomplete.

In general, these elements tend to be highly individualistic. As we have already seen, the notion of landscape has a strongly communitarian edge, since landscapes are cultural creations. The cultural element is so important that the landscape in the idea of the human right to landscape is typically constricted to cultural landscapes. Therefore, we face the problem of naming the cultural community whose traces in the landscape are to be protected and enhanced.

All cultural landscapes are multi-layered. Thus, the landscapes are usually not a product of any single cultural community but result from the accumulation of traces from several human generations and different cultural communities. Thus, there are often conflicts over the right character of landscape and what elements it should contain. Some of these controversies are global, since the value of certain landscapes is internationally recognised (consider the UNESCO's world heritage listing and the protection it provides merely through branding and reputation), but the value of foreign opinion can also be insignificant. Such conflicts can also be national conflicts if the landscapes being addressed are of national importance. A typical argument for landscape protection stems from national sentiments, but it is far from obvious that these sentiments override the economic use-values, the realisation of which can compromise the protected values. Often landscape controversies are expressions of (non-benign) cultural encounters within nation-states. Such conflicts are more than ordinary conflicts where the conflicting parties are individuals, both natural and legal, since they involve cultural characteristics; rather they are conflicts over cultural identity and the right to (cultural) landscape is the right to decide what matters to the cultural community.

Michel Pimbert and Jules Pretty explicate the meaning of 'cultural' as follows:

> Designating landscapes and the species they contain as 'cultural' has a num-ber of important implications for community-based conservation and the concept of rights over biological resources. Local communities may therefore claim special rights of access, decision, control and property over them. This historical reality should be the starting point of community-based conserva-tion whenever local people have shaped local ecologies over generations.
>
> (Pimbert & Pretty 1999, 208)

In many parts of the world, the indigenous and traditional communities' interests in landscapes are not legally recognised and they have to carry the political com-bat in this direction. The idea of a human right to landscape can then serve as an important way to secure that recognition.

In the Finnish context, this issue arises in the north where the indigenous Sámi peoples live along with the ethnic Finns. For the Sámis, the northern landscapes are cultural landscapes where they have exercised subsistence economy and rein-deer herding from time immemorial. For the Finns, this kind of human-centred understanding about the region is also not foreign as it is manifest in the Finnish concept of *erämaa* – a place for subsistence economy outside the historical vil-lages and modern towns (Kokko & Oksanen 2016). The continuation of tradi-tional economy is the requisite for maintaining the cultural landscape and vice versa. Therefore, to alter these landscapes without due processes that include the negotiation with the Sámi parliament (*saamelaiskäräjät*) can be considered as a violation of their right to culture. Despite many progressive steps, the question has remained highly contentious (see Heinämäki, Herrmann & Neumann 2015).

In general, the issue of cultural identity associated with landscapes brings up a crucial point regarding the debate on a human right to landscape. Namely, the substantial right to landscape requires procedural rights, which concern the right to information, participation and access to justice. This is recognised also in the European Landscape Convention: both the right to the landscape and the responsibility to protect and manage the landscape are mentioned in the preamble of the Convention. To fulfil their responsibilities, the members of the public – and the other stakeholders – have to have true possibilities to participate in the planning and implementation processes. The Convention emphasises the procedural rights and participation. It obliges, for example, the States to establish procedures for the participation of the general public, local and regional authorities, and other parties with an interest in the definition and implementation of the landscape policies (Article 5).

Concluding remarks

The concept of landscape has been addressed in scientific and public debates over centuries: what it has been, what it can be and how it should be understood and, in particular, what kinds of landscapes there are. In this article, the focus has been on cultural dimensions of the landscapes and cultural landscapes. Legally recognised cultural landscapes are peculiar commons – they are in many cases in private ownership but accessible to the public and there is a significant public interest in their protection. How can all these aspects be integrated into one policy?

The European Landscape Convention contains only one reference to human rights. Despite this probably deliberate omission, the idea of the human right to the cultural landscape has been discussed in the literature. As we see it, the two aspects of the notion of landscape adopted in the Convention – the human presence and the human look – seemingly associate landscape protection more with procedural rights than with substantial rights. This implies the importance of process in how landscape policies are formed and adopted. This is also reflected by Arler in his discussions on landscape democracy. Should we consider the right to landscape as mainly substantial rights, it can entail requirements for arresting the organic change in the landscape. In a world that changes incessantly, such a requirement is gibberish. The protection of the landscape is retrospective, conservative – and this can produce tensions between the protection and the aims to change or develop the landscape. That is the main reason for the importance of the processes where the landscape policies are defined and implemented.

There are other relevant issues such as whether the (assumed) human right to landscape is reducible to cultural rights that protect identity and to the cultural heritage of a locality or indigenous people, such as the Sámi, or individual rights that constitute a shield against harming. Thus considered, the landscape in itself, strictly understood, is not at the thrust of concern. Rather the protection of such a right inadvertently protects "valuables" that are labelled as "landscapes". Considering the history of landscape protection policies, it is obvious – with the exception of religious or sacred sites – that mundane landscapes that result from ordinary, everyday activities are being experienced after being jeopardised. This is most obvious in contexts where the continuation of traditional lifestyle is in danger. Thus, the defence of certain qualities in a landscape are also defences against external pressures to the cultural identity of a locality. Thus, the talk of the human right to landscape is political talk with aims to cultural conservation in tandem with ecological conservation. In this situation, the procedural nature of the right to landscape emphasises that landscapes belong to the world of significance that is produced and maintained by a group of people. Likewise, this world of significance can be shattered by some other group. Therefore, should there be the human right to landscape, it is fundamentally tied to these processes of making the world of significance.[12]

Notes

1 For example aircraft noise was considered by the European Court of Human Rights such as in the *Powell and Rayner v. the United Kingdom* case, Series A No.172 (1990) and *Hatton and Others v. the United Kingdom*, R:2003/VIII.
2 Cf. Beitz's practice-based approach to human rights according to which the conception of human rights is based on source material found in international political life (Beitz 2009, 102).
3 European Court of Human Rights has had cases in which the idea of landscape has played an important role. Amy Stecker (2011) has explained these cases as public interest vs. property rights cases, and in these decisions the right to landscape has not been "seen as a right in and of itself" (Stecker 2011, 60).
4 www.ymparisto.fi/en-US/Nature/Landscapes/National_landscapes.
5 The northern landscapes of the indigenous Sámi peoples are recognised as well as the urban, industrial landscape of Tammerkoski in Tampere resulting from actions by the Scottish manufacturer James Finlayson in the early 19th century.
6 www.ymparisto.fi/en-US/Nature/Landscapes/Nationally_valuable_landscapes.
7 www.ymparisto.fi/en-US/Nature/Landscapes/National_landscapes.
8 www.ymparisto.fi/en-US/Nature/Landscapes/Nationally_valuable_landscapes.
9 Thanks to John O'Neill for the Emerson reference.
10 Aesthetic and cultural considerations are not separated here, although it might be possible to do so if we assume that there is a culturally neutral aesthetic standpoint. For the purposes of this paper, the landscapes named in the two programmes are of aesthetic value in the conventional sense of the term that does not make such a neutrality assumption.
11 Much of the critical public debate on windmills in Finland have been based on alleged detrimental health impacts but the official view currently is that these claims are scientifically unconfirmed. This, however, opens up two interesting issues: the conflict between two understandings about the precautionary principle – between *in dubio pro natura* and *in dubio pro persona* – and the distribution of the burden of proof. As we have been pursuing here, the health-related aspects are outside our scope in our attempt to flesh out a strict sense of landscape.
12 We would like to thank Eerika Albrecht, Ashley Dodsworth and Selina O'Doherty for their useful comments.

References

Arler F. (2011) "Landscape Democracy in a Globalizing World: The Case of Tange Lake" *Landscape Research*, 36, 487–507.
Arler F. and Mellqvist H. (2015) "Landscape Democracy, Three Sets of Values, and the Connoisseur Method" *Environmental Values*, 24, 271–298.
Beitz C.R. (2009) *The Idea of Human Rights*. Oxford University Press, Oxford.

Déjant-Pons M. (2011) "The European Landscape Convention: From Concepts to Rights" in Egoz S., Makhzoumi J. and Pungetti G. eds., *The Right to Landscape: Contesting Landscape and Human Rights*. Ashgate, Farnham, 51–56.

Emerson R.W. (Orig. published 1836) *Nature* (www.emersoncentral.com/nature.htm).

Grammatikopoulou I., Pouta E. and Salmiovirta M. (2013) "A Locally Designed Payment Scheme for Agricultural Landscape Services" *Land Use Policy*, 32, 175–185.

Grant R.W. (2012) *Strings Attached: Untangling the Ethics of Incentives*. Princeton University Press, Princeton.

Heinämäki L., Herrmann T.M. and Neumann A. (2015) "The Protection of the Culturally and Spiritually Important Landscapes of Arctic Indigenous Peoples under the Convention on Biological Diversity and First Experiences from the Application of the Akwé:kon Guidelines in Finland" *The Year of Polar Law*, 6, 189–225.

Hiedanpää J. (2002) "European-Wide Conservation vs. Local Well-Being: The Reception of Natura 2000 Reserve Network in Karvia, SW-Finland" *Landscape and Urban Planning*, 61, 113–123.

Ignatieff M. (2001) *Human Rights as Politics and Idolatry*. Princeton University Press, Princeton.

Kokko K. and Oksanen M. (2016) "Wilderness Protection in Finland" in Bastmeijer K. ed., *Wilderness Protection in Europe: The Role of International, European and National Law*. Cambridge University Press, Cambridge, 314–336.

Kühne O. (2015) "Historical Developments: The Evolution of the Concept of Landscape in the German Linguistic Area" in Bruns D., Kühne O., Schönwald A. and Theile S. eds., *Landscape Culture: Culturing Landscapes: The Differentiated Construction of Landscapes*. Springer VS, Wiesbaden, 43–52.

Maijala, E.-M. (2014) Kirjallinen kysymys [Eduskunta written question] 454/2014 vp. Valtakunnallisesti arvokkaiden maisema-alueiden päivitys- ja täydennysinventointi.

Oksanen M. (forthcoming) "Property" in Hale B. and Light A. eds., *Routledge Companion to Environmental Ethics*. Routledge, London.

Pimbert M.P. and Pretty J.N. (1999) "Diversity and Sustainability in Community-Based Conservation" in Posey D.A. ed., *Cultural and Spiritual Values of Biodiversity: A Complementary Contribution to the Global Biodiversity Assessment*. Intermediate Technology Publications, London, 206–211.

Pungetti G., Oviedo G. and Hooke D. eds. (2012) *Sacred Species and Sites: Advances in Biocultural Conservation*. Cambridge University Press, Cambridge.

Raivo P.J. (2002) "The Finnish Landscape and Its Meanings" *Fennia*, 180, 89–98.

Rixecker S. (2011) "Re-Conceptualising Human Rights in the Context of Climate Change: Utilising the Universal Declaration of Human Rights as a Platform for Future Rights" in Egoz S., Makhzoumi J. and Pungetti G. eds., *The Right to Landscape: Contesting Landscape and Human Rights*. Ashgate, Farnham, 23–38.

Sandel M. (2012) *What Money Can't Buy: The Moral Limits of Markets*. Penguin, London.

Schuler M. and Dessemontet P. (2013) "The Swiss Vote on Limiting Second Homes" *Journal of Alpine Research | Revue de géographie alpine Hors-Série 02 février 2013*, http://rga.revues.org/1872; DOI: 10.4000/rga.1872.

Stecker A. (2011) "The 'Right to Landscape' in International Law" in Egoz S., Makhzoumi J. and Pungetti G. eds., *The Right to Landscape: Contesting Landscape and Human Rights*. Ashgate, Farnham, 57–67.

Tuan Y.-F. (1990) *Topophilia: A Study of Environmental Perception, Attitudes, and Values; with a New Preface*. Columbia University Press, New York.

Ympäristöministeriö. (1992) *Maisemanhoito: Maisema-aluetyöryhmän mietintö I*. Mietintö 66/1992. Painatuskeskus, Helsinki.

7 What's so good about environmental human rights?

Constitutional versus international environmental rights

Daniel P. Corrigan

Over the past few decades there has been increasing development of environmental rights at both the national (constitutional) and international levels, with a corresponding increase in the number of cases involving environmental rights being adjudicated in both constitutional courts and international human rights courts (hereafter cited as IHRCs). This raises the question as to whether it is better to develop and adjudicate environmental rights at the national or international level. I seek to show that international environmental human rights (hereafter cited as IEHR[s]) offer some unique advantages that systematically benefit environmental protection and that IHRCs and adjudication are a key part of that process.

May and Daly (2015) argue that environmental rights are best developed at the national constitutional level, and that constitutional courts are the most effective and appropriate institutions for adjudicating such rights. Their case is based on a number of purported problems with advancing environmental claims via international human rights, and the comparative advantages of advancing these claims via constitutional rights and adjudication in constitutional courts. I respond to this challenge and also show there are unique benefits that only IEHRs can provide. This involves drawing on Buchanan's argument (2013), which seeks to provide a justification for a system of international legal human rights by appealing to the benefits such a system can provide. I develop this argument to show that it not only justifies a system of international legal human rights, but provides an even stronger justification for adjudication of IEHRs in IHRCs. More specifically, I develop the argument by showing how adjudication can provide both a mechanism for realizing the benefits, while also facilitating a mutually supportive or reinforcing relationship among them, and in this way enhance the realization of these benefits and the value that they yield. I refer to this as a "value added" approach, as it explores the value that adjudication of IEHRs can add to environmental protection. I conclude that IEHRs and the adjudication of such rights in IHRCs have a valuable and legitimate role to play in environmental protection.

It is obvious that IHRCs, with their limited mandate and capacities, will not be able to address *all* environmental concerns. I claim simply that IHRCs currently have a unique and justifiable role to play in environmental protection, not that they are sufficient institutions for addressing all environmental concerns.

Environmental rights in international and constitutional legal systems

When the Universal Declaration of Human Rights (UDHR) was adopted in 1948, environmental concerns were not yet a focus of the human rights movement. Thus, the UDHR contains little mention of the environmental dimensions of human rights. Even by 1966, when the legally binding International Covenant on Civil and Political Rights (ICCPR) and International Covenant on Economic, Social, and Cultural Rights (ICESCR) were drafted, environmental concerns were still largely absent from the human rights agenda.

Public awareness of global environmental problems began to emerge during the 1960's, prompted by a number high-profile ecological disasters and the publication of Carson's *Silent Spring* (1962). By the 1970's, world leaders had convened the first global eco-summit in Stockholm, Sweden. This summit produced the Stockholm Declaration of 1972, which marks the first formal recognition of the human right to a healthy environment in an international treaty. Principle 1 of the Declaration states:

> Man has the fundamental right to freedom, equality and adequate conditions of life, in an environment of a quality that permits a life of dignity and well-being, and he bears a solemn responsibility to protect and improve the environment for present and future generations.

However, as with the UDHR, this document is merely a declaration, and hence is hortatory rather than legally binding.

During the 1970's and 1980's a number of specialized international human rights treatises, which are legally binding, recognized environmental rights. The Convention on the Elimination of All Forms of Discrimination Against Women (1979), in the course of discussing the rights of rural women, requires that such women "enjoy adequate living conditions, particularly in relation to housing, sanitation, electricity, and water supply" (Article 14). The Convention on the Rights of the Child (1989), as part of the human right to health, recognizes that children are entitled to "the provision of adequate and nutritious food and clean drinking water, taking into consideration the dangers and risks of environmental pollution" and that they have knowledge of "hygiene and environmental sanitation" (Article 24). In addition, as part of the right to education, the treaty requires that a child's education shall include "development of respect for the natural environment" (Article 29).

Another milestone came from the 1992 United Nations Conference on Environment and Development (UNCED), also known as the Earth Summit, which produced the Rio Declaration. The Declaration recognizes a human right to sustainable development (Principle 3), and also asserts that people should have procedural entitlements to public participation, access to information, and access to judicial remedies in the case of environmental matters (Principle 10). Like the UDHR and Stockholm Declaration, the Rio Declaration is a hortatory document that is not legally binding.

However, many of the most important developments in IEHRs have occurred not at the global level, but within regional human rights systems. The African Charter on Human and Peoples' Rights (1981) was the first regional human rights treaty to explicitly recognize a human right to a satisfactory environment. The African human rights system includes a court, but has not issued any rulings in environmental cases.

While the European Convention for the Protection of Human Rights and Fundamental Freedoms (1950) predates the environmental movement, and as a result lacks explicit recognition of the environmental dimensions of human rights, in 1998 the European human rights system adopted the Aarhus Convention on Access to Information, Public Participation in Decision-Making and Access to Justice in Environmental Matters. This convention is a legally binding treaty that explicitly recognizes procedural environmental human rights. Furthermore, the European system includes a court that has not only adjudicated cases involving these procedural environmental rights, but has also developed jurisprudence recognizing the substantive environmental dimensions of human rights included in the European Convention. Perhaps most notably, the court has developed the environmental dimensions of the right to private and family life.

The American Convention on Human Rights (1969) was also adopted before environmental issues were on the human rights agenda; however, in 1988 the parties to the Inter-American system of human rights adopted the Additional Protocol to the American Convention on Human Rights, which recognizes a human right to a healthy environment. The Inter-American system includes both a commission and a court. While the Additional Protocol is not legally binding, as is the American Convention on Human Rights itself, the Court has nevertheless cited the right to a healthy environment in a few of its decisions. Furthermore, the Inter-American Court has developed jurisprudence concerning the substantive environmental dimensions of traditional human rights, notably in the area of the human right to property as it concerns indigenous peoples and the right over their traditional lands.

The newest regional human rights treaties, The Arab Charter of Human Rights (2004) and the ASEAN Human Rights Declaration (2012), both include a right to a healthy environment. However, both systems lack a court and have not developed this right.

The 1970's were also a period when environmental constitutional rights began to be adopted. The first countries to constitutionalize a right to a healthy environment were Portugal (1976) and Spain (1978). As of 2012, 147 of 193 UN member states have a constitution that addresses environmental matters in some form (May and Daly 2015, 55–56). More specifically, 76 nations have constitutions that recognize a right to a quality environment (May and Daly 2015, 56), while 60 nations have constitutions that recognize rights or state duties relating to issues such as sustainable development, future generations, and climate change (May and Daly 2015, 329–342). When we consider constitutional environmental provisions, beyond simply environmental rights, we find that 108 nations have constitutions that impose duties on the state to protect the environment (May and Daly 2015, 304–324), and 13 nations have constitutions that recognize environmental protection as a national policy matter (May and Daly 2015, 325–328).

The case for constitutional environmental rights

May and Daly strongly advocate for environmental constitutionalism, which "embodies the recognition that the environment is a proper subject of protection in constitutional texts and for vindication by constitutional courts worldwide" (2015, 1). Environmental constitutionalism obviously involves a broader agenda relating to the valuation and protection of the environment, with environmental constitutional rights merely one aspect of this agenda. The broader goals of environmental constitutionalism may involve preservation and protection of the environment for its own sake. However, like human rights, constitutional rights tend to focus on protecting the interests of human individuals and groups. So both IEHRs and constitutional environmental rights are concerned with environmental issues as they relate to the interests of human individuals and groups. The focus of this chapter will be confined to the matter of environmental constitutional rights, rather than the broader agenda of environmental constitutionalism.

May and Daly repeatedly insist they are not claiming that constitutional law and constitutional environmental rights should predominate over international law and IEHRs (2015, 3, 54). However, they argue at some length for the advantages of the former over the latter. They recognize three general problems with advancing environmental claims via IEHRs:

1   International human rights were never designed to address environmental rights. Global (but not regional) human rights systems lack any direct right to a healthy environment. Therefore, referencing human rights conventions will largely fail as a means to advance environmental rights (2015, 26–28).
2   In order for environmental claims to be seriously considered in existing

human rights regimes, they must be linked to a recognized human right (2015, 27). If an environmental claim cannot be linked to such a right, then it will not receive serious consideration.

3   While international human rights regimes are formally enforceable, they involve weak compliance mechanisms.

(2015, 27)

In contrast, environmental constitutionalism presents a number of advantages. First, about three-quarters of the world's nations have a constitution that addresses environmental matters in some form (May and Daly 2015, 55–56). This can provide a good framework for advancing environmental rights. Second, the fact that so many constitutions contain rights explicitly pertaining to a quality environment or to other environmental issues such as sustainable development or climate change means that for environmental claims to be seriously considered, they do not have to be linked to more traditional rights. Finally, May and Daly contend that national courts are much better institutions for ensuring compliance with environmental rights (2015, 46).

The basis for this last claim comes in large part from a deeper criticism of IEHRs than those mentioned so far. May and Daly suggest that environmental rights are inherently intertwined with cultural relativism because there is no universal value that underlies the concept of environmental protection (2015, 29). Each nation has its own values concerning the balance between economic development and environmental protection and governing the allocation and use of natural resources.

Each nation will want to calibrate these matters in its own way, according to its own political calculations, cultural and economic history, and contemporary needs; each nation has a slightly different commitment to development, and ways of protecting against excessive privatization on the one hand and nationalization on the other. And each nation has its own political discourse . . . Naturally, this affects public and political discourse concerning environmental protection.

(2015, 46)

These contrasting values become especially apparent when we view the world in terms of the global North-South divide. The values of the global North have come to predominate over the values of the global South, facilitated by international economic institutions, such as the International Monetary Fund and the World Bank, which favour "privatization and development over ecological and cultural values" (2015, 29).

According to May and Daly, this issue of cultural relativism explains why constitutions and constitutional courts are best placed to develop and adjudicate environmental rights. Constitutional courts avoid cultural bias by allowing domestic judges to interpret and apply constitutional environmental rights in terms of their own domestic values and priorities, in contrast with international tribunals attempting to develop and impose uniform values in the form of IEHRs (2015, 46). Furthermore, since the judgments of national courts are likely to conform to the values and political culture of domestic society, these judgments are more likely to be followed by other domestic judges and to be accepted by domestic stakeholders. Finally, national courts are more accessible to those asserting environmental claims. Those who wish to assert environmental rights are more likely to have access to local lawyers who can bring suit in such courts (2015, 47). Thus, they conclude, "National courts are better suited to implement the norms that have been articulated at the international level, given their ability to translate those universal values into local vernaculars and to do so with authority and impact" (2015, 8).

Taking all of these factors into account, May and Daly contend that developing environmental rights at the constitutional level is the best approach:

> Constitutionalizing the environmental debate (as opposed to relegating it to the international level) avoids the problems of cultural bias that internationalization presents by allowing each nation to develop its own discourse with its own vocabulary and based on its own priorities and commitments.
>
> (2015, 46)

There is an additional aspect of May and Daly's case that bears mentioning. They rely on the method of comparative constitutionalism in their study and advocacy of environmental constitutionalism (2015, 3). However, they emphasize that comparative constitutionalism is not only the methodology for their research, but also "the practice by constitutional courts of comparing and contrasting texts, contexts, and outcomes elsewhere" (2015, 4). Thus, comparative constitutionalism is an approach that can be employed by constitutional courts in adjudicating and developing constitutional environmental rights. This method offers the distinct advantage of allowing a court to look not only at its own national history, constitutional origins, and best practices, but also at the "best practices among nations" (2015, 5).

The case that May and Daly develop in favour of a constitutional approach raises the following question: Do IEHRs have any value to add, or are environmental rights best developed at the constitutional level, perhaps in conjunction with the method of comparative constitutionalism? Given the possibility of such an approach, and its advantages as outlined by May and Daly, it may seem that IEHRs have little to offer. For this reason, the rest of this chapter will defend an international human rights approach to environmental rights, by more precisely identifying the value that such an approach can add. I do not argue that we should develop IEHRs instead of constitutional environmental rights, but simply that there are some benefits which can only be realised through IEHRs.

Are international environmental human rights problematic?

Before exploring the benefits that IEHRs can provide, let us first consider May and Daly's criticism. The first problem is that many international human rights treatises do not explicitly address environmental rights and that in order for environmental claims to be given serious consideration under this framework they must be linked to a recognized human right. A number of things can be said in response: First, the fact that many international human rights treatises were drafted prior to the emergence of environmental protection as a political objective does not prevent the subsequent recognition of their environmental dimensions. Second, many of the rights included in these treatises do not differ from the environmental rights found in constitutions. The most notable exception is the right to a safe, healthy, or adequate environment. However, while it is true that this right is not included in the major global human rights treatises, such as the UDHR, ICCPR, or ICESCR, it is included in some regional international human rights treatises, including the African Charter on Human and Peoples' Rights, the Additional Protocol to the American Convention on Human Rights, the Arab Charter of Human Rights, and the ASEAN Human Rights Declaration. Very few constitutions include more specific environmental objectives, and if they do, these typically take the form of state duties, rather than of individual rights. Therefore, the primary difference seems to revolve around the right to a safe, healthy, or adequate environment. My argument supports the idea that the right to a clean, healthy, or adequate environment should be added to global human rights treatises, but it is important to recognize that the inclusion of this right in many regional human rights treatises goes a long way towards realizing the benefits that this particular IEHR can offer.

Another purported problem concerns the claim that while international human rights regimes are formally enforceable, they involve weak compliance mechanisms. There are a variety of ways in which international human rights are enforced, ranging from "naming and shaming" states that fail in their human rights responsibilities, to review and reporting mechanisms, to economic and military sanctions. The argument I present in this chapter will focus on the role of IHRCs. Judgments by IHRCs are perhaps one of the stronger mechanisms for the enforcement of international human rights. States will generally want to avoid the reputation that comes with shirking a formal judgment by an IHRC. Furthermore, if a particular state disregards the judgment of an IHRC, it may be doubtful that the judgment of a domestic court would be more effective. Such a state may have a general disregard for the rule of law. Thus, enforcement of environmental rights through the judgments of IHRC may be as likely, or nearly as likely, to succeed as enforcement of such rights through domestic courts.

Perhaps the deepest aspect of May and Daly's case is the claim that environmental protection is a culturally relative idea or value. The reason this aspect is so important is not merely because it underpins the purported benefits that derive from the sensitivity and understanding of domestic practices with regard to national values and political contexts, but also because of its implications for the formulation and development of IEHRs. IEHRs cannot embody a multitude of incompatible conceptions of environmental protection, if in fact there are varying conceptions found in societies around the world. Rather, the development of such rights requires the creation and development of uniform rights that can be recognized and shared by all nations. Alternatively, there could be creation and development of IEHRs at the regional level, so that different regional systems have different environmental human rights. But even with this structure, there would need to be a uniform conception of IEHRs that could be recognized and shared by all nations within a given regional human rights system.

May and Daly's claim of cultural relativism seems to rest on the idea that different nations choose to balance the competing values of development and environmental protection/preservation in different ways. But balancing values is not the same thing as values themselves, and so differences in choices about how to balance these values is not the same thing as differences concerning the values themselves. Thus, it is possible that both development and environmental protection are objective universal values, but that different nations simply make different choices about how to balance these objective values. Based on their relatively brief comments, May and Daly have certainly not established the relativity of the values themselves. Rather, they seem to point to different social and political institutions for implementing these values, different "ways of protecting against excessive privatization on the one hand and nationalization on the other . . . [of] including notions of separation and sharing of powers, federalism, and individual rights and responsibilities" (2015, 46). There is no doubt that different nations have different institutions, processes, and political frameworks for implementing such values. But this simply implies that a system of IEHRs will need to take these factors into consideration; it does not show there is relativism about the values that underpin IEHRs.

Since nations have different institutions, processes, and political frameworks for realizing the competing values of development and environmental protection/preservation, this will tend to press for a minimalism in the formulation and development of IEHRs. Minimalism has been a common theme in the work of many human rights theorists.[1] To claim that something is a human right is to invoke a powerful political vocabulary, and hence many political movements seek to have their concerns framed as a human rights issue. If these claims are too prolific and include claims that are implausible, this will devalue the currency of human rights more generally. Due to this concern, many theorists have advocated for a human rights minimalism, a position that holds only the most basic human interests as rising to the level of a genuine human right. This same line of reasoning can be employed in the case of IEHR. Despite the aforementioned differences, there are likely to be basic objective interests of human beings relating to each of these values that can provide the basis of IEHRs. Identifying such a basis for IEHRs will allow us to conceptualize rights that can be universally recognized and shared by all nations, while recognition of political and institutional differences will help to keep the content of these rights minimal.

The case for international environmental human rights

After examining May and Daly's case for constitutionalizing environmental rights, and raising the question of whether this approach, in conjunction with the method of comparative constitutionalism, is best for instituting environmental rights, let us now turn to the case for IEHRs. In *The Heart of Human Rights*, Buchanan presents "The Argument from Benefits" (2013, 107–121) to justify a system of international legal human rights. I will develop The Argument from Benefits and apply it to environmental human rights in particular. In this way, I hope to identify the distinct contributions that IEHRs, in contrast to constitutional environmental rights, are able to make.

Before a justification can be offered for the existing system of international legal human rights, it is first necessary to provide a characterization of that system. Buchanan characterizes the general function as follows: "to provide a set of universal standards, in the form of international law, whose primary purpose is to regulate the behaviour of states towards individuals under their jurisdiction, considered as social individuals, and for their own sakes" (2013, 86). The final phrase, "for their own sakes," is meant to point out that the system is aimed at regulating state behaviour for the sake of individuals, not states. Buchanan believes that we can also identify two more particular aims, based on the content of the human rights norms themselves. These more particular aims are called the well-being function and the status-egalitarian function. The well-being function aims at regulating state conduct in order to help ensure that individuals have an opportunity to lead a minimally good life by providing protections and resources generally needed to lead such a life, and the status-egalitarian function aims at regulating state conduct for the purposes of affirming and promoting the equal basic status of all people (2013, 87).

It is worth pointing out the well-being function and the status-egalitarian function may provide a basis for conceptualizing and developing IEHRs that all nations can recognize and share. The idea would be that regardless of how nations choose to balance and implement the competing values of development and environmental protection/preservation, these choices are constrained by the considerations of well-being (opportunity to lead a minimally good life) and status-egalitarianism (equal basic status of all people) embodied in international human rights. This approach would involve identifying the environmental-related protections and resources generally needed to lead a minimally good life, as well as the environmental-related regulation of state conduct necessary to affirm and promote the equal basic status of all people, and formulating IEHRs that embody these requirements. Certainly some uniform environmental human rights can be developed on the basis of these functions. For example, we can formulate a uniform human right to water, which is an essential requirement for human well-being, by determining what the state is required to do with regard to access to potable water. Beyond meeting these basic universal constraints and requirements imposed by IEHRs, each nation would be free to balance the competing values of development and environmental protection/preservation as it sees fit, using the institutions, processes, and frameworks that it chooses.

The motivation for Buchanan's Argument from Benefits juxtaposes nicely with the case presented by May and Daly. One reason it is important to provide a justification for a system of international legal human rights, Buchanan contends, is because we can imagine alternative approaches to achieving the goals this system is designed to achieve. For example, in the wake of World War II, when the existing international legal human rights system was founded, there were some domestic constitutional rights systems that seemed to be doing a good job of protecting the interests of individuals. Given these examples, powerful states might have pressured states that lacked a system of domestic constitutional rights to create and implement one. So the question arises, what justifies developing a system of international legal human rights, rather than taking some other approach (Buchanan 2013, 106)? This is precisely the issue raised by May and Daly's case for constitutional environmental rights. In answer to this concern, Buchanan's Argument from Benefits appeals to six benefits that a system of international legal human rights can provide:

1) Improve and develop the understanding of domestic constitutional bills of rights[2]
2) Play a back-up role when domestic rights protections fail
3) Contribute to the legitimacy of states
4) Provide a resource for the development of international humanitarian law
5) Provide a unified framework for coping with global problems
6) Correct an inherent flaw in democracy

Furthermore, Buchanan mentions an additional benefit that the system has the *potential* to offer:

7)   Provide a potential resource for the regulation of international economic institutions

I outline how six of these benefits are supposed to justify a system of international legal human rights. I then argue that these benefits are realized in the case of IEHR. In other words, I show that (most of) the benefits which justify the system as a whole are also realized through this part of the system, or this family of rights. Finally, I show that five of these benefits are not merely realized, but also realized in an enhanced way through adjudication of IEHR in IHRC. This is because adjudication facilitates mutual reinforcement among the benefits, a possibility Buchanan does not fully explore. If these benefits justify the international legal human rights system as a whole, and the degree to which the benefits are realized is enhanced by adjudication of IEHR, then the Argument from Benefits provides an even stronger justification for adjudication of IEHRs. This is because the value added by the benefits is even greater in the case of adjudication of IEHRs in IHRCs.

The added benefits from adjudication of international environmental human rights

1. Improving and developing domestic constitutional rights

There are at least three ways in which a system of international legal human rights can improve domestic constitutional rights by establishing international legal obligations. First, the international human rights system establishes a list of recognized human rights that impose legal obligations on states. This can encourage states that lack a domestic bill of rights to create one and include these rights. Second, international human rights provide model rights for states to emulate (2013, 109). Third, it helps to counter-act a tendency in international law that Buchanan refers to as a "veil of sovereignty" (2013, 110), which gives states robust rights against outside interference in domestic affairs, so that they have broad discretion in terms of how they may treat individuals within their jurisdiction (2013, 122). If a state is encouraged to incorporate the list of international legal human rights into its system of domestic constitutional rights, this helps to remedy the "veil of sovereignty" by creating standards that limit how a state may permissibly treat those within its jurisdiction.

A system of international legal human rights can also contribute to a better understanding of domestic constitutional rights. It has sometimes been questioned whether international human rights express a cultural bias rather than genuinely universal rights (2013, 113–114). Buchanan suggests a number of reasons to believe this is not the case. First, there is ample evidence that the drafters of the UDHR took strong efforts to avoid cultural bias. For example, the drafters included a wide range of cultural perspectives, the initiative for an international bill of rights came from weaker states in the face of opposition from stronger states, and certain anti-colonial views were incorporated into the document. Second, the international human rights system has continued to be developed with the participation of people from many different cultures (2013, 115). This inclusion of participants from diverse cultural backgrounds gives the system what Buchanan calls an "epistemic advantage" (2013, 116), because it creates safeguards against parochial bias.

May and Daly's concern is not that the concept of rights represents "Western" values, but that the notion of environmental protection – which may serve as a basis for environmental rights – is culturally relative. They may be sceptical that we can develop uniform IEHRs on the basis of participation of people from diverse social and cultural backgrounds, because they believe that cultural relativism pervades the values of development and environmental protection/preservation and would therefore prevent agreement. However, as argued previously, differing ways of balancing competing values are not the same thing as the underlying values themselves. Give this distinction, we might retain confidence that including the perspectives and participation of people from diverse backgrounds will allow us to identify fundamental environmental values – in the form of rights – that all nations must comply with when striking the balance between these competing goods.

Buchanan's model treats international human rights as a sort of "global learning platform," as it is inclusive of people from many different cultures and perspectives. While May and Daly's comparative constitutional approach merely offers national courts the possibility of observing and incorporating "global best practices" into their decision-making, Buchanan's global learning platform seeks to embody those global best practices in the form of international human rights themselves, through the participation and input of people from a diversity of cultures and societies. Sometimes this input will take the form of a domestic constitutional right. In such cases, there is a reflexive relation between constitutional rights and international human rights. If a particular society's constitutional right represents a "global best practice," this can inform the conceptualization and development of an international human right. The international human right can in turn provide a model for other constitutional systems to emulate.

Buchanan suggests that rather than be concerned about parochial bias in international human rights, we should instead be concerned about such bias in domestic bills of rights. The most influential and widely imitated domestic bills of rights have been the U.S. Bill of Rights and the French Declaration of the Rights of Man and the Citizen. Yet these documents originated in particular historical-cultural contexts. By contrast, the "epistemic advantage" of the international human rights system can lead to a better understanding of domestic constitutional rights, because it helps to limit such bias as it influences either the initial formulation or subsequent interpretation of domestic constitutional rights (Buchanan 2013, 114). So, while May and Daly praise the domestic values and understanding that can be embodied in constitutional environmental rights and informs national courts, Buchanan raises the concern that these rights and institutions have a higher likelihood of involving a parochialism, which the international human rights system can help to rectify.

Now consider this benefit in the case of IEHRs. When IEHRs are part of the system of international legal human rights, this can encourage revision of domestic legislation accordingly. First, IEHRs make it clear that states have legal obligations with respect to environmental matters that impact individuals' rights. This can be particularly important in societies where protecting the environment is seen as a laudatory goal, rather than a legal obligation. Furthermore, IEHRs create the possibility of holding states accountable for such obligations through legal institutions. Second, inclusion of IEHRs in the list of international human rights can provide a model for states to emulate. The issue is, however, more complex. Many IEHRs, both substantive and procedural, involve more general rights that have implications when it comes to environmental matters. This implies that the modelling of rights involves not just those rights whose object is some aspect of the environment, such as the right to water, but also appreciating the potential environmental dimension of the objects of rights more generally. Human rights can be formulated in ways that either encompasses or fails to appreciate the environmental dimensions of a right. For example, the right to health can be formulated with or without taking into account a healthy environment (see Committee on Economic, Social, and Cultural Rights 2000). Third, IEHRs help to counteract the "veil of sovereignty," as states are encouraged to incorporate domestic constitutional rights that prohibit the state from neglecting or threatening the environmental interests of individuals within the state's jurisdiction.

IEHRs can also be particularly important in developing new understandings of domestic constitutional rights, if domestic legislation was formulated before the current awareness of environmental problems. In other cases, domestic constitutional rights may have been formulated or developed in ways that reflect only the experiences and interests of members of certain classes or groups within society, and fail to fully account for the environmental dimensions of these rights as they affect all individuals, especially the members of marginalized groups. IEHRs provide a model that can be emulated in the formulation and development of domestic constitutional rights. In this way, the "epistemic advantage" embodied in international human rights can also be instantiated in the formulation of domestic environmental rights, so as to genuinely recognize and protect the environmental interests of all.

Adjudication of environmental human rights in IHRCs can facilitate this benefit in at least two ways. First, the process of adjudication serves the purpose of norm specification, as the precise duties and obligations associated with these rights are determined by applying these norms in particular cases. As IHRCs carry out this process, they further develop the model provided for domestic constitutional rights. Second, the process of adjudication can help to identify the environmental dimensions of various human rights, which may not have been specified in human rights treatises or the interpretations of treatise bodies. For example, the European Court of Human Rights has identified the environmental aspects of the right to private/family life. This has been the chief right appealed to in the European human rights system when contesting environmental pollution. In *Lopez Ostra v. Spain*, the Court declared "severe environmental pollution [from a waste treatment facility] may affect individuals' well-being and prevent them from enjoying their homes in such a way as to affect their private and family life adversely" (*Lopez Ostra v Spain* [1995] 20 EHRR 277). The Court has built on this precedent in subsequent cases, continuing to develop the jurisprudence concerning the environmental dimensions of this human right.

As discussed above, adjudication in IHRCs can provide a mechanism for the interpretation and specification of these norms. This mechanism involves an "epistemic advantage" through its inclusion of judges from different regions and cultural backgrounds who bring internationally diverse perspectives to these courts. Furthermore, adjudication in IHRCs allows human rights norms to be applied to a diverse range of cases, drawn from the experiences of different societies and cultural settings. These aspects of adjudication in IHRCs help to ensure that IEHRs avoid parochial bias. For example, the Inter-American Court of Human Rights has developed the human right to property as it relates to indigenous peoples and natural resource extraction. Beginning with *Mayagna (Sumo) Awas Tingni v. Nicaragua*, the Inter-American Court recognized that the human right to property can constitute a communal right to ancestral lands, which protected the Awas Tigni against a timber concession the state had granted to a logging company. In subsequent cases, such as *Saramaka People v. Suriname* and *Kichwa Indigenous People of Sarayaku v. Ecuador*, the Court has gone on to determine that the human right to (communal) property of indigenous peoples requires consultation and participation, receipt of a reasonable benefit, and an environmental impact assessment if natural resources are to be extracted from their lands. So adjudication of IEHRs in IHRCs plays a fundamental role in facilitating the "epistemic advantage" that the international legal human rights system can provide.

2. The back-up role

Another area of added value derives from the back-up role that international human rights can play when domestic rights protection fails. Even in societies that have a system of domestic constitutional rights, there are often failures to implement these rights. Historically, this has been especially true when it comes to the rights of members of certain groups, such as women, racial and ethnic minorities, migrants, and indigenous peoples (Buchanan 2013, 110–111). International human rights can remedy these failures by providing a back-up. This back-up role can function even where there are no international institutions to enforce human rights, as for example, when domestic courts appeal to international human rights in their rulings and states comply with such rulings. Domestic courts are able to make such appeals because international human rights are part of international law (2013, 111–112).

May and Daly's comparative constitutional approach merely allows a national court to consider or examine jurisprudence from other countries, but this jurisprudence is not legally binding on the domestic court. On the other hand, international human rights involve norms that are legally binding on all nations, and thus must be taken into account by domestic courts. Similarly, domestic individuals or groups might appeal to the constitutional environmental rights of a foreign nation, but such an appeal is unlikely to create much pressure in the domestic context, whereas appeals to IEHRs involve international standards, and thus are much more likely to create pressure within the domestic context.

In the case of IEHRs, the benefit provided by the back-up role can be particularly important. States can have strong interests in, for example, development projects that threaten the environmental interests of individuals. Furthermore, powerful private interests, such as corporations, often have great resources and influence in society, and may be able to pressure the state to proceed with such projects. In such cases, IEHRs function as back-ups that explicate the state's legal duty to respect and protect the environmental interests of individuals within their jurisdiction. This can be particularly beneficial in the case of members of marginalized groups.

While Buchanan emphasizes that the back-up role does not require external enforcement mechanisms, adjudication in IHRCs provides one of the strongest forms the back-up role can take. IHRCs are able to render a legal judgment that explicitly declares a state's obligations in a given case. This enforcement mechanism and the related external pressure can be especially important in the case of IEHRs. It helps to ensure compliance with the IEHRs obligations of the state in cases where the state or powerful private agents can have strong interests, and in the case of members of groups who have traditionally borne environmental harms.

The back-up role is well illustrated by *Kawas Fernandez v. Honduras*, which involved the murder of a Honduran environmental activist and human rights defender. Ms. Kawas Fernandez formed a foundation to improve the lives of the people of the Tela Bay region of Honduras through protection of the environment and preservation of natural resources. Through the work of her foundation, she succeeded in having the Punta Sal area designated as a national park, reporting

cases of illegal wood exploitation and damage to the national park, and orga-
nized demonstrations against state initiatives to grant land titles and economic
development projects in the area (*Kawas Fernandez v. Honduras*, para. 50–52). In
1995, Kawas Fernandez was murdered in her home. The subsequent investigation
of the case involved obstruction by police authorities, threats against investiga-
tors and witnesses, and the cover-up of evidence (ibid, para. 85–89). There was
also groundless annulment of arrest warrants issued by a domestic court (*ibid*,
para. 57, 65–66). In 2009, when the Inter-American Court finally ruled on the
case, the investigation was still stalled at the preliminary stage (*ibid*, para. 68).

In 2003, a petition was filed with the Inter-American Commission on Human
Rights. The Commission was unable to reach a settlement with Honduras in the
matter, and eventually submitted the case to the Inter-American Court seeking a
judgment. The Court found that Kawas Fernandez was murdered in connection
with her work as an environmental activist (*ibid*, para. 98), that state agents had
colluded with private interests who caused her murder (*ibid*, para. 99), and that
the state failed to properly investigate the case (*ibid*, para. 100–108). Furthermore, the Court recognized that the murder of Kawas Fernandez occurred within
the context of a series of murders of environmental activists in Honduras (*ibid*,
para. 5, 69).

The Court held that there was a violation of Kawas Fernandez's right to life
(American Convention on Human Rights, art. 4), as well as her right to freedom
of association (American Convention on Human Rights, art. 16),[3] connecting
the violation of her right to life with the violation of her right to freedom of association (*Kawas Fernandez v Honduras*, para. 150). After affirming a positive duty
of the state to protect the right to freedom of association, the Court specifically
articulates this duty with regard to the activities of human rights activists (*ibid*,
para. 145). Furthermore, the Court treats environmental activism as a form of
human rights activism, stating that:

> there is an undeniable link between protection of the environment and the
> enjoyment of other human rights . . . The recognition of the work in defense
> of the environment and its link to human rights is becoming more promi-
> nent across the countries of the region, in which an increasing number of
> incidents have been reported involving threats and acts of violence against
> and murders of environmentalists owing to their work.
> (*Kawas Fernandez v Honduras*, para. 147, 149)

As remedies in the case, the Court required that the state pay compensation to
Kawas Fernandez's relatives, hold a public ceremony recognizing responsibility
in the matter, conclude the investigation and have it settled within a reasonable
period, and "carry out a national awareness and sensitivity campaign regarding
the importance of the work performed by environmentalists in Honduras and

their contribution to the defense of human rights" (*Kawas Fernandez v Honduras*, para. 162–214).

The *Kawas Fernandez* case provides an excellent example of how adjudication of IEHRs in IHRCs can provide a back-up role. This case involved collusion between Honduran authorities and private interests concerning environmentally threatening projects, which ultimately led to the murder of Kawas Fernandez for her activism against these projects. Adjudication of this case in an IHRC allowed recognition that her rights were violated and led to a judgment against the state. Furthermore, it demonstrates the severe limitations of domestic courts in some countries, particularly when it comes to the rights of environmental activists who may create problems for powerful economic and political interests.

Now let us consider the way in which adjudication of IEHRs facilitates a mutually supportive or reinforcing relationship between the first and second benefits. In the case of the first benefit, adjudication allows for the development and specification of human rights, which can then contribute to improving and developing the understanding of domestic constitutional rights. As human rights are developed and specified through adjudication, they are better able to provide the second benefit, the back-up role. This shows that adjudication facilitates a supportive relationship from the first benefit to the second, but it can also facilitate support in the other direction, from the second benefit to the first. If individuals bring claims in IHRCs when domestic rights protections fail, adjudication of such cases helps to develop and specify human rights. In other words, pursuing the back-up role through adjudication in IHRCs helps to develop and specify better model rights. Better model human rights can then contribute to the improvement and understanding of domestic constitutional rights, through inclusion and emulation of these model rights. So, adjudication facilitates a mutually supportive or reinforcing relationship between the first and second benefits.

3. Contributing to a state's legitimacy

State legitimacy partially depends on providing adequate protection of its citizens' human rights. There are two types of legitimacy: normative and sociological. Normative legitimacy refers to the actual authority of a state to rule, and involves a public standing that warrants certain types of respect. Sociological legitimacy involves widely held belief that a state has such authority and warrants respect, which can be important when it comes to the ability of an institution to properly function (Buchanan 2013, 112). The back-up function of international legal human rights can contribute to both types of legitimacy. The back-up function can contribute to a state's normative legitimacy by ensuring that a state does provide adequate protection of its citizens' human rights. It can contribute to a state's sociological legitimacy by allowing citizens to know that the state is not arbiter in its own case when human rights claims are made against the state (Buchanan 2013, 113).

This benefit also applies in the case of IEHRs. Since the state itself can have strong interests in development projects that threaten the environmental interests of individuals, and there can also be pressure and influence from powerful private agents with interests in projects that threaten the environmental interests of individuals, both the normative and sociological legitimacy of the state can be in doubt. The back-up role can contribute to a state's normative legitimacy, by helping to ensure that a state does respect and protect the environmental rights of its citizens, and can contribute to a state's sociological legitimacy by allowing citizens to know that the state will not be arbiter in its own case when environmental rights claims are brought against the state. Thus, the back-up role can make an important contribution to a state's legitimacy in the case of IEHRs. If environmental rights are developed only at the national level and adjudicated by constitutional courts, the added contribution to the normative and sociological legitimacy of the state could not be realized.

As discussed previously, adjudication is one of the strongest forms that the back-up role can take, and thus can make some of the greatest contributions to the legitimacy of the state. Adjudication in IHRC can make a powerful contribution to the normative legitimacy of a state by creating an external enforcement mechanism and external pressure to ensure that the state does fulfil its human rights obligations, including IEHR obligations. Adjudication in IHRCs can contribute to the sociological legitimacy of a state by providing an institution where citizens can bring claims against the state, including IEHR claims, and know the state is not arbiter in its own case. After the ruling in the *Kawas Fernandez* case, Honduras recognized responsibility in the matter and paid compensation to the next of kin. In this way, the normative legitimacy of the Honduran government was enhanced, because there was recognition and compensation for the human rights violation that occurred. Furthermore, the sociological legitimacy of the Honduran government was enhanced because this ruling by an IHRC allows the citizens of Honduras to know that the state is not the ultimate arbiter in its own case in such situations.

Now let us turn to the relationship between the third benefit and the first and second. Buchanan discusses the relationship between the second and third benefits: The back-up role enables the system of international legal human rights to contribute to the legitimacy of states. This relationship works in just one direction; the second benefit supports the third. However, as with the first and second benefits, adjudication can facilitate a mutually supportive relationship between the first and the third benefits. As discussed above, adjudication in IHRCs contributes to the legitimacy of a state by ensuring that the state respects and protects the human rights of its residents, and by allowing citizens to know that the state is not arbiter in its own cases when human rights claims are brought against it. In the process of adjudicating these cases, IHRCs develop and specify human rights, which in turn creates better model rights that can contribute to the improvement and understanding of domestic constitutional rights. So adjudication facilitates a supportive relationship from the third benefit to the first. It can also facilitate support in the other direction, from the first benefit to the third. If adjudication in IHRCs helps to develop and specify better model human rights, it can then contribute to the improvement and understanding of domestic constitutional rights. If domestic constitutional systems include and emulate these model human rights, this makes it more likely that states will respect and protect the human rights of their residents, which is a key component of normative legitimacy. So adjudication facilitates a mutually supportive relationship between the first and third benefits.

4. Provide a unified framework for coping with global problems

Human rights can provide a unified legal framework for coping with global problems. In particular, this applies to problems which involve harms states are unable to cope with individually, but that it would be inappropriate to hold them responsible for in the absence of any voluntarily assumed international legal obligation. The solution to these sorts of problems requires states to cooperate and coordinate using a single set of standards. Human rights provide an excellent standard for this purpose, both because they have greater legal weight than goals, and because they allow for the enlistment of the extensive political and legal resources of the international human rights system (Buchanan 2013, 118).

Environmental degradation is often a problem of this variety. Many environmental threats transcend national borders. Furthermore, they can present problems that states individually are unable to solve, and would thus be inappropriate to treat as the responsibility of a single state. Human rights will not always be the best set of standards for coordinating state action concerning environmental problems. However, there are certainly some types of pollution that negatively affect populations and may be usefully dealt with in terms of IEHR protections. In such cases, IEHR offer a number of advantages: They provide a way of conceptualizing the impacts as harms and create a presumption that such harms should be remedied, in addition to the greater legal weight of these norms and the ability to enlist the extensive political and legal resources of the international human rights system.

In order for environmental rights to provide a framework for coping with global environmental problems, uniform IEHRs will be required. If environmental rights are developed only at constitutional level, they will lack uniform norms that are capable of facilitating international coordination and cooperation among nations. Once again, while nations may choose to balance the values of development and environmental protection/preservation differently, IEHRs should be able to embody basic environmental interests that can be recognized and shared universally. It is these universal values that can facilitate international coordination and cooperation.

Adjudication of IEHRs in IHRCs provides a mechanism to help ensure that states comply with these coordination norms. Furthermore it allows for the enlistment of individuals as part of the enforcement structure, as individuals can bring suit in IHRCs. Thus, this approach enables individuals to become a part of the policing structure that ensures states comply with their obligations.

Climate change is an example of an environmental problem that is global and cannot be treated as the responsibility of a single state. Human rights may be able to offer a legal framework for coordinating action to deal with this problem, or at least comprise part of such a framework. Indeed, there have been attempts to bring the issue of climate change before a human rights tribunal. For example, in 2005 Shelia Watt-Cloutier, International Chair of the Inuit Circumpolar Council, along with 62 Inuit elders, filed a petition before the Inter-American Commission on Human Rights concerning the impact of climate change on the human rights of the Inuit (Earthjustice 2005). The Inter-American Commission declined to consider the petition, stating that it had received insufficient information for making a decision. However, the Commission decided to hold hearings on the impact of climate change on human rights, and invited representatives of the Inuit communities to testify at these hearings in 2007.

Subsequent to the Inuit petition to the Inter-American Commission, the UN Human Rights Council adopted a number of resolutions recognizing the impact of climate change on human rights. Resolution 10/4, adopted in 2009, recognized that "Human rights obligations and commitments have the potential to inform and strengthen international and national policymaking in the area of climate change, promoting policy coherence, legitimacy and sustainable outcomes" (United Nations Human Rights Council 2009). In 2011, the UN Framework Convention on Climate Change arrived at a set of decisions, known as the Cancun Agreements, which included a number of references to human rights, and "emphasizes that Parties should, in all climate change related actions, fully respect human rights" (United Nations Framework Convention on Climate Change 2011). Finally, the Paris Agreement of 2015 includes in its Preamble the first mention of human rights in an international environmental treaty, which states

> *Acknowledging* that climate change is a common concern of humankind, Parties should, when taking action to address climate change, respect, promote and consider their respective obligations on human rights.
> (United Nations Framework Convention on Climate Change 2015)

These developments show progress towards incorporating a human rights approach into international action to deal with climate change, including recognizing that human rights can provide norms for policy coherence, legitimacy, and determining appropriate outcomes, as well as acknowledgment that actions dealing with climate change must respect, promote, and consider human rights. While more precise obligations need to be defined, this demonstrates the potential for human rights to provide a standard or benchmark for coordinating state actions in response to climate change and setting permissible limits on emissions.

Adjudication of human rights relative to climate change could provide a mechanism for helping to ensure compliance with these norms. This is true with respect to both substantive and procedural IEHRs. In the case of substantive IEHRs, right-holders could bring suit when their substantive human rights have been violated or impacted by the effects of climate change and receive redress for such impacts. In the case of procedural IEHRs, suit can be brought to gain access to governmental information and to demand public participation, which can enlist individual right-holders to help ensure that states comply with their climate change–related human rights obligations through transparency and participation.

5. Correcting an inherent flaw in democracy at the national level

Democracy makes governments almost exclusively accountable to their citizens, and leads them to disregard the legitimate interests of non-citizens (Buchanan 2013, 119). A system of international legal human rights provides a mechanism for exerting pressure on governments to take account of the legitimate interest of foreigners and to counter-act the bias of democracy. This shows that a system of international legal human rights provides added value even for states where the back-up function is rendered superfluous because the state has such a good record of domestic rights implementation (Buchanan 2013, 120). While current human rights law is more successful in assigning duties to states regarding individuals under their jurisdiction, there has been development in the direction of assigning extraterritorial duties. This can be particularly seen over the past decade, with the elaboration of the Responsibility to Protect (R2P) doctrine, which entails both an obligation to help other states build capacity to protect the human rights of those under their jurisdictions, as well as an obligation of the society of states to act when a state egregiously fails to protect the human rights of those under its jurisdiction (Buchanan 2013, 121).

If environmental rights are only realized at the constitutional level, they will remain subject to this inherent flaw in democracy and fail to take into account the legitimate environmental interests of non-citizens. This is not a problem that can be corrected through comparative constitutionalism, which simply allows a domestic court to consider the judgments and legal opinions of foreign courts that bear on the constitutional rights of citizens of the country. While May and Daly believe it is an advantage that national courts can make decisions which are sensitive to domestic values and political contexts, this can involve a bias on the part of such courts that allows them to ignore the legitimate environmental interests of foreigners.

Counter-acting this bias in democracy can be particularly important with regard to environmental concerns, since environmental problems are commonly trans-boundary. If the structure of democracy causes governments to be accountable to the interests of their citizens while ignoring the interests of foreigners, IEHRs provide a set of universal international norms that protect the interests of all people beyond national boundaries. The R2P doctrine could be particularly useful in the case of environmental human rights concerns, where certain states either are not concerned with environmental harms affecting their citizens' human rights or lack the resources to address such issues. Thus, IEHRs, as they develop, have the potential to mobilize international resources and action regarding environmental harms related to these rights.

Adjudication of IEHRs in IHRCs provides one of the best mechanisms for exerting pressure on democratic states to recognize the legitimate environmental interests of foreigners. These institutions enable suits to be brought by individuals against a state, regardless of a plaintiff's citizenship. Further, IHRCs can render legal judgments against a state, making it clear the state has a legal obligation to address violations of the environmental human rights of foreigners.

So far, there have been no extraterritorial environmental human rights cases decided by IHRCs. However, John Knox, UN Special Rapporteur on Human Rights and the Environment, states that "there is no obvious reason why a state should not bear responsibility for actions that otherwise would violate its human rights obligations, merely because the harm was felt beyond its borders" (UNHRC 2013, para. 63). Furthermore, most of the human rights instruments that he reviewed indicate that states have "obligations to protect human rights, particularly economic, social and cultural rights, from the extraterritorial environmental effects of actions taken within their territory" (UNHRC 2013, para. 64). He cautions that the application of human rights in cases of trans-boundary environmental harms will not always be clear, due primarily to the fact that different human rights instruments treat the issue of jurisdiction differently (UNHRC 2013, para. 63). Thus, Knox's report offers support for the idea that adjudication of IEHRs can indeed provide the benefit of counter-acting the bias inherent in democracies.

Now let us consider the way in which adjudication can facilitate a mutually supporting relation between the last two benefits. The first three benefits are ultimately concerned with the role of human rights in the relationship between states and their domestic residents. The fourth and fifth benefits, by contrast, are internationally focused. Thus, it is not surprising that we would find supportive relations among the first three benefits on the one hand, and the latter two on the other. Adjudication of IEHRs can facilitate a mutually supportive relationship between the fourth and fifth benefits. It can function as a policing mechanism to ensure that states comply with human rights when they are used as coordination norms for addressing global or international problems. When such cases involve issues that affect the human rights of foreigners, adjudication can also help to correct the inherent bias in democracy and lead states to address the legitimate interests of foreigners. This shows that adjudication facilitates a supportive relationship from the fourth benefit to the fifth. It can also facilitate a supportive relationship in the other direction, from the fifth benefit to the fourth. Adjudication in IHRCs provides a mechanism for ensuring that states respect the legitimate interests of foreigners, by allowing individuals to bring suits against foreign states. In cases where the human right concerned also serves as a coordination norm for addressing a global or international problem, such adjudication can be used to police and ensure state compliance with the coordination norm. Thus, adjudication can facilitate a supportive relationship from the fifth benefit to the fourth.

Now that we have discussed these five benefits, we can see that adjudication of IEHRs in IHRCs actually enhances most of these benefits, and thus provides additional value. Adjudication enhances the benefits in at least two ways: First, it provides a stronger mechanism for realizing some of the benefits; and second, it facilitates a mutually supportive or reinforcing relationship among some of the benefits. Given that adjudication is able to enhance the benefits in these ways, it is likely to increase the degree to which the benefits are realized, and thus the value that they add. If the benefits are realized to a greater degree by adjudication of human rights in IHRCs, then the Argument from Benefits provides an even stronger justification for adjudicating IEHRs than it does for having a system of international legal human rights as whole, which may or may not include such courts. Buchanan emphasizes that many of these benefits could be realized, at least to some degree, in the absence of external pressure or an external enforcement mechanism, such as IHRCs. However, we should recognize the way in which adjudication of IEHRs in such courts can enhance these benefits, and thus the greater value that it can add.

6. Provides a potential resource for regulating global economic institutions

Finally, let us consider an additional potential benefit that a system of international legal human rights could contribute. Buchanan points out that a limitation of existing international human rights law is that it allows only for the regulation of states, and not for the regulation of other international actors, such as international economic organizations and multi-national corporations. However, in principle there is no obstacle to an agreement among states to modify the international human rights system in this way. Thus, the international legal human rights system has the potential to provide the benefit of imposing obligations on international economic institutions, such as the International Monetary Fund and World Bank (Buchanan 2013, 283–284).

This potential benefit could be very important in the area of IEHRs. May and Daly argue that the terms of the global environmental debate have been dictated by the values of the global North, and that these terms have been facilitated in particular through the policies and actions of global economic institutions such as the International Monetary Fund and World Bank. International human rights law could be modified to constrain and regulate the policies and actions of these institutions. Obviously, this benefit could only be realized through uniform

IEHRs, and could not be achieved if there are only a myriad of different constitutional environmental rights. Furthermore, the fact that international human rights are developed with the input of people from a variety of cultures and societies means that IEHRs can embody environmental values that are non-parochial, and thus provide constraints on these institutions that do not merely represent the values of only certain cultures or societies.

Conclusion

In this chapter, I have outlined how a cosmopolitan environmental theory can be realized through a system of international human rights. It should be clear that the Argument from Benefits provides a very strong justification for IEHRs and the adjudication of such rights in IHRCs. Most of the added value that helps to justify the international legal human rights system generally is also manifested in a particular family of rights which are a part of that system, namely, IEHRs. Furthermore, these same benefits are realized, and enhanced, by adjudication of IEHRs in IHRCs. So the benefits that justify the system of international legal human rights also justify to an even stronger degree the adjudication of IEHRs in IHRCs. The justification works all the way down. This is because the same benefits add value in all of these domains. Therefore, since the Argument from Benefits offers good reason to create and implement a system of international legal human rights, it also provides strong justification for the adjudication of IEHRs in IHRCs. Furthermore, it demonstrates why environmental constitutional rights alone cannot provide the benefits that a system which includes IEHRs has the ability to offer.

Notes

1 See for example (Nickel 2007, 10).
2 Buchanan actually characterizes the Argument from Benefits as appealing to seven benefits. However, two of these benefits are so closely related, improving domestic constitutional bills of rights and developing a better understanding of domestic constitutional rights, that I have combined them and treat them as a single benefit.
3 The Court also found that Fernandez's next of kin had suffered violations of their right to due process and right to judicial protection (Article 8(1) and Article 25 of the American Convention on Human Rights).

References

Association of Southeast Asian Nations (2012) *ASEAN Human Rights Declaration* (http://www.asean.org/storage/images/ASEAN_RTK_2014/6_AHRD_Booklet.pdf).
Buchanan A. (2013) *The Heart of Human Rights.* Oxford University Press, Oxford.
Committee on Economic, Social, and Cultural Rights (2000) *Substantive Issues Arising in the Implementation of the International Covenant on Economic, Social, and Cultural Rights, General Comment No. 14* (http://tbinternet.ohchr.org/_layouts/treatybodyexternal/Download.aspx?symbolno=E%2fC.12%2f2000%2f4&Lang=en).

Council of Europe (1950) *European Convention for the Protection of Human Rights and Fundamental Freedoms* (http://www.echr.coe.int/Documents/Convention_ENG.pdf).

Earthjustice (2005) *Petition to the Inter American Commission on Human Rights Seeking Relief from Violations Resulting from Global Warming Caused by Acts and Omission of the United States* (http://earthjustice.org/sites/default/files/library/legal_docs/petition-to-the-inter-american-commission-on-human-rights-on-behalf-of-the-inuit-circumpolar-conference.pdf).

Kawas Fernandez v. Honduras (2009) Series C No. 196.

Kichwa Indigenous People of Sarayaku v Ecuador (2012) Series C No. 245.

League of Arab States (2004) *Arab Charter on Human Rights* (http://hrlibrary.umn.edu/instree/loas2005.html).

Lopez Ostra v Spain (1995) 20 EHRR 277.

Mayagna (Sumo) Awas Tingni v Nicaragua (2000) HRL 1450.

May J. R. and Daly M. (2015) *Global Environmental Constitutionalism*. Cambridge University Press, Cambridge.

Nickel J. (2007) *Making Sense of Human Rights*. 2nd ed. Blackwell, Oxford.

Saramaka People v. Suriname (2008) HRL 3058.

Organization on African Unity (1981) *African Charter on Human and Peoples' Rights* (http://www.achpr.org/instruments/achpr/).

Organization of American States (1969) *American Convention on Human Rights* (http://www.oas.org/dil/treaties_B-32_American_Convention_on_Human_Rights.htm).

Organization of American States (1999) *Additional Protocol to the American Convention on Human Rights in the Area of Economic, Social, and Cultural Rights* (http://www.oas.org/juridico/english/treaties/a-52.html).

United Nations (1979) *Convention on the Elimination of All Forms of Discrimination against Women* (http://www.ohchr.org/EN/ProfessionalInterest/Pages/CEDAW.aspx).

United Nations (1989) *Convention on the Rights of the Child* (http://www.ohchr.org/EN/ProfessionalInterest/Pages/CRC.aspx).

United Nations (1972) *Declaration of the United Nations Conference on the Human Environment* (http://www.un-documents.net/unchedec.htm).

United Nations (1966) *International Covenant on Civil and Political Rights* (http://www.ohchr.org/EN/ProfessionalInterest/Pages/CCPR.aspx).

United Nations (1966) *International Covenant on Economic, Social, and Cultural Rights* (http://www.ohchr.org/EN/ProfessionalInterest/Pages/CESCR.aspx).

United Nations (1948) *Universal Declaration of Human Rights* (http://www.ohchr.org/EN/UDHR/Pages/Language.aspx?LangID=eng).

United Nations Framework Convention on Climate Change (2011) *Report of the Conference of the Parties on Its Sixteenth Session* (http://unfccc.int/resource/docs/2010/cop16/eng/07a01.pdf#page=2).

United Nations Framework Convention on Climate Change (2015) *Paris Agreement* (http://unfccc.int/files/essential_background/convention/application/pdf/english_paris_agreement.pdf).

United Nations Conference on Environment and Development (1992) *Rio Declaration on Environment and Development* (http://www.un.org/documents/ga/conf151/aconf15126-1annex1.htm).

United Nations Human Rights Council UNHRC (2009) *Resolution 10/4* (http://ap.ohchr.org/documents/E/HRC/resolutions/A_HRC_RES_10_4.pdf).

United Nations Human Rights Council UNHRC (2013) *Report of the Independent Expert on the Issue of Human Rights Obligations Relating to the Enjoyment of a Safe, Clean, Healthy, and Sustainable Environment*, John H. Knox (www.ohchr.org/EN/Issues/Environment/SREnvironment/Pages/MappingReport.aspx).

8 Environmental human rights – concepts of responsibility

Selina O'Doherty

"There is nothing 'natural' in natural disasters."

– Joaquín Toro (2011)

It is widely accepted that without major changes in human actions, huge amounts of people will have their human rights violated by the effects of environmental harms. By 2100 Kiribati, a Pacific island nation, will disappear due to rising sea levels. The Po Valley in Northern Italy will suffer increased flooding and draught on its most fertile agricultural land. Millions of people will be permanently displaced from their homes and become climate refugees. The forecasted resource shortages are predicted to cause, among other things, major increases in famine and war. Many of these events have already begun happening and are slowly accumulating, which will result in these ever more devastating effects. As the causes of this human suffering are known, this chapter focuses on identifying who is responsible for preventing it.

In the absence of adequate air, water and soil, human beings cannot thrive. Any deliberate threat to the ongoing provision of those resources may be construed as existential threats to humans and therefore as a violation of environmental human rights.[1] Environmental human rights in this chapter refer to environmentally-affected human rights, that is, the basic human rights which are impacted by environmental harms such as climate change, rather than independently recognised rights to a particular type of environment for its own sake, or the assignation of human rights to environmental features such as rivers and glaciers (Agence France-Presse 2017).

Although I do not oppose the framing of environmental rights as a separate and specific branch of rights, the types of intervention covered in this chapter are justifiable without the creation of a new stand-alone branch of rights as the current rights, entitlements and interests of people who are affected by anthropogenic climate change are already protected by many laws and rights. Rights which fall under this umbrella of environmentally-affected human rights, such as basic subsistence rights and welfare interests, are contingent on the availability of certain environmental conditions, namely air, soil and water. Therefore these fundamental rights to air, soil, and water are grouped here as environmental human rights (for a brief introduction to the embeddedness of existing rights to environmental security see Collins-Chobanian 2000; Shue 1980). For example, the existing right to an adequate standard of living which encompasses the rights to food shelter and water, is heavily affected by the availability of adequate soil and water, which are threatened by a myriad of anthropogenic climate change issues, including flooding, drought and heatwaves, increased extreme weather incidents and pollution; cultural and language rights are also environmentally-affected human rights, being violated indirectly via climate change–related migration or displacement; and the right to life itself, including the entitlement to protection from clear and present danger, is also dependent on provision or pursuit of adequate air, soil and water.

The global politics of the environment has increasingly been highlighted and framed as a politics of transnational harm. In order to address the harms stemming from climate change, it is necessary to identify agents who can (or must) manage, contain and prevent that harm – to identify those who have responsibilities linked to that harm. While the very phrase 'anthropogenic climate change' identifies humankind in general as accumulatively responsible for causing climate harms, complex issues regarding who is responsible for what, or for whom, and how they can meet that responsibility arise.

Responsibility

Where there are such recognised rights, there are thus responsibilities to act – on behalf of the victims in a humanitarian capacity, against the perpetrators violating those rights or, in some cases, against the actor allowing the perpetrators to commit those acts. For purposes of clarity in this chapter, I have differentiated between blame-responsibility and obligation-responsibility. The difference in simplistic terms being that the responsibility for causing something is referred to as *blame-responsibility* (for example, in the case of environmental human rights, being responsible for carrying out an action which harmfully affects an environmental human right). Being blame-responsible may also mean the actor(s) is liable for any mitigation or retribution owed in addition to being blameworthy for directly causing the harm. However as it is impossible to pinpoint individual actors who are directly blame-responsible for violations of environmental human rights caused by cumulative harmful actions such as climate change, this chapter is focussed on identifying which actor(s), in practice, can be held responsible for taking action to provide and protect basic human rights from anthropogenic environmental harm. This is referred to as *obligation-responsibility* – being obliged to take certain enforceable actions in reaction or pre-emption of a harm-causing action being carried out. This obligation can apply to an actor needing to address their own actions (obligation-responsibility for ones-self), but is also applicable to an actor being obliged to take action on behalf of those being affected by other actors (obligation-responsibility for others – humanitarian intervention or the Responsibility to Protect doctrine exemplify this).

This chapter considers who has the authority to legitimately enforce moral and ethical responsibility upon other actors within the complexities of pre-empted harms, future victims and indirect unintentional harm which affect environmental human rights. As the rights violations considered in this chapter are predicted, pre-empted harms which are being caused now but will occur at a later date, the rights-bearers who will become the victims of these violations are all future victims. These future victims will comprise both inter- and intragenerational members, as the pre-emptive obligation-responsibility is to protect those who would otherwise be affected at a later date, including both people who are not yet conceived (intergenerational) and people presently living who will still be alive when the harms occur (intragenerational). They should be considered (and protected) as current rights-bearers given the nature of the causes and the harms.

The following fable by novelist E. Lockhart (2014: 53–54) highlights the nuances and potential conflicts between the two particular types of responsibility, including where they may overlap. Imagine a terrible dragon is laying siege to an ancient kingdom. The king offers a vast reward to anybody who can slay it. However, no would-be hero is successful; each and every one is eaten by the dragon. The king then thinks perhaps sending a maiden to reason with the dragon may be effective where warriors and weapons have failed. The king also happens to have three daughters, and so he sends the eldest princess to try to stop the dragon. Before she manages to say a single word, the dragon simply swallows the girl up. The king then sends his second daughter, hoping she will succeed where her sister failed, but no – the dragon also swallows her before she could say a word. The king still reasons that his youngest, loveliest and cleverest daughter will surely charm the dragon, but the dragon simply gobbles her up too. So consider this: who was responsible for killing those girls – the dragon or the king?

Unravelling all the different threads of responsibility contained in the fable illustrates both blame-responsibility and obligation-responsibility. For the purposes of my argument the dragon may be exempt of responsibility. Although he is certainly to blame for burning the kingdom and eating the subjects, he is simply doing what a dragon does and cannot be bargained with or make a reasoned sentient choice to stop his ruinous behaviour. Let's consider the dragon as a parallel with the environment in this case – certainly it is the water which drowns people during a flood or the lack of food which starves people during a famine, but in the case of, say, anthropogenic climate change, an actor can be identified for causing the flood or the famine, essentially using the environment as a weapon.[2] It is the king who assumes responsibility from all angles of this situation. It is his obligation-responsibility to protect his kingdom and his subjects from the dragon, to provide them with human security,[3] and so he is responsible for taking action against the dragon. If he fails to meet this obligation-responsibility by acting against the dragon, he then becomes blame-responsible for ongoing serious harms to his subjects. The many attempts by heroes to kill the dragon were unsuccessful so, ideally, what was the king to do? Furthermore, he sent his daughters to the dragon believing, naively or otherwise, that each one would be successful. In short he sent them to their deaths, but not deliberately – he pleads manslaughter rather than murder.

Likewise, the many actors who incrementally cause climate change on a daily basis act deliberately, but without the premeditated purpose of causing climate change and the subsequent harms. Nevertheless, knowingly causing a human rights violation is still a violation, whether that violation was the intended purpose of an action or simply accepted as collateral damage. Knowledge of a situation would certainly appear to make a continuing harm a graver violation than just the original harm (for example, the king has committed a graver wrong against his third daughter than against his first daughter). After all, he inexplicably expected the first daughter to succeed in stopping the dragon, but certainly when the first and even second daughters were killed, he could not convincingly plead the same expectations by repeating his action for a third time, following two failed attempts. However, it may be the case that those responsible for providing future human security via environmentally-affected human rights will be blame-responsible for harming one group by fulfilling their obligation-responsibility to another. For example, the daughter-sacrificing king, had he done nothing, would have been blame-responsible for the continuing deaths and constant threat to human security of his subjects. Yet by attempting to fulfil his obligation-responsibilities to protect his kingdom and subjects, he caused harm, harm which he was arguably aware of, to some of his subjects, including his own children.

As the fable illustrates, responsibility can be multi-directional and diffused as well as direct. One actor being responsible for doing or causing something may create further responsibilities for either themselves or another actor, to do something. Several actors may be responsible in varying degrees for the same thing, and there may be an obligation-responsibility not to do something. Doctors have a responsibility not to harm their patients; parents/guardians have a responsibility to look after their children (although in turn, authorities such as the State are responsible for ensuring these responsibilities are met). As noted, it is widely agreed that much of the predicted harmful climate change is caused by human activity, thus humankind as a collective has been identified as the culprit for (environmentally-affected) rights violations. However, acknowledgement of this blame-responsibility creates an obligation-responsibility for action to prevent[4] or mitigate climate change and prevent further harm-causing behaviour. If we presume that environmentally-affected human rights are certainly being harmed by anthropogenic climate change, then it is also plausible to presume that there are agents responsible for taking protective action on behalf of the victims who are being harmed. With the accumulative causes and delayed manifestation of climate change and its subsequent rights-violating harms, and with the varied agential capacities of potential actors, identifying the responsible agents requires consideration of chains of cause and effect in relation to responsibility.

'The "innocent" agents' – individuals and civil society

As human beings, we make ourselves fit to be held responsible.

(Pettit 2015)

While every individual on earth may be accused of adding to the causes of climate change through using resources (and indeed through simply creating CO_2 while breathing), this minimal causal individual behaviour is not wherein the ultimate blame- or obligation-responsibility lies. When dealing with cumulative causes such as those of climate change, no individual responsibility can usefully be assigned to private individuals for either causing the harm, or for taking enforceable action. Let us take the premise that actions essential to survival, such as breathing, shelter or heating cannot be restricted because they are also protected by virtue of their being necessary for providing basic rights.[5] However, what can be curbed without impinging upon basic human rights are luxury lifestyle emissions (Shue 1993).[6] Restrictions on how large each individual's or family's or business's carbon footprints may impinge upon travel, or trade, but reductions in collective emissions carried out this way rather than insisting nobody reproduces or heats their houses or feeds their children make it possible to provide basic environmental human rights both currently and pre-emptively.

Identifying individuals as being obligation-responsible for the causal actions of climate change is an unfeasible method of addressing imminent environmental human rights violations. Certainly a group can be identified as being the blame-responsible collective for causing harm – regardless of intention, or even awareness of accumulation of their acts (Cripps 2013; Jarvis-Thomson 1986; May 1987, 1992). However, it is both implausible and unworkable to tackle on a collective transnational basis without imbuing the authority to regulate, enforce and govern the meeting of each responsibility upon a higher authority which can tackle the collective consequence via the individual aggregate members. For example, I, as an individual citizen, have no way to calculate exactly how much energy or resources I can physically use before crossing the harm-causing threshold without being provided with essential information from an authority on which I can base my carbon-neutral lifestyle. Even with information on how to live an individually carbon-neutral life, as it is my individual contribution to a cumulative harm, the impact of my behaviour is dependent on how much carbon my neighbour (or my neighbourhood) creates.

This is commonly referred as the free-rider problem, wherein any member who does not do their share of a particular collective action still benefits from the outcome of that action as enough other members of the collective do meet their obligation-responsibilities. It may be surmised as follows: if each of us reduces our carbon footprint by flying less and eating only locally sourced food there are long-term (and transboundary) benefits for everyone due to the reduction in greenhouse gases. However if a small amount of individuals within the collective striving for this environmental good realise that the good will still occur if they do not lessen their carbon footprint *because everyone else is lowering their emissions by enough* then they will benefit from the collective good without contributing a fair or equal share to it. Essentially they are free-riding on the beneficial actions of others. The problem with this is that if enough members of the collective realise that they can free-ride at no cost to themselves, then the collective good is never created as not enough actors will meet their obligations (for an overview on this problem see Hardin 2013; Vanderheiden 2016). The free-rider problem is not necessarily a deliberate position the free-riders take; without a reliable governing authority to inform citizens, each individual has no way to ascertain the limits of what they may produce – how boiling a kettle is linked to emissions levels, or how may miles can one drive before exceeding their fuel emissions allowance. Furthermore, there needs to be a legitimate authority which can prevent free-riding, as well-meaning green-living peers cannot enforce a free-rider to act in any particular way.

The crucial point for my argument here is that if the responsibility remains simply at an individual and voluntary level, without a higher central authority to enforce it, it is too thinly distributed to be manageable or effective. Furthermore, if there are no restrictive laws or policies regulating individual citizens' behaviour, then the governing authority is also somewhat blame-responsible for allowing harmful actions to occur. I am not breaking any laws by driving my car to the airport, buying imported plastic-packaged food, and then taking a long-haul flight, every week. Certainly there is information available to me and campaigns asking me to be mindful of this and be a greener citizen and decrease or offset my carbon footprint, but there are no involuntary restrictions forced upon me to regulate this harmful behaviour. Hence, surely that makes the regulatory authority where I am driving, shopping and flying blame-responsible for allowing me to act in such a harmful way. Maybe I am also indirectly to blame for releasing a huge amount of pollutants into a river, being aware of the damage that will do – but my boss has authorised it and he is not breaking any laws and is in full compliance with all policies of the jurisdiction the company is under. Again, that authority is then blame-responsible for allowing me to pollute.

In the above scenarios, the governing authorities allowing the harmful behaviour of individual citizens may also not be breaking any laws in allowing me to pollute at work or create a huge carbon footprint. My central claim is that the obligation-responsibility lies with them because although there may be no specific legal instrument prohibiting them from allowing these harmful behaviours which accumulate to violate environmentally-affected human rights, there are certain obligation-responsibilities on them to provide human security en masse. Therefore, although there is arguably a strong case for individual moral responsibility and a duty of assistance, the obligation-responsibility of each individual to not cause future environmental human rights violations could, as the following section will illustrate, be fulfilled through States meeting their own obligation-responsibilities to enforce and regulate non-harmful lifestyles on each citizen.

State agency and authority

As the individual blame-responsible actors cannot take the necessary actions to prevent or mitigate climate harms, the angle of responsibility to focus on in order to protect environmental human rights is obligation-responsibility. It is worth noting that as with many aspects of international politics, due primarily to global structural inequalities, despite all having agency and the concurrent responsibility which that creates, different States and institutions have different capacities which must be taken into account when assessing which agent has the obligation-responsibility to take action. With regard to climate change this is well captured by the UNFCCC principle of Common but Differentiated Responsibilities and Respective Capacities (CBDR-RC).[7]

These differing capabilities lead to unequal agency, even from two entities which legally hold the same agency. From a practical perspective this inequality must be taken into account: for example, some smaller States are less able to take action on their own behalf than larger stronger States (for example, Kiribati is less able to take action to protect itself against rising sea levels than perhaps the Netherlands or the US). Or a less developed country such as Sudan may be less able to employ actions to mitigate or prevent environmental human rights violations via future climate harms if those actions will also cause current socio-economic harms (in turn violating other human rights) due to its lower socio-economic development level. In such circumstances, under humanitarian principles and practices, the obligation-responsibility then falls to second- or third-party institutional actors (either States or intergovernmental actors) as the first responsible agent is either unable or unwilling to act.

In order to exercise agency, one must have both the capacity to act, and the freedom to do so. Having the capacity to act encompasses the ability for understanding, reasoning and action, while the freedom to exercise that capacity. The primary reason why I frame States as the main agents here is because they possess both the capacity to qualify as an agent, and also the independent conditions necessary to exercise or enforce that agency. Individuals, or civil society as a collective, certainly possess the capability to be a moral agent but as they are bound by the jurisdiction of institutions of governance (including their own States) they lack the freedom, certainly at least in part, to take enforceable pre-emptive actions on behalf of future generations. By this I mean, that despite the moral duty of activism which individuals can be said to have, an individual does not possess the freedom – or indeed the capability in cases as accumulative, transnational and severe as that of climate change – required to take effective pre-emptive action to fulfil obligation-responsibility to victims of rights violations. Just as the problem of climate change is complex and accumulative, the protective actions taken to pre-emptively deal with the harms and injustices it creates are also accumulative chains. Individuals can effect action via organisation(s) (such as activist organisations, or corporate polluters) to impact on the State. This may include where they spend their money, how they use resources, decisions regarding their own carbon footprint, protests and their political engagement from how they use their vote to standing for election, and so on (Klotz 2002; Epstein 2005; Guthman & Brown 2016).

The State then can affect international society or governance but also has the freedom to be effective and active *within* that society, which has become greater than the sum of its parts regarding authority to over-rule sovereignty. As climate change is an international issue requiring transnational actions, identifying those with suitable agency to act requires a consideration and interpretation of the many complex actors within the global system, those actors and subjects who form 'international society'. One of the main criticisms levied against identifying these agents is that within international relations and within the international system, there is the presumption/premise that States are still the main international actors. States act upon, interact and react in both directions, engaging with and being affected by other collective actors – 'downwards' with civil society, and 'upwards' with intergovernmental/international and multinational institutions.[8] However, despite States being viewed as persons in international law as well as politics (see Wendt 1999 for a good description of socially treating States as persons in international relations; Crawford 2006 for a legal treatise on States as persons), describing a State (or indeed a company or multinational institution, or even a collective of persons) as having *moral* agency as opposed to simply authority to act, is a somewhat controversial claim. It is, nonetheless, one I make given that the State (and corporate or collective actors) can be prescribed praise, blame, and most importantly in this case, obligation (Erskine 2003).

Returning to the fable of dragons and kings, we are now looking for the actors who hold the obligation-responsibilities to bring the king, the dragon, or indeed the village, to justice after the princesses and (would-be) heroes have died. Taking the premise that anthropogenic climate change is cumulative, and the majority of causal actions are deliberate, albeit not carried out with the explicit purpose of producing the subsequent environmentally-affected human rights violations, it is then necessary to question the division and duty of responsibility to act. Although many actors create a collective of blame-responsible actors, the greater duty in this case is reactive in practice as it is the actors who have the agency to enforce pre-emptive action who also have the obligation-responsibility to use that agency to do so.

'International relations', 'the global system', 'world order' or any other synonym depicting the current state system, the arena in which international politics plays out, has long been considered – indeed characterised – as anarchic: "at the top, there is no identifiable regime of dominance" (Cox 2005: 109). International society according to the English School[9] claims a society of states exists where

> a group of states, conscious of certain common interests and common values, form a society in the sense that they conceive themselves to be bound by a common set of rules in their relations with one another, and share in the working of common institutions.
>
> (Bull 1977: 13 as cited in Linklater 2005: 90)

This notion of an international society is no different in its illusions of anarchy, and despite alluding to the socialisation of relations between states, this is considered to occur within an anarchy – "sovereign states form a society, albeit an anarchic one in that they do not have to submit to the will of a higher power" (Linklater 2005: 84). Furthermore, a quintessential feature of membership in this society is that it is comprised of "sovereign equals". Both sovereign co-existence and co-operation are key strategies in the exercise of state sovereignty within international society. This is perhaps especially valid within the parameters of environmental politics, as territorial sovereignty has never been whole – for example sovereignty over a territory's own air (and so the pollution levels within that air) can only be a claim, never an indisputable fact, as the implications and referent object are both moveable and uncontainable – and it is on this precept that Marauhn (2007: 729–730) claims the Westphalian State system of international relations is often misinterpreted and over-estimated in not only a de facto, but also a de jure way.

International society, with these States-agents as its subjects, is not anarchic but has a self-governing 'higher power' – based on the conglomerate collectives of intergovernmental organisations (IGOs) which perpetuate and regulate global norms and standards. The importance of these IGOs is that the norms and standards they create and employ are based largely on protecting or pursuing human rights or human security, which both create the obligation-responsibilities and legitimise the State's role in taking the actions required to meet those obligation-responsibilities. Interstate conflict and self-promotion are not the defining characteristics of international politics, rather there is an interstate authority based on rules, norms and law which regulates relations and interactions between States (Linklater 2001) and also imbues obligations and duties between those States, the majority of which have their basis in modern human rights. The cosmopolitanist international society aligned with here holds that there are numerous influences (such as security, culture and economy) driving international relations. The relative importance of these influences is not based exclusively on relevance to State autonomy or sovereign security, but rather on necessary co-operation and human security. This shift in international relations, from the traditional focus on State independence and sovereign territory to a more interdependent world order has been identified as being due to globalisation, the increased movement of people and capital. This has simultaneously constrained and expanded the remit of State authority, and thus agency, most noticeably in areas such as humanitarian intervention and the growth in power and agency of international organisations such as the EU and the ICC.

Although it has much in common with liberalism regarding international relations as a benefit, and international society as not being anarchic, liberalism and cosmopolitanism are clearly distinct regarding the authority of States in the global hierarchy. Intergovernmental institutions are not only useful for settling disputes, but are a move towards de-nationalising States and their perceived monopoly of power – "States are not the law; they are subjects of it" (Benning 2007: 180). This international 'authority' is comprised of the mechanisms of governing created by multi-lateral co-operation and is a 'transactional' reality – something that is real and functioning, with visible agency, but does not exist outside of producing itself, in which there is no theoretical distinction between the imagined and the real; reality is due simply to a matter of practice (Lemke 2007). One way in which international society creates an international authority of behavioural norms presiding over States is through instruments of legitimisation such as institutions. The UN itself is a prime example of an instrument of legitimisation which produces international norms and values, such as the ones this chapter takes as premises, like the Human Rights Charter, or the notions of what is a 'just war', and in the case of environmental human rights, the framework which policies tackling climate change must be produced within. The United Nations Framework Convention on Climate Change – and its sub-divided internal instruments – approach to governing climate change serves as implementer of international norms and standards regarding environmental governance as well as being a producer and perpetuator of them. Although these institutions legitimise and enforce the governing of apparently sovereign and autonomous States, they are formed by the mutually constitutive relationship between these societies and their subjects – wherein the norms become accepted through practice, become institutionalised and self-perpetuate thereafter.

Although this system of governance is nothing more than an effect of strategies and regulations, this central authority is also irreducible to existing as an independent actor without the institutionalised strategies or political programmes legitimised by the subjects comprising it, thus is simply a result of recognition of practices. This can be clearly illustrated through the practices of intervention such as the Responsibility to Protect doctrine (ICISS 2001) invoking obligation-responsibilities to prevent other States or governments from not meeting the internationally agreed (or implied) norms of refraining from behaviour such as crimes against humanity – including behaviour which will violate environmentally-affected human rights.

While a State, in the physical sense we are used to thinking of it as, is depicted as little more than a patch of land with defined territorial and borders, the State as an entity is rather more than that. As with the environment the State is technically a non-sentient actor, despite being anthropomorphised, which functions as a conglomerate collective (French 1984). The State creates and then perpetuates authority, continuity and self-identity via continuous transferable government (for a detailed case on the creation of State 'personalities' in international relations see Bond 2006). Each State is also a subject of both international law and society, and as an entity must then respond to the commensurate obligation-responsibilities. Thus it may be straightforward to view a State as holding the necessary de jure agency to invoke pre-emptive action against climate change's threats environmental human rights. However, assigning any sort of moral agency to a State or to any collective is a more complex and contested claim which is relatively neglected.

A useful distinction made by Erskine (2003) (although the definitions which follow are my own application of the terms and though not without its own exceptions) is that of viewing individual agency as 'natural' and collective agency as 'artificial'. That is to say in simple terms, 'natural' agency held and employed by individuals is driven by direct reasoning and purpose, having the capacity to understand and react to reason, thus implying that they can then incur responsibility, while artificial agency is one that is created – such as that held by a conglomerate collective. A conglomerate collective is defined as a subject – possessing a unified being – and is "formally constituted as an organisation with an internal structure, rules, offices, and decision procedures" (French 1984: 13). Essentially, one member leaving or a new member joining does not affect the existence of the collective; it may be comprised of individual members which it needs (as representatives, citizens or managers for example) but it is not necessarily reducible to its individual members (Newman 2004). Generally this category of groups is seen as the only one which can bear rights, and this 'natural' agency can be extended to institutions, including the State and bodies such as the IPCC and the UN, considering the internal structures, rules, offices and decision procedures each enduring collective institution displays. In turn this frames them as being not only the most relevant but the obligated- responsible actors to take up the enforceable pre-emptive action which is needed in order to uphold the future obligations climate change threatens.

As such, in the case of climate change, the actors causing the climate change may be blame-responsible for the harm, but on the other hand, those authorities allowing the causal actions to be done are accountable for not stopping those actions. For example many of the industries responsible for huge levels of dangerous emissions, which in turn cause temperature increases and sea level rises, may not the accountable ones – the States (or other authoritative agent) may be the accountable ones. On the other hand, the accountable actors may then in turn, by virtue of being accountable, become obligation-responsible for taking action to stop those actors carrying out the causal harms. Alternatively, in the case that there is no accountable actor as no binding or agreed instrument is being broken and no harm is being deliberately carried out, the State may become responsible for protecting the victims of the harm, therefore being obligation-responsible for acting against the blame-responsible.

Furthermore, rather than being the obligation-responsible agent of providing or protecting environmental human rights solely on a State-citizenship basis, both the duty to assist and the presence of numerous responsibilities to provide and protect human rights recognise these as being owed to humans *qua* humans, thus extending the responsibilities and obligation to protect rights beyond a State's own territory (Deng et al. 1996). Holding an entitlement to the rights which States are bound to provide is based on an entitlement citizens in any jurisdiction possess because of their universal humanity as opposed to because of their citizenship, and as such, if a State is failing to provide (or pursue) security for their own citizens, an external actor is obliged to intervene and take responsibility for those citizens.[10] While not every right is owed universally,[11] (or violated universally even in the case of climate change and environmental human rights) human security and its intrinsic welfare interests *are* owed universally, as are the consequent obligation-responsibilities.

Conclusion

As recognised, there is a difficulty in identifying the individuals blame-responsible for causal harms at their most basic level (May 1987, 1992; Caney 2005; Cripps 2013). Ultimately, while certain causal actions may be traced to identifiable actors, several actors must be prohibited from continuing to cause certain harms for any intervention to be effective and to successfully protect environmental human rights. An individual State can limit its emissions and lessen its resource use by regulating the behaviour of the individual actors under its jurisdiction. This creates a trickle-down effect of addressing individual actions indirectly, which will then accumulate to prevent further harm-causing behaviour. This does not just apply to individual citizens, but even certain collective actors are difficult to single out (for example which corporation is responsible for *x* amount of pollution, whose level of emissions cross the threshold of being a harmful amount and so on). Nevertheless, in addition to States' legitimate authority at an international level, enforceable limits and regulations must be placed on the actions of the citizens of the State. I do not have the liberty or legitimate authority to enforce my neighbour to stop creating greenhouse gas emissions or using fossil fuels any more than I have the authority to stop him from neglecting his children.[12]

The State, however, does hold this authority. It can legitimately regulate the actions of its citizens through policy and law, restricting certain actions and enforcing others. The provision of basic human security and the embedded human rights are already ensured through State-regulated practices, many of which already indirectly apply to the environment and thus to environmentally-affected human rights. Severe and obvious violations of the human right to life such as killing or grievous bodily harm are illegal, while on the other end of the scale citizens are obliged to separate and recycle their waste and may incur financial penalties or refusal of waste services if they do not comply with these waste regulations despite no law being broken by not separating one's waste. It then is not too great a stretch to justify directly protecting environmentally-affected human rights from being violated by regulating the causal actions of citizens by regulating their individual carbon footprints through policy and law – for example, petrol, oil, air travel, imported goods and so on could be rationed for individuals.

Hence although there may be individuals who collectively cause harm – and essentially everything can be broken down to individual responsibilities if this chain were followed – it is inappropriate and unnecessary to hold them obligation-responsible for themselves, particularly considering the lack of intent. Again as noted, that is not to overlook the moral obligations of what individuals perhaps *should* do, but it does remove the responsibility of regulating what the individual *must* do, projecting them from self-regulation based on personal preferences up to State level via IGOs. Whether an individual wants to lessen their carbon footprint or not based on their personal principles becomes irrelevant, as their relevant actions are regulated by a legitimate authority. Ultimately, individuals (or small collectives such as activist groups, or citizens of a particular area of a city) are a less suitable agent of responsibility for three reasons: i) they hold no authority over each other, whether members of the same collective or not;

ii) they are what May (1992: 106–112) refers to as a "putative group", that is, one without any decision-making structure or ability; and iii) individual enforceable actions may be restricted or insisted upon, but these will be arbitrary at best if every individual and internal collective do not contribute to the overall necessary action of the entire collective.

Due to reason ii, if individuals are deemed the primary responsible agents to provide environmental human rights, there is no authority to oversee or ensure this responsibility is fulfilled. Certainly if individuals organised themselves in functioning groups, reporting to one central authority, they could aggregate their individual obligation-responsibilities to ensure prevention of environmental rights violations. This arrangement is essentially already in practice, with groups of citizens reporting to the central authority of the State they reside in, and the States in turn organised into a global society reporting to a central authority of, say, the UN or ICC. Thus in this sense (and only in this sense), if individuals are to be held responsible for their own actions they are already fulfilling those obligation-responsibilities by enforcing their legitimate authorities to fulfil their obligation-responsibilities. Essentially, States as the obligation-responsible agent are working not as sovereign independent actors to enforce whimsical or random behavioural regulations on any citizens if or when it simply pleases them. Rather they are working as co-operative agents by enforcing behavioural regulations, in order to create compliance with the instructions or rules of a higher power – despite the fact that they are the constituent parts of that higher power.

There are several compelling reasons why I argue that States are the most capable central agents obliged to take pre-emptive action to provide and protect environmental human rights. The State is a fitting actor which can meet – or ensure the meeting of – many obligation-responsibilities; in addition to having authority to enforce the necessary acts of commission or omission from their own subjects (or their own peers) they can project influence both upwards to IGOs and downwards to citizens and domestic societies. They can take pre-emptive enforceable action to protect against climate change via lifestyle-regulating policies, which can be enshrined in law. This is an important characteristic regarding how States, when justified, are the most capable of intervening, having both the agency and right authority to do so. In short, although the environment is a transnational entity, it is actually the State which is the primary obligation-responsible agent for providing environmentally-affected human rights.

Notes

1 Although a right to something does not automatically equate to a right to all *preconditions* necessary for provision of that security or right, the deliberate (or at least conscious) threat or harm to preconditions does constitute a threat or harm to the actual right or security.

2 For work on the politics and criminalisation of famines see (Edkins 2007).

3 The human security paradigm is a concept wherein the lives of individuals are secured as ends in themselves, not a means to any other ends – the human being the referent object of security (or more often in the literature, the lives of the body politic being the object of security, the paradigm thus being primarily applicable to humankind as groups). It is more generally defined as the protection and empowerment of people caught up in extreme violence and underdevelopment (Owens 2012: 547) – and as such anything creating (or threatening) extreme violence, or being regressive to socio-economic development may be framed as a threat to human security and therefore warrant humanitarian intervention. While it is divisible from human rights and humanitarian threats there is a multi-directional relationship between them, as threats to human security are often created by harms, risks or abuses of both, and vice versa.

4 This may be through an agent stopping others (or ensuring others are stopped) from acting in harm-causing ways, or through abstaining from particular behaviour oneself.

5 Certainly, as previously stated, if oxygen pills or plastic trees with photosynthesising abilities were created and readily available, or if the human body's needs for hydration or for its core to remain within a certain temperature range were to become obsolete to human life, then perhaps 'natural' oxygen or clean water would become a luxury which could be amended or rationed in order to prevent future HCCs. However, based on current scientific possibilities and availabilities, basic sustainable rights are embedded within current human rights discourse and are an essential component to securing human life.

6 Luxury emissions here taken to be those emissions created in pursuit of a decent lifestyle in addition to both survival and subsistence emissions. There is much debate about those luxury emissions which are embedded in people's lifestyles, particularly in Western lifestyles, which may be necessary to engage in one's contemporary life. However as they are not essential to biological survival or basic lifestyles they are the most justifiable emissions to adapt or restrict in order to avoid harmful emissions levels.

7 Common but Differentiated Responsibilities and Respective Capabilities (CBDR-RC) is the first principle of the United Nations Framework Convention on Climate Change (UNFCCC 1992). It acknowledges the different capabilities and differing responsibilities of individual countries in addressing climate change: "the global nature of climate change calls for the widest possible cooperation by all countries and their participation in an effective and appropriate international response, in accordance with their common but differentiated responsibilities and respective capabilities and their social and economic conditions." (Article 3 first principle). The principle has been further developed through negotiations and conferences of the parties and the 2015 Paris agreement maintained the principle.

8 A full exegesis of State authority in a global society is beyond the scope of this chapter but see on civil society Burgerman 2001; Khagram et al. 2002; Anheier, Kaldor et al. 2005, and Kuehls 1996; Held & McGrew 2002; Karkkainen 2004; Conca 2006; Bernstein & Cashore 2007 on transnational governing.

9 The English School is a theory of international relations, the underlying tenet of which is the existence of an international *society* of States (rather than an international *system* of fiercely independent States). Essentially this global society of States becomes greater than the sum of its parts, functioning as a society via political norms and etiquette observed by (theoretically) equal sovereign States.

10 This may be by the external actor providing or pursuing human security on the unwilling/unable State's behalf, or conversely, intervening indirectly to compel the unwilling State to pursue or provide this security.

11 For example the right to vote is not universally owed (exclusions apply to minors and prisoners in many electorates), and there are specific branches of rights recognised for ethnic minorities, children and women.

12 Certainly according to what is commonly accepted to be morally right I ought to
inform authorities of neglect or abuse, or intervene if the child is in clear and present
danger. But my individual responsibility lies in 'passing the buck' to the higher authorities, and if I were to choose to leave my moral responsibility unfulfilled, I would not
be in breach of any rule or regulation bestowed on me by governmental agents. For
example, on a more administrative scale I can call the relevant government agency to
report a neighbour for committing benefit fraud or for people trafficking, but I cannot
enter their property and physically take the money from them, or physically restrain
them from going to the welfare office every week. If this bad neighbour siphons water
from the pipe in my yard I can physically cut off the source, but I cannot dole out
retribution to him in any higher way, save for reporting him. I am not authorised to
take such actions (vigilantism is actually a crime in itself), and am not even obliged to
report such crimes and infractions, although I am encouraged to. Thus both the power
and responsibility afforded to or available to individuals is too weak, too thin, to work
feasibly on the scale at which rights violations and their causes and harms occur (and
thus must be tackled). Furthermore, although I may have responsibilities for my own
harm-causing actions and it may be morally right for me to only buy local produce and
not travel beyond anywhere within walking or biking distance, it is the responsibility of the State to provide limitations to ensure that I *meet* the required behaviour
regardless of my own moral compass. For example, some towns have gone completely
fair trade or some supermarkets are entirely organic – this enforces every individual
to comply with certain policies or regulations. This is another reason why a collective
agent must be responsible for regulating and enforcing the meeting of whatsoever the
individual obligations are deemed to be.

References

Agence France-Presse (2017) Himalayan Glaciers are granted 'rights of human beings'
for protection (www.pri.org/stories/2017-04-01/himalayan-glaciers-are-granted-rights-
human-beings-protection) Accessed April 17 2017.
Anheier, H. K., Kaldor, M. & Glasius, M. (2005) *Global civil society 2005.* SAGE, London.
Benning. J. F. (2007) "Cosmopolitanism" in Bevir M. ed., *Encyclopaedia of Governance.*
Sage, Thousand Oaks, 178–180.
Bernstein S. & Cashore B. (2007) "Can Non-State Global Governance be Legitimate?
An Analytical Framework" *Regulation & Governance,* 1, 347–371.
Bond P. (2006) *Talk Left, Walk Right South Africa's Frustrated Global Reforms.* University of
Kwazulu Natal Press, Scottsville.
Burgerman S. (2001) *Moral Victories: How Activists Provoke Multilateral Action.* Cornell
University Press, Ithaca NY.
Caney S. (2005) "Cosmopolitan Justice, Responsibility, and Global Climate Change"
Leiden Journal of International Law, 18, 747–775.
Collins-Chobanian S. (2000) "Beyond Sax and Welfare Interests" *Environmental Ethics,*
22, 133–148.
Conca, K. (2006) *Governing Water: Contentious Transnational Politics and Global Institution
Building.* MIT Press, Massachusetts.
Cox, R. W. (2005) "Civil Society at the turn of the millennium" in Amoore, L. ed, *The
Global Resistance Reader,* Routledge, Oxon, 103–123.
Crawford J. R. (2006) *The Creation of States in International Law.* Oxford University Press,
Oxford.
Cripps E. (2013) *Climate Change and the Moral Agent: Individual Duties in an Interdependent
World.* Oxford University Press, Oxford.

Deng F. M., Kimaro S., Lyons T., Rothchild D., & Zartman W. (1996) *Sovereignty as Responsibility: Conflict Management in Africa*. Brookings Institution Press, Washington DC.

Edkins J. (2007) "The Criminalization of Mass Starvations: From Natural Disaster to Crime against Humanity" in Devereux S. ed., *The New Famines: Why Famines Persist in an Era of Globalization* Routledge, Abington, 50–65.

Epstein C. (2005) "Knowledge and Power in Global Environmental Activism" *International Journal of Peace Studies*, 10, 47–67.

Erskine T. (2003) "Assigning Responsibilities to Institutional Moral Agents: The Case of States and 'Quasi-States'" in Erskine T., ed., *Can Institutions Have Responsibilities? Collective Moral Agency and International Relations* Palgrave, Houndsmills, 19–40.

French P. (1984) *Collective and Corporate Responsibility*. Columbia University Press, New York.

Guthman J. & Brown S. (2016) "I Will Never Eat Another Strawberry again: The Biopolitics of Consumer-Citizenship in the Fight against Methyliodide in California" *Agriculture and Human Values*, 33, 575–585.

Hardin R. (2013) "The Free Rider Problem" in Zalta E. N., *The Stanford Encyclopedia of Philosophy*. (https://plato.stanford.edu/archives/spr2013/entries/free-rider/) Accessed 20 November 2016.

Held, D. & McGrew, A. (2002) *Governing Globalization: Power, Authority and Global Governance*. Polity Press, Cambridge.

ICISS (2001) Evans G. & Sahnoun M. (Co-Chairs). The Responsibility to Protect, Report of the International Commission on Intervention and State Sovereignty, International Development Research Centre, Ottawa.

Karkkainen B. C. (2004) "Post-Sovereign Environmental Governance" *Global Environmental Politics*, 4(1), 72–96.

Khagram S., Riker J. V, & Sikkink K. (2002) *Restructuring World Politics: Transnational Social Movements, Networks, and Norms*. University of Minnesota Press, Minneapolis.

Klotz A. (2002) "Transnational Activism and Global Transformations: The Anti-Apartheid and Abolitionist Experiences" *European Journal of International Relations*, 8(1), 49–76.

Kuehls T. (1996) *Beyond Sovereign Territory*. University of Minnesota Press, London.

Lemke T. (2007) "An Indigestible Meal? Foucault, Governmentality and State Theory" *Distinktion*, 15, 43–66.

Linklater A. (2001) "Citizenship, Humanity, and Cosmopolitan Harm Conventions" *International Political Science Review*, 22(3), 261–277.

Linklater A. (2005) "The English School" in Burchill S. & Linklater L. eds., *Theories of International Relations*. Palgrave MacMillan, Houndsmill, 84–109.

Lockhart E. (2014) *We Were Liars*. Hot Key Books, London.

Marauhn, T. (2007) "Changing Role of the State" in Bodansky, D., Brunnie, J. & Hey, E. eds, *The Oxford Handbook of International Environmental Law*. Oxford Univesity Press, Oxford, 727–748.

May L. (1987) *The Morality of Groups: Collective Responsibility, Group-Based Harm, and Corporate Rights*. University of Notre Dame Press, Notre Dame IN.

May L. (1992) *Sharing Responsibility*. University of Chicago Press, Chicago.

Newman, D. G. (2004) "Collective Interests and Collective Rights" *American Journal of Jurisprudence*, 49(1), 127–163.

Owens P. (2012) "Human Security and the Rise of the Social" *Review of International Studies*, 38, 547–567.

Pettit P. (2015) *Incorporating for responsibility*. Keynote address. Unpublished. Collective Responsibility for the Future. School of Politics and International Relations, University

College Dublin and the Jean Beer Blumenfeld Center for Ethics, Georgia State University. 15 & 16 June 2015.

Shue H. (1980) *Basic Rights: Subsistence, Affluence, and U.S. Foreign Policy*. Princeton University Press, Princeton.

Shue H. (1993) "Subsistence Emissions and Luxury Emissions" *Law & Policy*, 15, 39–60.

Thomson J. J. (1986) "Imposing Risks" in Parent W., ed., *Rights, Restitution, & Risk*. Harvard University Press, Cambridge 173–191.

Toro J. (2011). There is nothing 'Natural' in Natural Disasters. *The World Bank*. (http://blogs.worldbank.org/latinamerica/there-is-nothing-natural-in-natural-disasters).

United Nations Framework Convention on Climate Change (1992) (http://unfccc.int/resource/docs/convkp/conveng.pdf).

Vanderheiden S. (2016) "Climate Change and Free Riding" *Journal of Moral Philosophy*, 13, 1–27.

Wendt A. (1999) *Social Theory of International Politics*. Cambridge University Press, Cambridge.

9 Future people's rights

Dispelling an ontological worry

Hubert Schnueriger

The meagre outcomes of climate conferences reveal how delicate a task it is to come up with viable provisions and policies to fight climate change. Other areas of fighting environmental perils are hardly better off. Undoubtedly, the reasons why it is so difficult to tackle these challenges are manifold and they arguably mutually reinforce each other (Gardiner 2011). An important reason is certainly that it is notoriously contested in what normative and conceptual framework environmental issues can and should be dealt with. Among the most fundamental issues is that of how the interests of future people can and should be accounted for at present. It is disputed, for instance, whether persons not yet living can have rights against moral agents living at present and whether expensive environmental policies can be justified by reference to future people's rights.

Being able to back up the fight against climate change and other environmental perils with future people's rights gives it an eminent political and rhetorical standing. This standing mirrors a widely held contention in academic literature that rights have a particular normative strength. They are often said to work like trumps (Dworkin 1984), even though this characterization is somewhat misleading. Rights do not have to trump every other consideration nor do they have to be very weighty. Their particular normative strength is due to the particular way they structure the practical realm. Invoking rights emphasizes the irreplaceability of individuals and their interests. It is, for example, irreconcilable with approaching environmental issues on a consequentialist or purely cost-benefit basis (Fitz-Patrick 2007, 385ff; Bell 2011, 100). The question whether future people can have rights is related to another conceptual question. It has been argued that presently living persons cannot stand in a relation of justice to persons not yet living exactly because the latter cannot have rights against the former (Beckerman and Pasek 2001, 13ff).

The aim of this chapter is to defend the conceptual consistency of the idea that people living in the future have rights against moral agents living at present. The background of the paper is constituted by anthropogenic impacts on the environment such as climate change or pollution. It is an open question among defenders of a rights-based approach whether environmental issues can and should be discussed on the basis of genuine environmental rights or whether they should be discussed on the basis of other, more familiar rights alone (Woods 2014, ch. 9). In any case, it seems obvious that environmental perils can adversely affect goods such as health, life, subsistence or physical integrity that are protected by familiar human rights. In order to keep the assumptions as moderate as possible, environmental perils will here be taken to pose a threat to familiar human rights such as the right to health.

Objections against the conceptual consistency of rights talk in the relationship between presently living moral agents and future living people have been brought up in different, partly interrelated guises (see, e.g. Tremmel and Robinson 2014, 145ff). The debate on future people's rights has proved helpful in shedding light on most of these objections (see, e.g. Caney 2006; Gosseries 2008; Bell 2011). Astonishingly enough, however, the most fundamental of these objections has not been dealt with adequately so far. The Non-Existence Objection maintains that people living in the future cannot have rights against presently living moral agents for the very reason that they do not yet live. The main idea behind this objection is that people living in the future would have to have rights now if the rights were to be respected now. This objection will be introduced in more detail in the first section. The second section critically discusses the predominant refutation of the Non-Existence Objection. In a nutshell, this refutation holds that the Non-Existence Objection misses its mark by presupposing that the rights at stake must be conceived of as present rights. Against this, scholars such as Lukas Meyer, Axel Gosseries and Derek Bell insist that it is the future rights of people living in the future that must be respected at present. They defend what may be called a Future-Rights-of-Future-People Conception. However, this suggestion faces problems of its own. It will be argued that it gives the Non-Existence Objection too much credit by trying to come to terms with its ontological presuppositions. Both proponents of the Non-Existence Objection and proponents of the Future-Rights-of-Future-People Conception go astray by conducting the debate on future people's rights on a problematic ontological basis. Instead of trying to steer between the Scylla of present rights of future people and the Charybdis of future people's future rights, it is more seminal to defend rights talk in intergenerational issues on the basis of a general theory of rights-ascriptions that escapes notoriously contested ontological commitments. Consequently, the third section investigates the conditions under which rights are commonly ascribed to persons. As will be argued, it is not particularly difficult or problematic to ascribe rights to future people that are immediately relevant for present policies and actions.

The Non-Existence Objection

The paradigmatic formulation of the Non-Existence Objection stems from Richard T. De George:

> Future generations by definition do not now exist. They cannot now, therefore, be the present bearer or subject of anything, including rights. Hence they cannot be said to have rights in the same sense that presently existing entities can be said to have them. This follows from the briefest analysis of the present tense form of the verb 'to have'.
>
> (De George 1981, 159; see also Beckerman and Pasek 2001,
15ff; Macklin 1981, 151f; Earl 2011, 69ff)

Before having a closer look at the argument, four preliminary remarks are in order. First, the Non-Existence Objection basically maintains that entities not yet living cannot have properties at present. Nothing depends on whether these entities are future generations or members of future generations. As it is notoriously contested whether collective entities can have rights at all, references to future generations will be understood here as a shorthand form for references to members of future generations. Second, the objection refers to people not yet living. It does not matter how far in the future these people will live. Third, the Non-Existence Objection must be distinguished from the much more extensively discussed objection against rights talk in the relationship between moral agents living at present and future living people based on what Derek Parfit has called the Non-Identity Problem (1984, 359). It bears on cases in which not only the future living people's quality of life may be affected by the actions of people living at present, but also their very existence and genetic identity. Actions affecting the identity of future people cannot harm them according to this objection as they would not exist if the action was not performed. Consequently, the future living people cannot be said to have a right against moral agents living at present not to be harmed by them according to this argument (e.g. Preda 2016, 98). This objection is obviously less fundamental than the Non-Existence Objection. It only applies in cases in which the relevant action indeed affects the genetic identity of the future living people. Even if one admits for the sake of the argument that political programmes and policies in general affect the genetic identity of the people living in the not-so-distant future, the same does not hold for most of the actions and behaviour of individual moral agents (Tremmel 2009, 39ff). A second consideration questions the objection against rights talk based on the Non-Identity Problem in a more general way. The objection presupposes a highly contentious concept of harm according to which an individual can only be harmed when the respective action makes her worse off than she would otherwise be. An alternative concept of harm identifies harmful actions by reference to a threshold. Harming someone means, then, causing this person to fall below a specified threshold (Meyer 2003, 147). For example, presently living moral agents can harm people yet to come into existence by causing or contributing to the causation of circumstances that damage the health of future living people. In what follows, this threshold conception of harm will be accepted. That leads to the fourth remark. Proponents of the Non-Existence Objection do not claim that the argument also shows that one can have no moral obligations or duties concerning people not yet living (De George 1981, 158, 163f; Macklin 1981, 151; Beckerman and Pasek 2001, 25f). They only claim that the future people cannot have rights correlative to such obligations.

The Non-Existence Objection can be reconstructed as follows, whereby 'nr' means 'no rights':

$P1_{nr}$ Entities that will live in the future do not exist now.
$P2_{nr}$ Entities that do not exist now cannot have any properties now.
$P3_{nr}$ Rights are to be conceived of as properties of entities.
C_{nr} Entities living in the future cannot have rights now.

The first premise is not as trivial as it may seem at first sight. It is a contested topic in the metaphysics of time whether there is any ontological difference between the past, the present and the future. For example, Willard Van Orman Quine suggests in his *Quiddities* to conceive of time as a fourth dimension in addition to the three spatial dimensions (1987, 197f). This would allow talking of every born person as real, independently from when she lives (1987, 74). Living at present is accordingly not 'ontologically privileged' to living in the future (see van Inwagen and Sullivan 2016). Consequently, future people are no less real than one's contemporaries. They are just spatiotemporally differently located. Interestingly, Quine emphasizes the implication of this metaphysical position for intergenerational issues. He contends that insofar as all born people are conceived of as real people they must also morally be treated as real people. That implies that one has to respect the interests of people not yet living (1987, 74f). The Non-Existence Objection, notwithstanding first appearance, is compatible with such an ontological position. The latter builds on a tense-less understanding of 'being', 'having' and 'existing' (1987, 75), whereas the Non-Existence Objection presupposes a tensed understanding of these verbs. It is one thing to argue that every entity has a spatiotemporal existence. It is another thing to maintain that a particular entity exists at a particular point in time (Unnerstall 1999, 35ff; Earl 2011, 64). This abstract and general consideration can be supplemented by the observation already hinted at that proponents of the Non-Existence Objection normally do not maintain to show thereby that people living at present cannot have any duties with regard to people living in the future. Insofar, they do not have to deny that people not yet living can be treated as actual or real people whose interests must be respected and considered in present actions and policies.[1]

The second premise states that an entity that does not exist now cannot have any properties now. It invokes a more general principle stating what has been called a Bearer-Attribute Contemporaneity Requirement (Gosseries 2008, 455). For example, maintaining that Frederick I, the medieval emperor also known as Barbarossa, has in the year 2017 an impressive red beard when he has died towards the end of the twelfth century is not possible. In contrast, it is possible to talk at present about Frederick I and his having a red beard using the grammatical present tense form of 'to have' without using it in a tensed form. The same holds for people living in the future. It is definitely possible to ascribe properties to persons not yet living. For example, the future children of the currently living rich people can be said to be the heirs of their wealth if they are entitled to inherit. The particular question at stake is whether they can have the properties at present.

The third premise is, in the form it is presented, unproblematic. Rights can be understood as normative properties. However, it is worthwhile to keep in mind that proponents of the Non-Existence Objection are inclined to treat rights as any other kinds of properties. Beckerman and Pasek explicitly argue that rights are to be treated as any other properties: "The crux of our argument that future generations cannot have rights to anything is that properties, such as being green or wealthy or having rights, can be predicated only of some subject that exists" (Beckerman and Pasek 2001, 15). Some caution here is necessary. The Bearer-Attribute Contemporaneity Requirement introduced above gains its intuitive plausibility against the background of physical properties. It is not evident whether it applies to non-physical properties as well.

The literature on future people's rights commonly distinguishes between two different ways to counter the Non-Existence Objection. They are, following a suggestion by Robert Elliot (1989, 160f), often distinguished as the Concessional and the Non-Concessional View. The Non-Concessional View rejects Premise $P2_{nr}$. Consequently, it maintains that rights can exist at present even though the right-bearers do not yet exist (Elliot 1989, 160; Partridge 1990, 54). The Concessional View, in contrast, accepts that people living in the future do not have rights at present. Insofar, it accepts all three premises as well as the conclusion but criticizes the argument for being practically irrelevant. When present policies and actions are justified or criticized by reference to the rights of people living in the future, it is their future rights that are referred to. It is the future rights of future people that must not be violated by present policies and actions. The Concessional View turns out to be a Future-Rights-of-Future-People Conception. Most proponents of a rights-based approach to intergenerational issues defend the Concessional View in this way. As will become evident in the next section, it proves highly problematic.

Future people's future rights

The paradigmatic defence of the Future-Rights-of-Future-People Conception relies on a necessary relation between rights and interests, holding that it is possible to affect the rights people will have in the future just as it is possible to affect the interests they will have in the future (Hoerster 1991, 98f). Lukas Meyer presents the argument in favour of this conception as follows:

> we can safely assume, first, that future people can be bearers of rights in the future; second, that the rights they have will be determined by the interests they have then; and, third, that our present actions and policies can affect their interests. Thus, if we can adversely affect future people's interests, we can violate their future rights.
>
> (Meyer 2003, 145)

The argument consists of four premises, 'fr' reading 'future rights':

$P1_{fr}$ Persons living in the future can have rights in the future, i.e. they can have future rights.

$P2_{fr}$ The rights persons living in the future will have will be determined by the interests they will have in the future.

$P3_{fr}$ Present actions can have an impact on the future interests of future persons.

$P4_{fr}$ A sufficient condition of an infringement of the rights determined by the interests of the right-holders is the negative impact on the respective interests.

C_{fr} The future rights of persons living in the future can be infringed by actions or policies at present.

The first premise seems unproblematic. Nobody partaking in the debate denies that actual people living in the future can and will have rights then.

The second premise invokes, together with the fourth premise, the thesis of a conceptual connection between rights and interests as is mainly characteristic for the so-called interest theory of rights. This theory, or better, this family of theories, holds that the function of rights consists in protecting or promoting an interest of the right-holder. It will be discussed in more detail in the last section. The last section also briefly introduces the traditional alternative to the interest theory of rights, the will theory of rights.

The third premise states that present actions and policies can affect the (future) interests of future people for the worse. They can harm future persons. As briefly discussed above, this premise is supposed to apply even to cases in which actions and policies contribute to the identity of the right-holder.

The fourth premise presents a criterion that allows establishing the infringement of a right. It contends that a right is infringed when the right-holder is (threatened to be) harmed. Not every infringement of a right is unjustified. In cases of rights conflicts for example, it may be justified to infringe the weaker of the conflicting rights. Hence, it is possible to distinguish between justified and unjustified infringements of rights (Thomson 1986, 40). Only in the latter case is it suitable to talk of rights violations.

Problematically, the conclusion does not immediately follow from the premises. It does not follow from the fact that an agent harms a person, that the agent infringes a right of hers not to be harmed. This only follows if she has a right against this agent not to be harmed by him, and whether such a right can exist is exactly what is being questioned. The argument plays down what proponents of the Non-Existence Objection insist on, namely that one cannot have rights against one's non-contemporaries.

In order to gain a clear understanding of the differences between proponents of the Non-Existence Objection and proponents of the Future-Rights-of-Future-People Conception, it is necessary to have a closer look at the structure of rights.

Future people's rights and the structure of rights

The Standard View: the correlativity of rights and duties

There is quite a broad consensus in the contemporary literature on the concept of rights that the framework of rights talk should be Hohfeldian in style. Wesley N. Hohfeld famously distinguishes between four atomic or fundamental kinds of rights: claim rights or 'rights in the strictest sense', privileges, powers and immunities (Hohfeld 1913). All of them exhibit a triadic structure: A right-holder has a right against the addressee of the right to something, namely the object of the right (Alexy 1985, 171f). Importantly, the object of an atomic right in this sense is always an action or an omission of an action. For the discussion at hand, only so called claim-rights are of interest. The object of a claim-right is always its addressee's action. At the same time, the addressee has a duty *owed* to the right-holder to act accordingly. This is commonly called the correlativity of rights and duties or the Correlativity Thesis. In this venerable tradition of rights talk, rights are best understood as relational normative properties (Stepanians 2005).

'Having a right' means accordingly to stand in a particular normative relationship to another entity. Quite common references to rights such as 'a right to subsistence' or 'a right to health' are elliptical according to this tradition. Either they are a shorthand form for a plethora of different atomic rights or for a singular atomic right. Most often, the shorthand form refers to the good protected by the rights. It may be helpful to illustrate this considering the 'right to health'. Without knowing who is obliged or allowed to do what, one does not know the content of the right. Does it entitle the right-holder to help in case of sickness or does it (only) forbid others from damaging the right-holder's health? Who would have to help the right-holder and who would have to abstain from damaging her health? It suffices for the purpose of this paper to assume that it only implies the negative right that one's health not be damaged. For convenience, this will often be referred to in what follows as the right not to be harmed. At the same time, it seems unproblematic to assume that it is a universal and general right. It is universal as every person has it and it is general as it consists against every moral agent.[2] Of course, this again is a shorthand formulation. Strictly speaking, having a general right not to be harmed means having as many atomic rights as there are moral agents having a correlative duty. In the example at hand, all these atomic rights are determined by the right-holder's interest in health. Crucially, if a person has a right not to be harmed against another agent and the other agent harms the right-holder, then the latter infringes her right. His harming the right-holder is a sufficient criterion for establishing his infringing her right.[3] For convenience's sake it can be said that the right to health is, then, infringed when at least one of the addressees harms the right-holder by damaging her health.

The Future-Rights-of-Future-People Conception and the Standard View

With these conceptual clarifications in mind, it not only becomes clear why the argument in favour of the Future-Rights-of-Future-People Conception fails to be conclusive but also why it may seem sound at first sight. It is certainly plausible to assume that every person living in the future will have a right to health, implying that no one is allowed to damage the right-holder's health. The people living in the future will have a universal and general right to health. Being a general and universal right, it holds against every moral agent. Consequently, every moral agent has a duty owed to each and every person not to harm her, in the sense of not damaging her health. Thus, it is possible to conclude from the fact that when a duty-holder causes damage to a right-holder's health that he infringes her right, held against him, not to be harmed by him. Now, the Future-Rights-of-Future-People Conception seems to presuppose that when the right not to be harmed can be conceived of as a right against everyone, it holds against everyone that can harm the right-holder. Insofar as one can not only be harmed by one's contemporaries but also by people that will have lived before, proponents of the Future-Rights-of-Future-People Conception conclude that one's right to health holds against them, too. This presupposition is far from trivial. It implies the rejection of what Axel Gosseries has called the Obligation-Right-Contemporaneity requirement according to which rights and their correlative duties must both exist at the same time (Gosseries 2008, 455).

This rejection of the Obligation-Rights-Contemporaneity Requirement presents two problems. First, if rights correlate to duties, they form constitutive parts of a normative relationship between the right-holder and the duty-bearer. Accordingly, proponents of the Future-Rights-of-Future-People Conception must accept that a normative relation consists between presently living duty-bearers and right-holders living in the future. Because they accept the Bearer-Attribute-Contemporaneity Requirement as well, they have to contend that the two relata, the rights and their correlative duties, exist temporally independently from each other. In consequence, they presuppose on the one hand the Bearer-Attribute-Contemporaneity Requirement but deny on the other hand the Obligation-Rights-Contemporaneity Requirement. It is far from evident that this is a consistent solution. The proponents of the Future-Rights-of-Future-People Conception have to back up their suggestion with an ontology of relations that makes clear why the relata of a relation do not have to exist at the same time even though the time of existence is conceived of as being crucial when it comes to the relation between individuals and their properties. The Future-Rights-of-Future-People Conception fails as an immediate answer to the Non-Existence Objection for a second but related reason. According to the Correlativity Thesis, the right and the correlative duty have the same object, namely an act of the duty-bearer. The Future-Rights-of-Future-People Conception holds that persons living in the future would have future rights against moral agents not living anymore who acted, or would have had to act, in a certain way in the past. The future persons would, accordingly, have a right in the future to something that does not and cannot be realized anymore (De George 1981, 160f; see also Beckerman and Pasek 2001, 18, 20). Hence, the Future-Rights-of-Future-People Conception does not really fare better in regard to ontological questions than the position the Non-Existence Objection attacks: How can someone have a property in the future if a constitutive and necessary element of this property does not exist anymore?

This objection against the Future-Rights-of-Future-People Conception presupposes that its proponents accept the Standard View on the correlativity of rights and duties. This assumption may be premature even though some of them explicitly refer to the correlativity of rights and duties (Gosseries 2018, 450ff; Bell 2011, 100 et passim). They may nevertheless have a different understanding of this relation in mind, building the Future-Rights-of-Future-People Conception, that way, on a different conception of the structure of rights. It is worthwhile to ponder on this possibility by investigating into the justification of the Future-Rights-of-Future-People Conception by Derek Bell. On the one hand, his justification of this conception can be understood as quite directly tackling the objection brought forward in the last paragraph. On the other hand, it seems to go together with an abandonment of the correlativity of rights and duties as introduced above.

The Future-Rights-of-Future-People Conception
and an alternative view on the structure of rights

The Future-Rights-of-Future-People Conception has been criticized for its implication that the people living in the future would have a right to something that is not accessible anymore. Neither the duty-holder nor the duty nor the conditions for its performance would exist anymore. The action of the subject of the correlative duty would have to have occurred in the past in order for the right to be respected. Bell's main line of reasoning aims at showing that this implication is not only less counterintuitive than it may seem at first sight but that it is also not confined to normative relations between non-contemporaries:

> insofar as the effects of all actions necessarily occur after the action, the 'problem' is quite general: all human rights-based duties are current duties grounded in the future rights of persons living in the future (even if it is the very near or immediate future). We are duty-bound not to act so that a person living in the future will have one of their human rights violated as a consequence of our actions.
>
> (Bell 2011, 107)

It is, according to this defence, a common feature of right-duty relationships that there exists a temporal difference between rights and their correlative duties (Bell 2011, 107f; see also Lawrence 2014, 41).

Bell's defence of the Future-Rights-of-Future-People Conception seemingly proceeds in two main steps, both of them being problematic. First, he distinguishes between the action that is the object of the duty and the action's effect on the right-holder, contending that there is a time lag between the occurrence of an action and its effects on the right-holder's interests. To be sure, it is not necessary to hold the view that there is always such a time lag. It suffices that it counts for paradigmatic and uncontested rights-duty relationships. The case of a company pouring sewage on a particular occasion into a river may serve as an illustration of this idea. It is certainly possible to distinguish the act of pouring toxic water into a river from its temporally delayed damaging effect on people living downstream. However, things look different if the description of the act changes. Arguably, the company is supposed to not pour toxic water into the river in order not to harm the people downstream. That raises the question at what point in time it harms the people in the example: Does it harm them at the moment it pours toxic water into the river? Or does it harm them at the moment the people bath in the toxic water? Or is the question misconceived altogether? Whatever the answer is, it is obvious that the first premise relies on a far from trivial identification of the relevant act. From a normative point of view, the effects of an act are not as easily detachable from its performance as Bell suggests. This point can also be put in terms of rights and duties. It is pertinent to distinguish between the abstract duty not to harm other people and the different concrete duties derived from it. The abstract duty not to damage another's health gives rise to more concrete duties to abstain from all the concrete acts that may have a damaging effect on others' health. This allows, of course, for different degrees of concreteness reaching down to so-called basic actions. It is, however, the abstract right and the abstract duty that identify the normatively relevant act-description.

Second, Bell presupposes that a right is infringed when the right-holder actually suffers the harm. That is, in light of the first step, supposed to show that the infringement of a right occurs later than the duty-bearer's breach of his correlative duty. Bell takes this to reveal that it is always a future right that is infringed by a duty-bearer's action even though it may be the very near or even immediate future (2011, 107f). Even having admitted that it is possible to distinguish between an act and its delayed effects, it does not follow that the respective duty and the respective right do not exist at the same time. It is one thing to argue that the breach of a duty occurs at another time than the infringement of a right, but another to argue that the duty and the right do not exist at the same time. The fact that someone's right not to be harmed is infringed at a certain point in time does not show that it only exists at this time. Residents living by a river hold a right against companies that they not pollute the river all the time, not only when it is infringed. Insofar, it is not possible to conclude by analogy that future people's rights are best understood as their future rights just as all of one's contemporaries' rights one infringes are, seen from the point in time the relevant action is performed, their future rights.

Bell's direct defence of the Future-Rights-of-Future-People Conception appears in a different light when his rather passing remarks on the grounding relation between human rights and their correlative duties are taken to imply a departure from the Correlativity Thesis as introduced above. Human rights are, according to him, supposed to ground their 'correlative' duties (2011, 107). The very idea of rights as grounding duties has famously been put forward in order to reject the Correlativity Thesis (MacCormick 1977, 201; Raz 1986, 170f). According to this understanding of the relation between rights and duties, rights can be understood as intermediate conclusions from ultimate values to duties (Raz 1986, 181). Rights and the duties they justify have their place not only on different levels of practical reasoning. They have also different contents. The content of the right is the good to be protected by the 'correlative' duties whereas the content of those duties are the actions that may harm the right-holder.

This understanding of the relation between rights and duties can indeed support the Future-Rights-of-Future-People Conception. Rights and duties can coherently exist at different points in time according to this understanding. The main costs of defending rights of future people on the basis of this alternative conception of rights consists in giving up the direct link between the content of a right and the content of the respective duties. According to this alternative view, maintaining rights of future people implies maintaining that their interests are important enough to justify duties of people living at present. Which duties that may be is left open. Arguably, this conception of rights assimilates rights and interests.

Instead of opting for this highly problematic deviation from the Standard View, it makes sense to take a closer look at its main alternative. The Future-Rights-of-Future-People Conception has been introduced above as the paradigmatic form of the Concessional View. It does not question the premises of the Non-Existence Objection but rejects the argument as being practically irrelevant. The Non-Concessional View, in contrast, rejects the second premise of the Non-Existence Objection, which states that entities that do not yet live cannot have any properties at present. It thereby rejects the Bearer-Attribute Contemporaneity Requirement. That does not imply that the rights exist totally independent of rights-subjects. It implies, however, that the rights do not have to exist at the same time as their bearers (Elliot 1989, 161). To be sure, the Non-Concessional View does not hold that the rights in question are the rights of possible right-holders. Quite on the contrary, they are the rights of actual bearers of rights living in the future. Whether there are such rights at present depends on whether there will be people living in the future. The rights are contingent on the future existence of their bearers. As it seems fair to assume that there will be people in the future, it seems fair to assume that there exist rights of future people now (Elliot 1989, 162). The Non-Concessional View has, so far, remained a minority position in the debate on future people's rights. The main reason for this may be that its proponents have not yet directly answered the ontological worry underlying the Non-Existence Objection. Elliot, for example, tries to dispel the ontological worry by reconstructing it as an epistemic worry. He defends the Non-Concessional View by arguing that it parallels a case in which a moral agent fires a missile onto a distant island. Whether she thereby violates the rights of people living on the island depends on whether there are people living on this very island. This case is supposed to be similar to the case of future people's rights. The reluctance to ascribe present rights to future people is, then, allegedly due to the fact that the people living in the future are in a sense epistemically inaccessible (Elliot 1989, 162). That is, however, not the worry underlying the Non-Existence Objection.

The Non-Concessional View's marginal role in the debate is nevertheless quite astonishing. It has already been mentioned above that it is quite unproblematic to ascribe at present properties to people living in the future. In order to make progress, it makes sense to step back and to question the terms in which the debate on the rights of future people has been conducted so far. Both proponents as well as opponents of the Non-Existence Objection accept that the debate should be conducted as a debate on the ontology of properties. In addition, both presuppose or, at least, do not question that normative properties are to be treated like non-normative properties. That is as amazing as it is problematic. The long-standing and ongoing debates in metaethics reveal that the ontological status of normative properties like 'good' or 'right' is notoriously contested. It cannot just be presupposed that rights have to be treated like non-normative properties. Interestingly, it is not necessary to go into this area of moral ontology in order to defend the conceptual possibility of future persons having rights that are relevant for present actions and policies. It suffices to have a closer look at the concept of (claim-)rights and the conditions under which entities can be said to have them.

Rights and reasons for action

The most promising method to find out under what conditions rights are ascribed to an entity is to ask under what conditions duties are *owed* to an entity, drawing that way on the correlativity of rights and duties.[4] It is most beneficial to perceive this directionality of a duty as a specific way a duty can be related to another entity. Not every duty that is related to another entity is a duty owed to it. It is, for example one thing to maintain a duty not to treat animals cruelly, but quite another to maintain that this duty is owed to them (see, e.g. Kant MS AA IV, 442). The different theories of rights differ in how to conceive of this directionality of duties. As mentioned above, two main families of rights theories are traditionally distinguished: the will or choice theory and the interest theory. Broadly put, the will theory holds that a duty is owed to a particular entity if that entity has a certain degree of control over it. The right-holder may, for example, be able to waive her right and thereby waive the performance of the duty or she may, quite on the contrary, demand the performance of the duty. Proponents of rights of future persons have not often referred to a will theory of rights (but see Baier 1981). That may be due to general reservations towards the will theory of rights or to particular difficulties of ascribing rights to persons not yet living on this basis as it is not obvious how future people could perform the relevant kind of control over the duty of people not living anymore (for general objections to the will theory, see MacCormick 1977, 195ff). It is by far more common to defend future people's rights in terms of the interest theory of rights. Meyer, Gosseries and Bell indeed argue for the Future-Rights-of-Future-People Conception on the basis of the interest theory.

The interest theory maintains that rights protect and promote interests of the right-holder. In order to exclude misunderstandings, it must be emphasized that it does not deny that the right-holder normally has a certain degree of control over the correlative duty. It denies, however, that this control necessarily forms part of the concept of rights. A viable version of the interest theory needs further qualification. Otherwise, it faces a contingency problem: Not every individual that benefits from a duty has a correlative right (Jhering 1906, 336; Lyons 1994, 29). An individual may indirectly and by hazard benefit from the performance of a duty. A widespread reaction to this problem consists in introducing what can be called a semantic criterion of qualification: According to this criterion, there must be a necessary relation between the content of the duty and the relevant interest (Kramer 1998, 81). However, all known versions of a semantic qualification lead to false positives and negatives. The reason for this extensional inadequacy consists in the fact that it undercuts the very distinction mentioned above as crucial for the concept of rights. A semantic criterion identifies the right-holder by relying on the content of the duty and thereby on the entity in regard of which the duty exists (if there is such an entity). It loses sight of the particularity of directional duties. A second version of a 'non-contingency criterion' fares better in this respect. It conceives of the relation between a duty and the protection of another's interest as a justificatory one. It clearly distinguishes between the justificatory basis of a duty and its content. That is not to deny that the content of a duty very often provides its justificatory reason.

According to this understanding, rights and rights talk express a specific justificatory structure of practical reasoning. Put in an abstract way, having a duty owed to an individual means that one has the duty for that individual's sake. Articulated differently, duties owed to others express what is demanded out of respect for others. To respect someone means, according to this justificatory version of the interest theory, to give her interests due concern. Accordingly, the interests provide the reasons for the other's duties. A simple example can illustrate this. Being healthy is in everybody's (objective) interest. A duty not to damage another's health is owed to the other person if her interest in health is the reason for this very duty. Interest theorists are inclined to take interests as the only morally relevant properties that can justify other's duties. This may be too strong a supposition, but nothing depends on it for the discussion at hand.

It is, now, possible to formulate an argument to defend the idea that future people can have rights against presently living moral agents:

P1   A person x has a right against a moral agent y that y performs act ϕ if the moral agent y has a duty to perform act ϕ owed to person x.

P2   Having a duty owed to a person x means having the duty for that person's sake.

P3   At least some of the duties owed to another person x are justified by x's interests. The interests provide the sufficient requiring reasons for the respective duties.

P4   Moral agents living at present can have duties for the sake of people living in the future justified by their interests.

C   Future persons can have rights against moral agents living at present.

The first premise expresses under what condition an entity can be said to have a right according to the correlativity thesis. People living by a river may have a right against companies that the companies forbear from every action that damages their health if the company has the duty owed to them to forbear from every action that damages their health. The second premise states the condition under which a duty is owed to an entity. The companies' duties to forbear from every action that damages the residents' health is owed to them if it is justified for their sake. The third premise adds that the content of the duty is often, and perhaps always, provided by interests of the addressee of the duty. It is, for example, the residents' interests in health that justify the companies' duties to forbear from every action that damages their health. Premise four is supposed to present the decisive step as it applies the concept of a duty owed to others to intergenerational relations. If moral agents living at present have a duty not to damage future people's health and if this duty is justified for the sake of the future people, this warrants the conclusion that the future people have a right against the moral agents living at present not to damage their health.

Conclusion

The Non-Existence Objection denies that people not yet living can have rights against people living at present because they do not yet exist. The underlying thought is that it only makes sense to attribute rights to people living in the future against people living at present if the rights would exist at present. The predominant defences of rights talk with regard to future people do so either by presupposing a highly contested and problematic structure of rights or by a way that cannot dispel the ontological worry motivating the Non-Existence Objection. The last section tried to address this worry directly. It defended the conceptual consistency of future people having rights against presently living moral agents on the basis of a particular concept of rights. It holds that rights exhibit a particular justificatory structure. This, in turn, may raise the suspicion that it remains too parochial as there is no consensus in the literature that rights indeed exhibit this kind of justificatory structure as a conceptual necessity. It is, therefore, pertinent to highlight that the decisive considerations do not depend on this particular conception of rights. The core of the argument consists in invoking the ontological conditions of rights-duty relationships among contemporaries and making evident that the same conditions hold in the case of rights-duty ascriptions among non-contemporaries. A right-duty relationship between two contemporaries exists if and only if it is justified. There is no need to introduce a further ontological condition when it comes to normative relationships between non-contemporaries.

This argument can be complemented by a consideration from a related, albeit slightly different angle. *Ex hypothesi*, proponents of the Non-Existence Objection do not deny that people living at present have duties to future people. Insofar, they have to accept that there exists a normative relationship between people living at present and people living in the future. They must accordingly attribute to the people living in the future the normative property of standing in a normative relationship with people living at present. Given that, it is not intelligible why this property cannot be a right understood as a relational normative property.

Proponents of the Non-Existence Objection may perhaps still be inclined to insist that future people's rights would have to exist at present in order to be relevant at present. This, however, is a superficial linguistic difficulty. The crucial point is that attributing rights to future people against moral agents living at present means that their future interests provide at present reasons for the latter to act accordingly. There is nothing ontologically mysterious about that.[5]

Notes

1 In other words, trying to solve the issue of future people's rights by generally referring to the problem of future contingents would not directly answer the ontological worry bothering the proponents of the Non-Existence Objection. Thanks to Christian Seidel for pressing me on this point.
2 'Moral agents' can be understood in the broadest possible way. Every entity that can be conceived of as a duty-bearer can be the addressee of a right.
3 Needless to say, the right may already be infringed when the right-holder is exposed to a certain threat to her health.
4 This section draws on thoughts developed in the course of the justification of a status theory of rights (Schnueriger 2014).
5 Many thanks for helpful comments to Selina O'Doherty, Ashley Dodsworth, Markku Oksanen, Angelika Krebs, Larissa Daetwyler and Jan Mueller. Rob Lawlor gave some encouraging and highly helpful hints at an early stage of the paper. Many thanks as well to the audiences at the conferences where early versions of this paper have been presented.

References

Alexy R. (1985) *Theorie der Grundrechte: Studien und Materialien zur Verfassungsgerichtsbarkeit.* Nomos Verlagsgesellschaft, Baden-Baden.
Baier A. (1981) "The Rights of Past and Future Persons" in Partridge E. ed., *Responsibilities to Future Generations: Environmental Ethics.* Prometheus Books, Buffalo, 171–83.
Beckerman W. and Pasek J. (2001) *Justice, Posterity, and the Environment.* Oxford University Press, Oxford.
Bell D. (2011) "Does Anthropogenic Climate Change Violate Human Rights?" *Critical Review of International Social and Political Philosophy,* 14/2, 99–124.
Caney S. (2006) "Cosmopolitan Justice, Rights and Global Climate Change" *The Canadian Journal of Law and Jurisprudence,* 19/2, 255–78.
De George R. T. (1981) "The Environment, Rights, and Future Generations" in Partridge E. ed., *Responsibilities to Future Generations: Environmental Ethics.* Prometheus Books, Buffalo, 157–65.

Dworkin R. (1984) "Rights as Trumps" in Waldron J. ed., *Theories of Rights*. Oxford University Press, Oxford, 153–67.

Earl D. (2011) "Ontology and the Paradox of Future Generations" *Public Reason*, 3/1, 60–72.

Elliot R. (1989) "The Rights of Future People" *Journal of Applied Philosophy*, 6/2, 159–70.

FitzPatrick W. J. (2007) "Climate Change and the Rights of Future Generations" *Environmental Ethics*, 29/4, 369–88.

Gardiner S. M. (2011) *A Perfect Moral Storm: The Ethical Tragedy of Climate Change*. Oxford University Press, New York.

Gosseries A. (2008) "On Future Generations' Future Rights" *Journal of Political Philosophy*, 16/4, 446–74.

Hoerster N. (1991) *Abtreibung im saekularen Staat: Argumente gegen den § 218*. Suhrkamp, Frankfurt am Main.

Hohfeld W. N. (1913) "Some Fundamental Legal Conceptions as Applied in Judicial Reasoning" *The Yale Law Journal*, 23/1, 16–59.

Jhering R. von (1906) *Der Geist des roemischen Rechts auf den verschiedenen Stufen seiner Entwicklung 3. Teil 1. Abteilung*, 5., unveraend. Auflage. Breitkopf und Haertel, Leipzig.

Kant I. (MS) *Die Metaphysik der Sitten* in Kant I *Gesammelte Schriften* hg. von der Preussischen Akademie der Wissenschaften. Georg Reimer, Berlin 1900ff, Bd 6, 203–493.

Kramer M. H. (1998) "Rights without Trimmings" in Kramer M., Simmonds N. and Steiner H. eds., *A Debate over Rights: Philosophical Enquiries*. Clarendon Press, Oxford, New York, 7–111.

Lawrence P. (2014) *Justice for Future Generations: Climate Change and International Law*. E. Elgar, Cheltenham.

Lyons D. (1994) "Rights, Claimants, and Beneficiaries" in Lyons D. ed., *Rights, Welfare, and Mill's Moral Theory*. Oxford University Press, New York, 23–46.

MacCormick N. (1977) "Rights in Legislation" in Hacker P. M. S. and Raz J. eds., *Law, Morality, and Society: Essays in Honour of H. L. A. Hart*. Clarendon Press, Oxford, 189–209.

Macklin R. (1981) "Can Future Generations Correctly be Said to Have Rights?" in Partridge E. ed., *Responsibilities to Future Generations: Environmental Ethics*. Prometheus Books, Buffalo, 151–5.

Meyer L. H. (2003) "Past and Future: The Case for a Threshold Notion of Harm" in Meyer L. H., Paulson S. L. and Pogge T. W. eds., *Rights, Culture, and the Law: Themes from the Legal and Political Philosophy of Joseph Raz*. Oxford University Press, Oxford, 143–59.

Parfit D. (1984) *Reasons and Persons*. Clarendon Press, Oxford.

Partridge E. (1990) "On the Rights of Future Generations" in Scherer D. ed., *Upstream/Downstream: Issues in Environmental Ethics*. Temple University Press, Philadelphia, 40–66.

Preda A. (2016) "Human Rights, Climate Change, and Sustainability" in Bos G. and Duewell M. eds., *Human Rights and Sustainability: Moral Responsibilities for the Future*. Routledge, London, 95–106.

Quine W. V. (1987) *Quiddities: An Intermittently Philosophical Dictionary*. Belknap Press of Harvard University Press, Cambridge/MA.

Raz J. (1986) *The Morality of Freedom*. Clarendon Press, Oxford.

Schnueriger H. (2014) *Eine Statustheorie moralischer Rechte*. mentis, Muenster.

Stepanians M. (2005) Rights as Relational Properties: In Defense of Right/Duty-Correlativity Unpublished habilitation thesis, University of Saarbruecken.

Thomson J. J. (1986) "Self-Defense and Rights" in Thomson J. J. ed., *Rights, Restitution, and Risk: Essays in Moral Philosophy*. Harvard University Press, Cambridge/MA, 33–48.

Tremmel J. C. (2009) *A Theory of Intergenerational Justice*. Earthscan, London.

Tremmel J. C. and Robinson K. (2014) *Climate Ethics: Environmental Justice and Climate Change*. I. B. Tauris, London.

Unnerstall H. (1999) *Rechte zukuenftiger Generationen*. Koenigshausen & Neumann, Wuerzburg.

van Inwagen P. and Sullivan M. (2016) "Metaphysics" (http://plato.stanford.edu/entries/metaphysics/) Accessed 17 August 2016.

Woods K. (2014) *Human Rights: Issues in Political Theory*. Palgrave Macmillan, Basingstoke.

10 Human rights–based precautionary approaches and risk imposition in the context of climate change

Eike Düvel

Why adopt a human rights approach in climate change ethics?

If the human rights of the most vulnerable future people are at stake in anthropogenic climate change, a robust case in favour of aggressive mitigation and adaptation could be made (Caney 2010, 163). A human rights approach would require us to prioritize life, health and subsistence of the most vulnerable before other considerations, such as welfare maximization, may come into play.[1] This is the idea of lexically prior entitlements, and it exists in different varieties. Caney (2009, 2010) has defended an approach based on human rights. Meyer (2009, 2003), Harman (2004, 2009) and others instead have defended a threshold notion of harm that gives priority to improving the well-being of individuals below a certain threshold. Despite minor differences, I will call these and similar theories basic rights theories the focus of which is on rights to, e.g., life, health and subsistence.

When it comes to future damages, risk and uncertainty play an important role. It has been argued that the uncertainties surrounding climate change are so extensive that it is hard to tell what the future costs and benefits of a given policy will actually be and how they are distributed (Gardiner 2011, 30). Thinking about our duties to cut greenhouse gas emissions in terms of basic rights marks a fundamental shift in perspective. Instead of focusing on optimizing the overall balance of costs and benefits, the basic rights approach directs us to first ensure that every person's basic rights are honoured and thus a robust case in favour of aggressive mitigation and adaptation would emerge.

Focussing on basic rights will also appeal to those who harbour general doubts about aggregative-consequentialist moral theories and related cost-benefit analysis (Caney 2010, 169–170). Rights approaches take the separateness of persons seriously by barring the justification of harming one person for the benefit of another without regard for what that means for the harmed person. Lenman (2008, 99–100) and Frick (2015, 175–176) mention the general distaste for the reduction of ethics to the production of value as another reason for such an approach.

The concept of rights also plays an important role in the international political and legal discourse. Such a theory may enable us to participate more easily in it. Furthermore, rights can be enshrined in international treaties; one can demand their fulfilment and they make it easier to point out what the wrong in delayed climate change mitigation consists of, apart from the uncertain effects on the balance of costs and benefits (Caney 2010, 171–172).

Unfortunately, though, the anti-aggregative leanings of rights theories come at a considerable price. Because rights are absolute claims but (numerical) risk comes in degrees, a naïve basic rights theory will run into what has been called the problem of paralysis (Hayenhjelm & Wolff 2012, 1; Holm 2016). As risk is pervasive, virtually all actions may violate some right and thus naïve rights theories will judge virtually all actions to be impermissible. This problem occurs because there is nothing in the concept of rights which says that merely risking a right is less objectionable than actually violating it. No one defends the no-risk principle, but replacing it is not as easy as it first seems.

I discuss two points in this chapter. The first is to explain how exactly the problem of paralysis arises out of rejecting certain forms of aggregative-consequentialist reasoning and why it shouldn't be taken lightly. The second is to show a way out of the problem of paralysis for basic rights theories. I think that a version of Scanlonian contractualism can stick to the spirit of rights approaches while avoiding the problem of paralysis. Part of the contractualist solution will be to allow a limited form of aggregative reasoning. I will then show how my results can be applied to risk impositions involving environmental rights. I will conclude that many of the risks imposed on people through anthropogenic climate change are not justifiable by contractualist reasoning.

The no-risk principle and the problem of paralysis

According to the no-risk principle, driving a car to buy groceries would be impermissible, because there is a chance that you will run someone over. Kissing your lover puts them at risk of acquiring a terrible transmissible disease – a disease which you didn't know that you had. A flower pot on your windowsill might fall on someone's head and injure her, and so on.[2] Since non-zero chances for rights violations are "easy to come by" (Jackson & Smith 2016, 284), virtually all actions would be impermissible if rights really were absolute and the no-risk principle held.

Let me be very clear here that I am not advocating for the no-risk principle. The implications of adhering to the no-risk principle verge on absurd, but it can be used as a starting point to think about rights and risk. Furthermore, rights-based theories can be distinguished by how they modify or replace the no-risk principle.

The main intuition against the no-risk principle is that the costliness of reducing risks is morally relevant. It seems the balance of costs and benefits should play some role; you should not be required to do everything physically possible to minimize risks. However, it is unclear what resources a rights view has to determine that point or whether that is possible at all, once aggregative-consequentialist reasoning has been rejected.

In contrast, consider again the tools aggregative-consequentialist theories have to tackle cases like the above: what counts for the moral evaluation of an action are the consequences. In the case of risk, expected consequences are considered. In the above cases, what we are comparing is the certain gain of a minor benefit (a joyride, a kiss, having pots on the windowsill) against the risk of grave harm. If the probability of the harm occurring is high, the action will be impermissible, if the probability is sufficiently low, it will be permissible. What action should be chosen depends on the expected balance of costs and benefits.

Rights and the problem of paralysis

We might think that the above examples – driving a car, kissing your lover, having pots on the windowsill – are extreme examples, because they are about astronomically small chances of rights violations. There are two answers to that: Firstly, that there is nothing to be found in the concept of a right that would tell us anything about when a risk is small enough to be negligible or when it is high enough to deserve attention. Secondly, in the case of policy decisions, even individually very small risks become very important. As very small risks are often imposed upon a large number of people, it is an "actuarial certainty" (Lenman 2008, 109) that for a few unlucky ones, risks will materialize and paralysis on the policy level would ensue. Consider the following example:

> **Vaccination:** In pursuit of immunizing the population against a very unpleasant disease, the government imposes on each of its 20 million citizens a 1 in a million risk of being killed by an allergic reaction to the inoculant.[3]

From the perspective of a naïve basic rights theory with the no-risk principle, it seems that such a vaccination scheme would be impermissible, since it puts people's right to life at risk. As we expect very few to die and the alternative would be to have many people suffering from the disease, this seems extreme.[4] Furthermore, it would be individually rational to participate in the vaccination scheme, since it is highly likely that they will therefore avoid a very unpleasant disease and there is only a tiny chance that they will die from an allergic reaction.

One might again object here that is precisely because a large number will benefit from the vaccination whereas only very few people suffer an allergic reaction that it is permissible to establish this scheme. One has to be very careful here, because limiting aggregative-consequentialist reasoning was the reason why basic rights theories were adopted in the first place. Without any further checks the door to full-fledged aggregation opens, leading to very implausible results in cases like the following:

> **Experimentation:** In pursuit of developing and then administering a vaccine to the population against a very unpleasant disease, the government randomly selects, rounds up, and then kills 20 of its 20 million citizens in medical experiments necessary for the development of the vaccine.

A theory should allow Vaccination and prohibit Experimentation. A basic rights theory *with the no-risk principle* will judge both policies to be impermissible, because in Experimentation, people's right to life will be violated and in Vaccination, their right to life will be put at risk. It fails because it cannot make sense of the fact that the probability to have an allergic reaction is very small. Aggregative-consequentialist theories will judge both policies to be permissible because the balance is the same in both. They fail because they don't take into account how the victims in Experimentation are affected.

The challenge I want to take up here is to formulate a view that can make sense of the importance of probability in Vaccination, and at the same time, takes the complaints against being treated in a certain way seriously. Some readers might think that all of this is, in the end, simply about the doctrine of double effect (DDE), which states that it is sometimes permissible to cause harm when this is an unintended but merely foreseen consequence of an action aimed at producing some good.[5] In some sense there are links, and contractualists have pointed out that there are affinities to the "roughly Kantian thought that the intending – foreseeing distinction embodies a certain way of respecting people that recognizes their special right to object and to demand justification from us when our actions aim at their harm" (Lenman 2008, 103–104). But the DDE does not help us all the way to the desired conclusion. For one, it has nothing to say on the probability in Vaccination: If the chance of an allergic reaction would be much higher, vaccination should not be permissible. Second, the DDE is often defended with reference to the intending/foreseeing distinction, but merely invoking it will not do any work. The contractualist solution I will sketch at the end puts the weight on whether the principle behind an action can be justified to those affected by it.

Explaining rights

Before we have a look at possible solutions for the problem of paralysis, let us consider the concept of rights in more detail and what it means to have a right.

Many approaches to rights are quite parsimonious. Alan Gewirth supports a Hohfeldian definition according to which a right "entails a correlative duty of some person or persons to refrain from acting in various ways required for the first person's having that to which she has a right" (Gewirth 1981, 12). Often, rights are thought to be grounded in certain features of the rights-holder. Raz (1984, 166) argues, "'X has a right' if and only if X can have rights, and, other things being equal, an aspect of X's well-being (his interest) is a sufficient reason for holding some other person(s)to be under a duty". Scholars working in a broadly deontological framework ground rights not in interests but, for example, human dignity. However, this need not be the case. To adopt the structure and language of rights, one need not have a theory which takes rights to be the fundamental normative notion. Rights can also be seen as pragmatic or legal instruments for achieving whatever one believes to be of moral value, such as the utilitarian aim of "the greatest happiness for the greatest number".

I will take basic rights theories as theories with three features: rights are entitlements of persons (ultimate normative category, anti-aggregative), there is a hierarchy of rights (trumping character, lexical priority), rights do not exhaust the normative-practical domain; they may often leave the question of what to do, all things considered, open to the agent.[6] Defining basic rights theories in this way emphasizes their opposition to aggregative-consequentialist theories to which they are often supposed to be an alternative. Each element is meant to block a certain feature of aggregative-consequentialist reasoning, as I will explain below.

When I speak of rights as claims of persons I mean that rights are non-instrumental (Nagel 1995, 86). In contrast, aggregative-consequentialist theories equip us with a single goal (maximize overall utility) and our actions can then be evaluated by how well they achieve this goal. The value or the values to be promoted are impersonal; persons come into play insofar as they are vessels for the valuable things, like happiness, welfare or preference satisfaction. With basic rights theories, on the other hand, what is valuable is intrinsically linked to persons. Rights are entitlements of persons. Acting in a way that fulfils one person's right while violating another person's right is impermissible in a basic rights view (unless the first person's right trumps the second person's right), whereas any redistribution of pure harms and benefits is permissible in aggregative-consequentialist accounts, as long as it does not lower the net sum of value. In contrast, on a basic rights view, it is difficult to decipher which person's right should be met if only one of two equal rights of two different persons can be honoured.[7]

Connected to this is another feature of basic rights theories, as I will understand them here: Basic rights theories have some resources to solve conflicts among rights. Rights come in a hierarchical order in which higher-ranking rights trump lower ranking rights and other considerations (Dworkin 2009). The hierarchy of rights may be quite complex, involving side constraints, exceptions, circumstance-sensitivity, non-transitivity and so on. Furthermore, it is often claimed that rights

are absolute. What is meant by that is certainly not that every right holds uncon-
ditionally all the time but that, as long as it is not outranked, a right constitutes an
absolute entitlement of the rights-holder to its substance. As mentioned before,
there is no weighing mechanism inherent in the concept of rights which would
allow us to determine the relative strength of rights to each other.[8] If a right out-
ranks another right or another consideration, it does so decisively.

As indicated before, rights are not exhaustive for the question of what one
should do. Behind this stands the idea that it is up to people to formulate a plan
of the good life, determine what they take to be valuable, engage in their own
projects and so on. The rights of others are side-constraints of one's freedom.[9]
Scanlon (1998, 95–96) famously describes this part of morality as the sphere
of what we owe to each other, which does not exhaust the practical-normative
domain or even the moral-normative domain. Griffin (2008, 63–66) gives two
examples for other normative domains, welfare and justice, and adds that there
may be many more.

It is worth pointing out how this sets basic rights theories apart from their
aggregative-consequentialist alternatives in yet another way. With basic rights
theories, the value of individual choice, often discussed under the headings of
autonomy or freedom, forms the normative basis of the theory. That freedom or
exercise of autonomy justify rights in basic rights theories will also be important
later on for the contractualist solution of the problem of paralysis.

Modifying or replacing the no-risk principle

The no-risk principle is prompted by the question of how uncertainty about possible negative consequences should affect the permissibility of an action. Suppose
you have two action alternatives A and B and you have to choose one. A risks
violating a right while B certainly violates a right. The right in A trumps the
right in B. Let us now vary the risk: If the probability in A is 1, then you should
certainly choose action A because the right in B is trumped by the right in A.
How small does the probability in A have to be for B to be permissible? Does it
have to be below a certain threshold, or does it depend on the case, the balance
of harms and benefits, or perhaps intent?

The no-risk principle says that, because the right in A is really important, any
risk of violating it trumps the certain violation of the lower-ranking right in B.
The no-risk principle is certainly wrong, but it is not easy to see what the correct answer here is. Vaccination suggests that an action can be permissible if the
probability of a violation of a higher-ranking right is >0. Experimentation shows
that it is not only about probabilities, but why is that? In the following sections,
I will discuss two of prominent approaches which are, however, not successful in
plotting a middle way between the protections of rights and allowing some risk
impositions to promote lower-ranking rights and other normative considerations.

Threshold approaches

The first approach I will discuss introduces probability thresholds, below which risks are negligible. A similar strategy has been discussed in the context of deontological moral theories and can be easily adapted to basic rights theories, since both share what Frank Jackson and Michael Smith call the on-off nature of moral claims. By this they mean that

> an action is or is not the breaking of a promise, the telling of a lie, the punishing of someone innocent, etc. . . . this contrasts with ethical theories that focus on the values of states of affairs associated with actions, where these values may be positive or negative to one degree or another
>
> (Jackson & Smith 2016, 16–17)

There is a similarity here with basic rights theories: there are rights and duties (not) to treat persons in a certain way and these, too, don't come in degrees.

Jackson and Smith locate a problem with deontological theories when it comes to implementation. An implementation rule, they write, tells us how to actually achieve the things a moral theory demands of us. For example, Kantians might think that one should not punish the innocent – but no one punishes the innocent as such, just as no one breaks promises as such and so on. What people do is to undertake certain actions which count as not punishing the innocent, for example by saying, as a judge, to an innocent defendant "I find you not guilty", or by being at a certain place at a certain time if one promised one would do so (Jackson & Smith 2016, 5–6). What is needed to get from the moral rule (what Jackson and Smith call constitution rules) to the appropriate action is an implementation rule. In the case of the deontological judge, such a rule ensures that the judge won't punish the innocent. At the end of the trial, her options are to either say "I find you guilty" or "I don't find you guilty". Since there is a *non-zero* chance that the defendant is *not* guilty, despite overwhelming evidence to the contrary, the judge should always acquit her, because that is the only sure way to not punish the innocent. This would lead the idea of a justice system ad absurdum (Jackson & Smith 2016, 7).

One intuitive solution to this problem would be to define a probability threshold below which the defendant's innocence is so unlikely as to be negligible. Apart from the practical problem of being able to pin down the numerical probability of a defendant being guilty, the usual problems of thresholds arise. The first is to agree on a specific threshold. It would be surprising if we could find a philosophical argument with the conclusion that anything less than 5% probability of being innocent makes it permissible to send someone to prison. Another typical problem for threshold approaches is that someone with a 4.9% probability of being innocent might incur 10 years in prison whereas someone with a 5.1% probability will be free. One could hold against these arguments that there is some considerable grey area around the threshold but also clear cases in which someone should be sent to prison and clear cases in which someone should not be sent to prison. I don't think that deontologists, or rights-theorists for that matter, have the resources to even give a range in which the threshold should lie. There is nothing in the concept of rights or duties which could inform us in doing that. This is no accident: Determining a threshold would require us to think about the value of a state of affairs which could be positive or negative to a degree – and this is the kind of reasoning we wanted to avoid in the first place. One might interject here that what I described is not a theoretical problem of some strands of deontological moral theory but a challenge judges face every day. Unlike deontologists, judges are not however bound by the rule that they should not punish the innocent, but by the rule that they should only punish those whose guilt is proven beyond a reasonable doubt. They have considerable leeway in deciding what constitutes a reasonable doubt and what doesn't.

Jackson and Smith note that threshold approaches also struggle with conjuncts of actions. When a threshold of probability is reached so that Φ becomes permissible and, independently, another threshold is reached so that Ψ becomes permissible, it could be the case that the complex action Φ-and-Ψ is impermissible, because multiplying the probabilities from both cases lowers the probability in the conjunct case, so that it may fall below the threshold required by threshold deontology. Whether doing one and the same thing is permissible would then depend on how to describe an action – a result we should want to avoid.[10] I don't think that these challenges to threshold deontology are insurmountable. Nevertheless, the difficulties of setting thresholds and identifying the morally relevant action descriptions can be avoided with a different but related approach I will present in the second part of this chapter.

Consent-based views

An alternative strategy to tackle the problem of risk starts very differently: There is one kind of risk imposition where it is hard to see why it should be impermissible, and that is pure risk imposition. A pure risk imposition is a case in which the harm does not materialize, the "victim" didn't know of the risk and would not have acted in a way that would have exposed her to the risk anyway (Oberdiek 2012, 340–341). What harm has been done to an agent in such case? The idea is to uncouple the wrong of risking from the harm which materializes.

Oberdiek claims that it is actually the person's autonomy that is harmed by imposing a risk on her. When referring to autonomy, Oberdiek follows Raz, who requires for personal autonomy certain mental capabilities, an adequate range of valuable options and being free of intentionally manipulating influences from outside. In the case of risk imposition, the last two points are of interest to us:

Imposing a risk on someone diminishes her range of valuable options and it does so in a specific way which can be interpreted as an outside manipulation.[11] Oberdiek compares imposing risks on someone to laying traps. Autonomy comes in degrees and even taking single options away from an agent may diminish her autonomy in meaningful ways (Oberdiek 2012, 352) and thus imposing risk may require justification.[12]

How could risk imposition be justified then? Oberdiek starts from the consideration that, in modern societies, imposing risks is "not just inescapable . . . but often appropriate" (Oberdiek 2012, 355) because of the cooperative and intertwined nature of our lives. Imposing the risks that emerge from the societal nature of human life requires fulfilling one's duties of due care. Oberdiek argues that someone who drives a car while drunk neglects her duty of due care, she takes the lives of others in her hands and this is what requires her to act with due care. Oberdiek's characterization of what exactly due care entails remains sketchy since his argument is mainly concerned with the harm in pure risk imposition and *why* it needs to be justified. On the topic of when it actually *is* justified, not much is said.

Oberdiek says that autonomy is important and that thus risk impositions can be harmful to an agent's interests. But agents have other interests besides autonomy and there can be trade-offs. How do we decide which trade-offs are permissible and which are not? Ferretti (2016, 13), who defends a similar position, is aware of this problem but says she can be agnostic about the trade-offs because "our judgements about risk imposition should be guided by the normative theory of freedom distribution that we favor". She continues that "one may want to equalize overall freedom, or rather maximize it, or merely guarantee a minimum of it at all times to all of the relevant persons" (Ferretti 2016, 13). She envisions a division of labour where respect for persons grounds the need for a theory on how to distribute autonomy and freedom but does not say anything specific on what that theory should look like. I doubt that one can mix and match any distributive theory with the Kantian assumptions present in these approaches. The notion of respect is usually invoked to block certain (re)-distributions and might thus be incompatible with, for example, aggregative approaches.

Thinking about risks first, rights second in Scanlonian contractualism

This chapter set out to find an alternative to aggregative-consequentialist theories because, in unrestricted forms, they tend to yield implausible results in cases in which mundane benefits to the many can be achieved by harming the few considerably. It turned out that without these tools, it is hard to keep the problem of paralysis in check. In the beginning of this chapter, I formulated the challenge as finding a theory which can make sense of the importance of probabilities and expected outcomes in Vaccination and which can, at the same time, explain what is wrong with the way in which we treat people in Experimentation, although the expected outcome is the same in both cases. My basic strategy is to re-appropriate the tools of aggregative consequentialism, in a restricted way.

A very short sketch of Scanlonian contractualism

Contractualism, as Scanlon defends it, is concerned with two interconnected ideas: first, the nature and justification of reasons and a certain form of practical reasoning; second, a theory of the rightness and wrongness of moral principles. For my purposes, especially the second part will be relevant.

Scanlon claims that "An act is wrong if its performance under the circumstances would be disallowed by any set of principles for the general regulation of behavior that no one could reasonably reject as a basis for informed, unforced general agreement" (Scanlon 1998, 153). Conversely, moral principles for the general regulation of behaviour are justified if those affected by them could not reasonably reject them. Justification is owed to those who are similarly motivated to find principles for the general regulation of behaviour (Scanlon 1998, 4–5). In other words: When considering the permissibility of an action the question is whether the principle from which this action derives is the one against which others would have the weakest objections. It will probably always be the case that someone has some objection against what you do, but it is not only their objections which count, but also your own objection against not undertaking the action.[13]

The contractualist solution to the problem of paralysis

A general principle allowing the imposition of risks of rights violations cannot reasonably be rejected, since the result of this rejection would be paralysis. Thus the rejection is not reasonable even from the point of view of those who are most affected by it in a negative way, i.e. those for whom the risk will materialize. To block a principle, one must be willing to endure the same limits to one's liberty that one demands from the risk imposer. Since this would mean paralysis for everyone, the rejection is not reasonable even from the point of view of those the risk is imposed upon.

A crucial part of this argument concerns the scope of principles for action. What I claim here is that there are some more general principles or at least that there are requirements of consistency among principles. Arguing in one case that a risk imposition is impermissible because it might result in harm would require the objector to accept the same kind of reasoning in structurally similar cases. I believe that this consistency requirement can do a lot of work. It connects all cases in which risks of serious harms are imposed for enjoying mundane benefits.

Another idea inherent in the above is that not only the reasons of the objector are important when considering a principle, but also those of the agent. For example: If you are starving and consider taking food from someone who has more than enough, the fact that he or she has an objection against you taking the food is not enough to make the principle guiding your action impermissible. It is precisely because you have a strong reason to do it, one stronger than the property claim of the other person, that the action is permissible. As mentioned earlier, the justification of our principles is aimed at those who are similarly motivated, so the objections they would level against us cannot be parochial, but must be general. They have to take into account what way of living together would result from their principle. Furthermore, the above reasoning has some similarities to aggregative-consequentialist accounts because it takes expected outcomes into account. Consider Vaccination again: In general, the above principle allows vaccination schemes because of the expected benefits they yield to the population. Yet if the numbers were different, if the risk of allergic reactions would be much higher or the individual benefits negligible, then the scheme would not be permissible.

Can the above principle make sense of the distinction between Vaccination and Experimentation? In Experimentation, the expected benefit for every citizen is also positive, so why should they object to this scheme? In literature, this problem has been discussed under the heading of ex-ante vs ex-post contractualism. It has been claimed that it makes a difference whether we count only those objections people have in advance (when the policy is proposed) or also those once the policy is underway. The option I prefer is to adopt ex-ante contractualism, but there are also a number of other features of contractualism which still make it impermissible to engage in experimentation, despite the expectation that one will be benefitted by it. One could call this ex-ante contractualism with side-constraints.

Here is one feature that could do this: Kumar argues that the principles we adopt can yield two kinds of implications, those of instrumental and intrinsic, against which may lead those affected to reject them. An instrumental implication "concerns a respect in which an individual stands to be benefited or burdened as a result of an activity being permitted" (Kumar 2015, 36). What is meant here are tangible benefits and burdens like gains and losses of goods, enjoyable activities or bodily harm. In other words, instrumental implications concern what is happening to a person as a result of a principle being adopted. The discussion of contractualism mostly revolves around these, which is also due to the fact that Scanlon uses examples involving instrumental considerations. (Scanlon 1998, 235)

An intrinsic implication, as Kumar (2015, 38) characterises it, "concerns the significance of a certain type of conduct being permitted, quite apart from either the possible consequences of the permission being exercised or other indirect consequences of it". This is exactly what is at stake in Experimentation: Everyone has reason not to cede to others "the authority to make decisions concerning how an individual's body may be used" (Kumar 2015, 38). Experimentation will be impermissible even though there is an expected benefit for everyone. Interestingly, Kumar believes that this has "nothing to do with the imposition of either harm or the risk of harm. The objection, rather, is that the experimentation requires that it be permissible to involuntarily involve individuals in it as experimental subjects" (Kumar 2015, 37–38). Thus although participation could appear to be attractive ex-ante, because individually, everyone has lots to gain and only stands a very small chance of being the unlucky test-subject, once we take this intrinsic implication into account, we see that we have good reason to reject the policy.

Lenman reminds us that we also have to keep the strains of commitment (also cf. Rawls 1999, §29) in mind from the ex-ante perspective. If a principle would require us to agree to sacrifice others or to agree to be sacrificed, we can't agree to that principle in advance because once we have to go through the implementation of it, it will be very hard for us, psychologically, to accept what is happening to us or what we now need to do to others. It is not that it is impossible to commit oneself to do it, but given human psychology, it is a promise which is likely not fulfillable. If we have trouble seeing ourselves to be able to follow what we agreed to once the dice have been cast, then we should not agree to Experimentation in the first place (Lenman 2008, 116).

There are other features of Experimentation which allow us to distinguish it from Vaccination. Lenman (2008, 101–105) mentions three of them: a) Vaccination is straightforward and all those upon whom the risk is imposed are potential beneficiaries. It is only because some also have an allergic reaction that they will not be benefitted. This is not the case in Experimentation. The test-subjects could not benefit from the procedure, even in principle.[14] b) What the government and its agents do in Vaccination is *being guided by the aim* of vaccinating the population. In Experimentation, they are, at some point, guided by the aim to kill someone. c) In Vaccination, the government takes reasonable precautions to protect *each* of its citizens; in Experimentation, at some point, there is more it could do to protect *each* citizen from harm, namely, it could refrain from killing them.

What the preceding discussion shows is the general commensurability of strong protections of individual claims, as contractualists among others envision them, with a way to allow risk imposition. The title of this chapter mentions the idea that contractualists think about risks first, rights second. By this I mean that the level of protection individuals enjoy depends on to what extent risks can reasonably be minimized. This involves a number of different considerations.

On the most basic level, absolute protections against risk imposition are rejected since they would lead to the problem of paralysis. In a second step, instrumental implications are weighed against each other and the principle is selected which yields the weakest individual complaint, taking into account the complaints from those who will be burdened, but also the complaints from those who would miss valuable opportunities if the action in question would be forbidden. At the same time, intrinsic considerations will be considered: If adopting a principle would undermine the possibility of a moral relationship of mutual recognition, which is the ultimate aim in Scanlonian contractualism, then it can be reasonably rejected, even though the balance in terms of benefits and burdens is positive. Only after we have gone through this process, we arrive at what can be identified as individual rights. Often these justified claims also protect against risk imposition, but they are not unqualified claims. They may require due care, compensation in the case of accidents and so on, but since there is always a non-zero chance that an action will result in catastrophe, none of these claims will be absolute.

Basic rights, the environment and climate change

At the beginning of this chapter, I hinted that a basic rights approach promises to ground a robust case for aggressive climate change adaptation and mitigation, especially in situations of extensive uncertainty. It should have become clear by now that this idea has to be qualified. Rights do not offer strong protection under uncertainty because they are insensitive to risk. If that were the case, the problem of paralysis would arise. It is rather because rights are sensitive to what happens to individual people that they preclude certain kinds of risk impositions. In this section I will briefly sketch what these findings mean for environmental rights.

Basic rights as I understand them here are entitlements of persons, not rights of animals or the environment. Protecting biodiversity, animal life, conservation and so on is seen here as a means to the end of protecting the preconditions for basic human rights to life, health and subsistence. Nickel calls environmental rights like these "human-oriented" (Nickel 1993, 283). Nickel himself argues for a Right to a Safe Environment (RSE) protecting against "substantial and recurrent threats" (1993, 295) to "health and safety" (1993, 284). Rights such as the above and the RSE are derivative. It may well be the case that there are further rights pertaining to animals and the environment directly, but these are outside the focus of this paper.

What are the implications of environmental rights such as the RSE? I will focus here on the case of anthropogenic climate change. Climate change is a global phenomenon in the sense that greenhouse gases emitted in one place disperse globally and lead to rising global temperatures. These in turn lead to heightened risks of floods, storms, heatwaves, etc. The effects differ locally; some areas will experience more severe effects of climate change while others will be less affected or even be positively affected (Field et al. 2014, 14). On balance though, the projected negative effects far outweigh the positive effects. Furthermore, the ability to cope with these effects differs, based not only on location but also importantly on socio-economic status: poor people in developing countries are most vulnerable and their interests in e.g. life, health and subsistence will be threatened the most (Field et al. 2014, 6).

Our case here is also markedly different from Vaccination or Experimentation in that the risks to fundamental interests are distributed very unequally (Field et al. 2014, 12). People in rich countries will probably mostly experience welfare losses through adaptation costs. This can be severe, like resettling whole communities in e.g. Florida or Venice, but the US and Italy will be able to still guarantee the basic rights of those affected by sea-level rights. People in poor countries, on the other hand, will very likely have their basic rights threatened – without any compensation. Even from the ex-ante perspective, their prospects are negative and thus they can reasonably reject a policy imposing these risks upon them. This grounds a strong case for combating global climate change, one which is not overruled by the fact that doing so will be very costly. What people in rich nations lose in terms of welfare does not outweigh the fundamental interests of the most vulnerable. This marks a key difference to cost-benefit approaches.

There is a further point concerning compensation. With aggregative-consequentialist approaches, burdens to one person can be compensated with benefits to another person. A basic rights theory will block such trade-offs. Compensation does play a role, but only once an unintended harm materializes although reasonable steps had been taken to minimize its risk and due care was exercised. Compensating the foreseen victims of one's action is not a way to avoid complaints. This has two-fold implications for a business-as-usual approach to climate change (that is, the approach of not lowering greenhouse gas emissions aggressively), since business-as-usual not only means knowingly violating e.g. the right to a safe environment, but also comes without any intent to compensate the ensuing harms.

Conclusion

The starting point for this chapter was the question how an otherwise promising basic rights approach can avoid the problem of paralysis. I argued that basic rights theories share three features, which set them apart from aggregative-consequentialist theories: Rights are entitlements of persons, they block the interpersonal aggregation of benefits and burdens in some cases and they describe only part of morality. Two approaches to solve the problem of paralysis have been found wanting. Threshold approaches face difficulties in finding a plausible way to identify probability thresholds and to evaluate complex actions. Approaches focussing on autonomy or freedom go some way in the right direction, but in this chapter, I put them to the side to focus on Scanlonian contractualism as a theory that can explain well why some risk impositions are permissible and some are not. The key idea of this approach is to take the problem of paralysis as a starting point for thinking about risk imposition. Since the no-risk principle leads to paralysis, it can be reasonably rejected. Thus we may impose risks upon each other. How much risk? This depends, first on the balance of burdens and benefits for those affected, is dependent on how much care is taken to minimize risks, and on whether the principle in question upholds the possibility of standing in a relationship of mutual recognition. I argued that while Vaccination meets these requirements, Experimentation does not. In the process, I also argued that adopting an ex-ante perspective allows us to understand why we may impose risks of severe harms on people to gain moderate benefits for a larger number of people. This is because the ex-ante prospects for each individual are positive.

Finally, I sketched what my findings mean for environmental rights. Using the example of a person-centric right to a safe environment, I argued that imposing risks of violations of the right to a safe environment, as it is the case with climate change, can't be justified with contractualist reasoning. First, because the distribution of risks is highly unequal, second because compensation for harms from climate change is neither intended nor will it even be applicable, insofar as basic rights are concerned, since these are not subject to trade-offs.

Notes

1 Caney argues that climate change threatens "in particular the human rights to life, health, and subsistence", (p. 172), that "Analyzing the impacts of climate change in terms of its effects on human rights enjoys advantages over other ways of evaluating the impacts of climate change" (p. 173) and that "Endorsing a human-rights framework for evaluating the impacts of climate change has implications for our understanding of who should bear the burdens of climate change and what kinds of policies are appropriate" (p. 173). In "Climate Change, Human Rights, and Moral Threshold" Caney explicitly endorses human rights as claims with lexical priority over other values.

2 See (Lenman 2008), 112 for some of these, and more, examples.

3 These are adapted from (Lenman 2008).

4 Some are uncomfortable with the fact that in Vaccination, no one might die whereas in Experimentation, 20 people will certainly die. From the point of expected utility, this does not make a difference. If you think it might make a difference for contractualists, think of the following example – Contaminated Vaccine: A terrible mistake has happened at the only pharmaceutical company and 20 vials of contaminated vaccine have been mixed up with the 19,999,980 vials of vaccine. Giving a dose of contaminated vaccine will technically vaccinate a person but also kill her. It would be very costly to find out which ones are contaminated, so the government decides to vaccinate the population anyway.

5 There are further conditions, the most important being that the good produced must be sufficiently large in relation to the harm.

6 This is important because it opens up a realm of personal projects and values which might conflict with the rights of others or might require risking them. Barbara Fried seems to hold that this antagonism between freedom of conduct and freedom of harm is what in the end will require contractualists to adopt some sort of interpersonal aggregation (Fried 2012, 65–66).
7 The discussion about whether the numbers should count, started by John Taurek, comes to mind here. Cf. (Taurek 1977).
8 Yooav Isaacs calls this deontology's lack of a decision theory, cf. Isaacs 2014.
9 This is how Nozick conceives of rights, though it is a matter of debate of how strict these side-constraints are. Cf. (Nozick 1974, 33–34, 49–50).
10 A counterargument to this line of thought can be found in (Aboodi et al., 2008, 262–263).
11 It seems to me that one might even leave this point aside. Maria Paolo Ferretti thinks that Oberdiek's conception only hinges on the range of options Oberdiek (2012, 353).
12 To quote the exact wording: "[A]utonomy comes in degrees and thus can be curtailed or diminished even when not outright annihilated. What this means is that even a single well-placed trap, or even foreclosing a single option, can conceivably diminish one's autonomy, which is far from saying that it necessarily does".
13 There is some debate on how exactly this should be understood. Johann Frick, for example, argues that contractualism employs a series of pairwise comparisons to identify the strongest objection. This is the usual way to understand the reasoning in situations where claims collide. Rahul Kumar (2015), though, is not so sure.
14 In **Vaccination**, the allergic reaction occurs in addition to the inoculation.

References

Aboodi R., Borer A. and Enoch D. (2008) "Deontology, individualism, and uncertainty: A reply to Jackson and Smith" _Journal of Philosophy_, 105, 259–72.
Caney S. (2010) "Climate change, human rights, and moral thresholds" in Gardiner S. M., Caney S., Jamieson D. and Shue H. eds., _Climate ethics: Essential readings_. Oxford University Press, New York, 163–77.
Caney S. (2009) "Climate change and the future: Discounting for time, wealth, and risk" _Journal of Social Philosophy_, 40, 163–86.
Dworkin R. (2009) "Rights as trumps" in Kavanagh A. and Oberdiek J. eds., _Arguing about the Law_. Routledge, New York, 335–45.
Ferretti M.P. (2016) "Risk imposition and freedom" _Politics, Philosophy & Economics_, 15, 261–79.
Field C.B., Barros V.R., Mastrandrea M.D., Mach K.J., Abdrabo M.-K., Adger N., Anokhin Y.A., Anisimov O.A., Arent D.J., Barnett J. et al. (2014) "Summary for policymakers" in _Climate change 2014: Impacts, adaptation, and vulnerability. Part A: Global and sectoral aspects. Contribution of working group II to the fifth assessment report of the intergovernmental panel on climate change_. Cambridge University Press, Cambridge, 1–32.
Frick J. (2015) "Contractualism and social risk" _Philosophy & Public Affairs_, 43, 175–223.
Fried B.H. (2012) "Can contractualism save us from aggregation?" _The Journal of Ethics_, 16, 39–66.
Gardiner S.M. (2011) _A perfect moral storm: The ethical tragedy of climate change_. Oxford University Press, New York.
Gewirth A. (1981) "Are there any absolute rights?" _The Philosophical Quarterly_, 31, 1–16.
Griffin J. (2008) _On human rights_. Oxford University Press, New York.
Harman E. (2009) "Harming as causing harm" in Roberts M. A. and Wasserman D. T. eds., _Harming future persons_. Springer, Dordrecht, 137–54.

Harman E. (2004) "Can we harm and benefit in creating?" *Philosophical Perspectives*, 18, 89–113.

Hayenhjelm M. and Wolff J. (2012) "The moral problem of risk impositions: A survey of the literature" *European Journal of Philosophy*, 20, E26–E51.

Holm S. (2016) "A right against risk-imposition and the problem of paralysis" *Ethical Theory and Moral Practice*, 19, 917–30.

Isaacs Y. (2014) "Duty and knowledge" *Philosophical Perspectives*, 28, 95–110.

Jackson F. and Smith M. (2016) "The implementation problem for deontology" in Lord E. and Maguire B. eds., *Weighing reasons*. Oxford University Press, New York, 279–92.

Kumar R. (2015) "Risking and wronging" *Philosophy & Public Affairs*, 43, 27–51.

Lenman J. (2008) "Contractualism and risk imposition" *Politics, Philosophy & Economics*, 7, 99–122.

Meyer L.H. (2009) "Intergenerationelle Suffizienzgerechtigkeit" in Goldschmidt N. ed., *Generationengerechtigkeit: ordnungsökonomische Konzepte, Untersuchungen zur Ordnungstheorie und Ordnungspolitik*. Mohr Siebeck, Tübingen, 281–322.

Meyer L.H. (2003) "Past and future: The case for a threshold notion of harm" in Meyer L. H. Paulson S. L. and Pogge T. W. M. eds., *Rights, culture, and the law: Themes from the legal and political philosophy of Joseph Raz*, Oxford University Press, New York, 143–58.

Nagel T. (1995) *Equality and partiality*. Oxford University Press, New York.

Nickel J.W. (1993) "The human right to a safe environment: Philosophical perspectives on its scope and justification" *Yale Journal of International Law*, 18, 281–95.

Nozick R. (1974) *Anarchy, State, and Utopia*. Basic Books, New York.

Oberdiek J. (2012) "The moral significance of risking" *Legal Theory*, 18, 339–56.

Rawls J. (1999) *A theory of justice*. Rev. ed. Harvard University Press, Cambridge, Mass.

Raz J. (1984) *The morality of freedom*, Oxford University Press, Oxford.

Scanlon T. (1998) *What we owe to each other*, Cambridge University Press, Cambridge, MA.

Taurek J.M. (1977) "Should the numbers count?" *Philosophy & Public Affairs*, 6, 293–316.

Index